EASTERN
CANADA

Welcome to Eastern Canada

Carole Chester

Collins
Glasgow and London

The author and publisher wish to acknowledge the generous assistance of the staff of Tourism Canada.

Cover photograph
Van Phillips

Photographs
Quentin Bell
pp. 21 top, 104 bottom, 108, 122, 123

Canadian High Commission
pp. 83, 90

J. Allan Cash
pp. 15, 34, 42, 100

Bruce Coleman
p. 87

Colorific
pp. 47, 69, 80, 85, 91

Dept. of Tourism, Govt. of Nova Scotia
pp. 99, 102, 104 top, 107, 113

Dept. of Tourism, Govt. of Ontario
pp. 30, 38, 39 top

Robert Estall
pp. 21 bottom, 31, 33, 39 bottom, 44, 48, 53 right, 96, 109

Photo Tourism Québec
pp. 57, 61, 70

Picturepoint
pp. 41, 45, 49, 89, 125

The Photo Source
pp. 11, 37, 53 left

Topham
pp. 13, 19, 24, 62, 103, 116, 119, 121

Van Phillips
pp. 8, 17, 63, 67, 68, 71, 74

Zefa
pp. 28, 71, 93

Regional Maps
Mike Shand, Kažia L. Kram, Iain Gerard

Town Plans and Area Maps
M. & R. Piggott

Illustration
pp. 6-7 Peter Joyce

ISBN 0 00 447512 7

HOW TO USE THIS BOOK

The contents page of this book shows how Eastern Canada is divided into provinces. The book is in two sections: general information and gazetteer. In the gazetteer each tourist region has an introduction and a regional map (detail below left). There are also plans of the main cities

(below right). The main entries in the gazetteer are shown on the regional maps. Places to visit and leisure facilities available in each region and city are indicated by symbols. Main highways, railroads and airports are shown on the maps.

Regional Maps

Town Plans

Museum/gallery
Main airports
Other airport
Theater
Interesting building
Fortress/old fort
Monument/NHP/NHS m
Religious building/shrine ✝
Spa
National/Prov. park 🌲
Park
Gardens

Amusement park
Zoo/Safari park
Wildlife/Wildlife reserve
Aquarium
Boating/sailing
Water sports
Scuba diving
Canoeing
Winter sports
Caves/mines
Hiking

Museum/gallery
Library
Garden
Car Park ℗
Information
Interesting building
Park
City Hall
Theater
Post Office
Religious building ✝
Bus terminal
Market

metres		feet
1000		3281
400		1312
200		656
0		0

======= four lane divided highway
—— principal highway
— railroad

Local airport
Hospital ⊕
Railway station

CONTENTS

HISTORY

The name 'Canada' is an Algonquian Indian word ('Kannata' meaning 'a settlement') and before the French settlers, the only inhabitants in this part of North America were Indian tribes such as the Hurons and the Algonkin. Canada's European history started in the East with sporadic visits by Vikings, who established a colony on the northern tip of Newfoundland at L'Anse aux Meadows around 1000 AD. The first explorer of note, however, was John Cabot who landed at Cape Breton Island on June 24, 1497, claiming it for Britain. On his second voyage that year, he traveled southeast along the coast of Labrador and Newfoundland, returning home to talk of great fishing grounds, the Grand Banks.

No doubt a number of European fishermen came this way, but the real discoverer of Canada's mainland was Jacques Cartier who, in 1534, set off from France with 60 men and two small boats. He reached Newfoundland and by way of the Strait of Belle Isle, entered the Gulf of St Lawrence. It was Cartier who named his discovery 'Kannata'. Like other explorers of his era, he was primarily seeking a route to the Pacific, the North West Passage. The following year he tried again, this time with three vessels, taking them up river some 800 mi into what is today Québec, and pushing on as far as Hochelaga (Montréal), before being literally stopped in his tracks by the Lachine Rapids.

That meant a return to Québec to suffer from frosts and blizzards and in constant fear of Indian attack. Not all the Indians were violent though, and when lack of fruit and vegetables caused scurvy among Cartier's men, friendly Indians showed him how to make medicinal tea from the bark of white spruce.

Cartier's third voyage took place in 1541 but this time under the leadership of Jean Francois de la Rocque, Sieur de Roberval, who was appointed by the French king as viceroy of a 'New France'. Roberval's efforts at colonization proved futile and France lost interest for another 60 years. Breton and Basque fishermen continued to come, as did others from SW England, at first on a seasonal basis, but later they stayed all year round. They discovered that they could trade with the Indians for beaver skins. It was the start of the fur trade which, as European demands for fashionable Beaver hats increased, began to develop at a considerable rate. Indeed, competition was so fierce that fighting broke out between the English,

French, Iroquois and Hurons, in an attempt by the colonial powers to safeguard their trade routes.

Interest in Canada was rekindled and the French, under the auspices of the Sieur de Monts, experimented with a settlement on the Bay of Fundy in 1604. But then explorer Samuel de Champlain established a trading post at Québec in 1608 as a base from which to search for the Northwest Passage. He did explore up river but he failed to find a way to the open sea. What he did do in 1609 was to ally himself with the Hurons and the Algonkin. What he should have done was ally himself with the Iroquois, who were better warriors. He also started the system of company monopolies for the fur trade, which eventually became the Company of the One Hundred Associates, and was entrusted with the government of the Québec colony in 1627.

The Iroquois became English allies and for a couple of decades in the 1640s wrought havoc on the line of French settlements along the St Lawrence, practically paralyzing the fur trade for the French, and dispersing their allies, the Hurons. Many of the Jesuit missionaries who had come out with Champlain were also killed. Among them was Father Jean de Brébeuf who died of slow burning at the hands of the Iroquois at St Ignace on the banks of the Sturgeon River.

Even before the Iroquois destroyed the Hurons, it looked as if Québec would not survive. Twenty years after its founding, it had a population of only 65 and when in 1628 reinforcements of people and supplies were sent out, they ran straight into the hands of a small English privateering squadron. Starving Québec was forced to surrender but was returned to the French in 1632 under the Treaty of St Germaine-En-Laye. The colony was again saved from disintegration when, thanks to Jesuit propaganda, the wealthy French formed Canada's first immigration agency — La Société de Notre Dame de Montréal. In

1641 it sent 47 people under Sieur de Maisonneuve to the island of Montréal which it had obtained by official grant. Soon this outpost was to become the focal center of the fur trade.

Canada's early pioneers had a tough time, what with the severe winter weather and Indian attacks. By 1663, there were still only 2500 French settlers mostly confined to Québec, Trois Rivières and Montréal, compared with some 40,000 British settlers in New England. The population of Acadia (an area covering much of the Maritime Provinces) was less than 400, mostly at Port Royal and vulnerable to English sea power. It was Louis XIV who decided to save his overseas possessions and in 1665 sent ships and troops to anchor below the Rock at Québec. By introducing a Sovereign Council composed of a governor, a bishop and an intendant with four local residents, Louis' chief minister, Colbert, laid the foundation for a permanent colonial bureaucracy responsible to the king.

Under this new regime, the governor, as administrative head, was responsible for military matters; the bishop found that moral welfare required political action; and the intendant had to deal with economic, financial and judicial affairs. The colony became fact.

During the next 30 years, state-aided immigration and subsidized industrial development led to expansion, largely due, it is true, to intendant Jean Talon, whose prime consideration was to increase the population. Marriage therefore became a duty and those who stayed single were penalized. Shipments of 'brides' arrived and by the end of the century, Talon had achieved what he had set out to do — the population had risen to 7000; the amount of cultivated land had doubled; and new industries had been launched. Even the foundations of a Canadian clergy were laid by Francois de Laval, whose seminary at Québec was later to become the University of Laval. Bishop de Laval

was too autocratic and puritanical not to have opposition and in this case it was Louis de Buade, Comte de Frontenac. Historians refer to Frontenac as Canada's most arrogant, bad tempered governor. His name has certainly lingered on.

New France at this time used the seigneurial system, developed by Talon whereby a *seigneur* (or squire) was granted a plot of land, looked after his tenants and was expected to build up a local community. The tenants could divide their land up among their children so that as time went by, the strips became narrower and narrower and more and more crowded with tiny houses. Also at this time, the adventurous fur trappers moved further and further into the backwoods as their prey retreated west, while French explorers and *coureurs du bois* cut new pathways over the Great Shield.

While the French were moving into Canada, the British, of course, were moving into America in even greater numbers, There were a number of border raids and counter raids between the two between 1688 and 1713, but of little consequence. For example, William Phips may have destroyed Port Royal in 1690 but failed to capture Québec in the same year. There were fights over Hudson and James Bay territory with the result that by 1713 only Fort Albany on James Bay remained in British hands. The Treaty of Utrecht regained the Bay for the British and ceded them Acadia. Port Royal became Annapolis Royal, but the new province of Nova Scotia received scant attention. Only in 1749 was Halifax established to keep an eye on Cape Breton Island where the fortress at Louisbourg guarded the mouth of the St Lawrence.

Aware of a potential British threat, the French built a chain of forts and military posts, at Niagara and elsewhere, gradually extending west. They were right to do so for William Pitt's objective was to destroy French power in North America. He envisioned a three-pronged attack: in Ohio country against Fort Duquesne, then to the St Lawrence Valley via Forts Niagara and Frontenac; in the center up the Lake Champlain route where Crown Point and Ticonderoga guarded the way to Montréal; and in the east to knock out Louisbourg in order to reach Québec. Duquesne and Niagara duly fell, opening the west to English enterprise. A costly defeat at Ticonderoga was a setback but in 1758 Louisbourg fell, opening the way to Québec, an operation that terminated on the Plains of Abraham in September of 1759 with victory for the British and the death of both the British general, Wolfe and the French general, Montcalm.

Replica of Cartier's ship

This was not the end of New France, however. In turn, General James Murray's garrison was beseiged by French forces and only the 1760 British relief squadron prevented surrender. Finally Murray and Amherst took Montréal and the Treaty of Paris in 1763 gave Britain everything east of the Mississippi save New Orleans.

For several years, the new military governors made no attempt to change the French Canadian situation. When Murray became the first head of civil government in the new province of Québec in 1764, he shelved the notion of a legislative assembly as unfit for a community whose Catholic electorate under English law would be at the mercy of a minority of Protestant merchants. He and his successor insisted that French laws and customs should be protected, yet as certain benefits of English commercial law became known, a hybrid developed, confusing to all.

To clear up the confusion, the Québec Act was passed in 1774, an act of expediency since there were rebellious murmurs to the south. When the American Revolution broke out, the French Canadians largely refused to have anything to do with it. But as a result of the war thousands of Loyalists flooded into Canada. For the more than 30,000 taking refuge in the Maritimes, there was no problem, they enjoyed traditional colonial self-government, but to the west it was a different situation. Those Loyalists who crossed into the St Lawrence Valley resented the restrictive constitutional system which had only been established to pacify a conquered people. The French Canadians already there certainly did not take too kindly to this new wave of fiercely loyal British immigrants demanding their accustomed liberties. It was the start of racial duality.

In 1791, the Constitutional Act tried to provide a solution by creating two separate provinces: Upper Canada and Lower Canada, separated by the Ottawa River. Each was given an elected assembly with the power to make its own law. In Upper Canada, credit goes to John Graves Simcoe, the first Lieutenant-Governor, who made York (Toronto) the capital and started building two great roads, one to Lake Simcoe and one to Montréal. Upper Canada also saw a steady flow of farmers and speculators arrive from the US in search of cheap land, eyeing it as future United States territory. By 1812, 80 per cent of the population of Upper Canada had come from the US and of these three-quarters were of non-Loyalist descent.

The United States design on Canada led to the inconclusive War of 1812. The War did not actually create a national Canadian consciousness but it did confirm Canada's tie with Britain rather than with the United States. On the other hand there were reformers who felt shut out from the privileges of the ruling cliques (known as the 'Family Compact'). Conflicts between the two led to rebellion in 1837 in both Upper and Lower Canada. Though they did not reach dangerous levels, the disturbances led to Britain's re-examination of colonial government vis-à-vis supreme authority in Westminster and finally the Great Reform Bill of 1832 set Canada on the way to becoming a classic experiment in self-government. Lord Durham, sent out to investigate the disturbances, recommended the two provinces be joined and this was done in 1840 with the Act of Union.

Problems continued as the French Canadians watched the English-speaking population increase and eventually surpass them in numbers. While they tried to protect themselves with complicated legislation, the English became more aggressive and by 1864, Parliament had ceased to function. This and the fear of invasion again due to the American Civil War, led to the British North America Act being passed in 1867 creating a Canadian Confederation of Ontario and (now separated) Québec, Nova Scotia and New Brunswick. Prince Edward Island entered the Confederation in 1873 but Newfoundland did not join until 1949.

Canadian participation in the First World War helped the nation to gain international recognition though at home there were still racial strains. Once the war was over, Prime Minister Sir Robert Borden insisted on membership in the Peace Conference, leading to a seat in the new League of Nations and the right of membership in the council.

During the 1920s and 30s, despite suffering the same turbulence the rest of the western world was experiencing, there was intense exploration in northern Ontario and development of natural and mineral resources. And a new boom took place after the Second World War. Immigration was encouraged once more and all types of people found a new home in Eastern Canada.

Today in Ontario, Toronto has become *the* financial and arts center. Orchards cover the Niagara Peninsula and in southwest Ontario there is some of the most productive agricultural land in Canada, while Québec, Canada's largest province, has historical Québec City and the international, cosmopolitan city of Montréal. Eastern Canada also boasts the national capital of Ottawa, the wilds of Newfoundland, and the holiday beaches and conference centers of the Maritime Provinces.

PASSPORTS AND PAPERWORK

Passports A valid passport is necessary for all UK visitors to Canada. No visa is required if the stay will be less than 3 months. If the visit will be for less than 3 months only a British Visitors Passport is needed. Visitors from other countries may also require a visa. US citizens and permanent residents do not require either passport or visa though they may be asked for proof of their status, *eg:* birth certificate, voter's certificate or Alien Registration Card. Travelers who are under 18 and not accompanied by an adult need a letter of permission to travel in Canada from a parent or guardian.

Customs regulations allow personal effects duty free including 1.1 litres/40 oz spirits or fortified wine or 8.2 litres/288 oz beer or ale plus 200 cigarettes, 50 cigars, and 0.9 kg/2 lb tobacco. Gifts of up to C$40 value may be brought in duty free. No plant material may be imported.

Sporting equipment may be imported free of charge providing it is declared at entry point. The same is true of rifles and fishing tackle.

Insurance Visitors should ensure that they are adequately insured for health, accidents and motoring before they leave home. If current policies do not cover travel to Canada, extra insurance should be taken out. This is especially true for UK visitors who will find medical services in Canada (while excellent) extremely costly. The British National Health Service does not cover medical care in Canada though doctors may be easily found by consulting hospitals or hotels. Those on prescribed medicines should take sufficient supplies with them or at the very least a copy of the original prescription in case renewal is necessary.

CURRENCY

The unit of currency in Canada is the Canadian dollar (C$) which is divided into 100 cents. Coins are issued as 1, 5, 10, 25 and 50 cent pieces plus one dollar in coin form. Notes come in denominations of 1 dollar, 2, 5, 10, 20, 50, 100, 500 and 1000 dollars.

The US dollar is currently worth more than the Canadian dollar but may be used for purchases when the difference will be given in Canadian change. Dollar travelers checks are the best bet for Europeans as sterling cash or travelers checks may not be exchanged everywhere.

Banks are to be found at airports and in cities. Normal hours are 1000-1500 Mon.-Fri. In some cases, there are extended hours on Thurs. and Fri., and in further cases, on Sat. At many transportation centers, there are exchanges which stay open almost 24 hours. Most transportation centers and most banks have an international exchange facility, as do some travel bureaux and hotels. Canada's largest foreign banknote broker is the Bank of Canada.

GETTING THERE

Almost all the provinces have an international airport for flights from Europe and/or the US. Getting there by sea is less easy since the major liners only make the occasional visit to Canada and ferry service to Yarmouth from the US is only available in summer. Travellers from the US can easily get to Canada via car or bus.

By Air

From the UK Air Canada provides scheduled year-round service to Gander, Halifax, Montréal, Ottawa and Toronto. British Airways has year-round scheduled service to Montréal and Toronto ex UK. Both airlines offer classes of seating with a range of fares. CP Air is the scheduled airline arm of the Canadian Pacific Corporation with departures from Amsterdam's Schiphol Airport to Halifax, Toronto and Montréal.

Wardair offers charter and scheduled service from the UK to Montréal and Ottawa from May-Oct., and year round to Toronto out of London Gatwick and May-Oct. to Toronto from Birmingham, Newcastle and Stansted and March-Jan. to Toronto from Manchester and Prestwick. A number of charter flight brokers also offer flights to Canada: Airplan to Toronto, April-Oct.; Border Travel Service to Toronto from Prestwick, April-Oct.; Chieftain Tours to Toronto from Belfast, Dublin and Shannon, April-Oct.; Enterprise Travel to Toronto from Belfast, April-Oct.; Globespan to Montréal, Ottawa and Toronto, from London, Manchester and Prestwick, May-Nov.; Jetsave to Montréal and Toronto from Manchester, London and Prestwick, year-round; Ulster Maple Leaf Travel to Montréal and Toronto from Belfast, April-Oct.

From the US Air Canada serves Halifax out of Boston, Los Angeles and New York; Ottawa from Chicago and Los Angeles; Montréal from Chicago, Los Angeles, Miami and Tampa; Saint John, New Brunswick from Boston; and Toronto from Boston, Chicago, Dallas, Houston and New York. Other major airlines with services from the US to Canada East include Eastern, American Airlines, US Air and Delta.

Airports The two main airports for British visitors are Toronto and Montréal. The Lester B. Pearson International Airport in Toronto is 29 km / 18 mi from downtown with a journey time of about half an hour when there is no rush-hour traffic. Taxis are costly — the most economical way is the airport bus which makes stops at major hotels. Courtesy minibus service is offered by hotels in the airport vicinity. Mirabel International Airport in Montréal is 53 km / 33 mi from the city center with a journey time of about an hour. Taxi fares are exorbitant — an express bus service is offered to the main bus terminal by the Queen Elizabeth Hotel. US Citizens fly into Dorval International Airport. (There is a shuttle service between the two.)

By Sea

Polish Ocean Lines has some departures to Montréal from Gdynia via Rotterdam and London six times a year from April to October.

By Bus

Greyhound and Trailways have frequent services from US cities to Montréal and Toronto as well as inclusive tour packages. It is also possible to travel by train to

Canada from the US.

Inclusive Tours

A number of companies feature inclusive holidays to Canada with escorted and unescorted itineraries, city packages, fly/drive programs etc. Specialists in Canada belong to CHTA (Canadian Holidays and Travel Associates), which was formed in 1977. They include: Albany Travel, All Canada Travel & Holidays, Canada Air Holidays, Caravan Abroad, Chieftain Tours, Thomas Cook, Discover Canada, Jetlink, Jetsave, National Holidays, Sonicworld and Trekamerica.

GETTING AROUND

Canada has a well organized transportation network that works efficiently so getting around the provinces is easy. Modern highways, scheduled and charter air service, rail and ferry links are all well geared to the traveler.

By Air

Internal air services are provided by three national airlines, five regional carriers and some 75 local service carriers providing a variety of scheduled and charter flights. The three national carriers are Air Canada, CP Air and Wardair. The main internal carrier for Atlantic Canada is Eastern Provincial Airways, for other parts of Eastern Canada there is Nordair, Ontario Air and Québecair.

By Rail

VIA Rail operates extensive passenger services across Canada and some of the routes are particularly scenic. Long distance trains are very comfortable with observation and dining cars, sleepers, reclining seats and picture windows. There is also good inter-city service between such cities as Québec, Toronto and Montréal.

VIA's 'Fare for all Plan' covers several schemes including Canrailpass which gives unlimited travel for a specified period at a fixed rate. The UK agent for VIA Rail is Thomas Cook.

By Ferry

Ferry services are not only a means of getting from destination to destination, but also add an extra scenic dimension. From the US, there are border crossings from Bal Harbour, Maine, to Yarmouth, Nova Scotia, and Portland, Maine to Yarmouth. Central Canada ferry service is available from Matane, Québec, to Baie Comeau, Québec; Matane to Godbout, Québec; Rivière du Loup, Québec to St Siméon, Québec; Trois Pistoles, Québec to Les

Escoumins, Québec; Tobermory, Ontario, to South Baymouth, Manitoulin Is., Ontario. In Atlantic Canada, ferries operate between Cape Tormentine, New Brunswick, and Borden, Prince Edward Island; Caribou, Nova Scotia, and Wood Island, Prince Edward Island; Digby, Nova Scotia, and Saint John, New Brunswick; North Sydney, Nova Scotia, and Argentia, Newfoundland; North Sydney, Nova Scotia, and Port aux Basques, Newfoundland.

By Boat

Eastern Canada's lakes and waterways lend themselves to a boating holiday. Craft may be rented at innumerable marinas and at a number of lakeside resorts short cruises are possible. Canoeing and rafting are equally readily available, and can often be combined with a camping trip.

The major waterways are in Ontario: the **Rideau Canal** was built in 1826 to provide a safe water route from Ottawa to Kingston in the event of another war between Britain and the United States. It was not actually completed until 1832 by which time it was no longer required for its original purpose. Today, this canal connects Ottawa with Kingston and is one of the most picturesque parts of Ottawa city. It is one of the Heritage Canals with a navigational season from mid-May to mid-October. Houseboats and cruisers may be rented for use on the Rideau.

St Lawrence Seaway Canada's early settlers, traders and trappers depended upon the original St Lawrence river route. The St Lawrence Seaway opened on 26 June 1959, finally allowing ocean-going vessels to bypass the rapids that formerly impeded progress between Montréal and Prescott in Ontario. Craft of less than six meters/20 ft long or 1000 kg/1 ton in weight are not permitted in this seaway's locks.

Georgian Bay is an incredibly beautiful resort area mainly for big boats. It has its own national park, Georgian Bay Islands National Park. For trailered boats, try the stretch from Port Severn to Parry Sound.

The **Trent-Severn Waterway** meanders for 384 km/239 mi from Trenton on Lake Ontario to Port Severn on Georgian Bay. It is navigable from mid-May to mid-October. There are 44 locks and also excellent fishing and lovely scenery. Minimum navigable depth is 1.83 meters/six feet. Houseboats and cruisers may be rented for use on this waterway.

The **Great Lakes** provide excellent boating. In addition to the major ports, there are many small harbors with good facilities for pleasure craft.

Lake of the Woods has a shoreline that twists for 104,000 km/65,000 mi and is dotted with thousands of islands. Ideal for the boating enthusiast who brings his trailered craft or rents a houseboat or power boat. Launching ramps, cranes and berths are all available.

By Road

Eastern Canada is well served with bus lines, many of which offer stop-over privileges. Besides Greyhound, major companies for Atlantic Canada are Acadian Lines in Halifax, Nova Scotia; Terra Transport Roadcruiser Service in St John's, Newfoundland; SMT (Eastern) Ltd., in Saint John, New Brunswick. In Central Canada there are Canada Coach Lines, Hamilton, Ontario; Charterways, London, Ontario; Gray Coach Lines, Toronto, Ontario; Travelways, Lindsay, Ontario; Voyageur, Montréal, Québec; Voyageur Colonial, Ottawa, Ontario.

Car and camper rental is readily available (see *If You Are Driving*) and all roads are clearly marked by the individual provincial highway authority and each bears its provincial road number. The finest highway of them all is the Trans-Canada Highway which crosses the country from Victoria, British Columbia to St John's, Newfoundland for 8000 km/5000 mi, and is marked throughout by a maple leaf emblem.

Rideau Canal locks, Ottawa

City Travel

Montréal and Toronto are both served by good public transportation — buses and metro. One of the best ways to get around the old quarter of Québec City is by *calèche* (horse-drawn carriage). Taxis operate in all cities and at all airports. You can phone for one or find one at a taxi stand. In Montréal and Toronto, one ticket pays for travel on bus and/or metro.

IF YOU ARE DRIVING

Accidents In the case of an accident, call the Canadian Automobile Association. Or dial the operator 'O' and ask for a specific service. *NB* Québec offers no-fault insurance but Ontario does not.

Breakdown Call the CAA. Major cities have a branch office of this association, *eg:* the Montréal Motoring Club.

Car Rental is easily available throughout Canada. Major companies like Hertz and Avis or Budget have desks at airports and in the cities but there are also local companies listed in the phone books. Almost all offer special deals and packages depending on rental duration and time of year. Minimum age is 21. Driving is on the right.

First Aid Stations are clearly posted along Ontario highways.

Gasoline Regular unleaded and premium unleaded gas are sold at service stations, most of which will accept credit cards. There are no standard hours — some may close at 1900, some may be open 24 hours, but watch out for Sunday closings. In remote areas stations often close on weekends and in many communities opening hours are on a rotation basis. Remember gas is sold in litres, with about 4 litres to one US gallon.

License A valid driver's license from any country is good for driving in Canada for any period up to three months. US citizens driving across the border need to bring with them a Non-Resident Insurance Card available from the insurance agent, or the policy itself. Drivers of rental cars coming across the border need a copy of the rental contract with them.

Police Municipal and provincial forces patrol highways and other areas, in Ontario and Québec. Each city has a separate police number listed in public phone booths. Or dial 'O' and ask for the police.

Restrictions Seat belts must be worn at all times by adults and children. Windshields and side-front windows must allow a clear view of the vehicle's interior. Studded tires are forbidden, from about April-Nov.

Road conditions Information on road conditions is available from the Road Information Centre in Toronto, (416) 248-3561 all year round, as well as from district offices listed on Ontario's Official Road Map. Each province has its own travel centers.

Speed Limits for controlled access highways are 90-100 kph/55-62 mph, other highways 80 kph/50 mph, urban and other populated areas 40-60 kph/25-37 mph or as posted.

Tolls are charged at international bridges, tunnels and ferries. Ontario's and Québec's highways are toll-free.

Rules of the Road for camping vehicles A recreational vehicle may not be more than 4 m/$13\frac{1}{2}$ ft high, 2.5 m/$8\frac{1}{2}$ ft wide. The combined maximum length of car plus recreational vehicle must not exceed 19 m/65 ft.

All recreational vehicles must be fitted with:

a safety chain to couple trailer with towing vehicle,

a breakaway switch if a trailer weighs more than 1200 kg/3000 lb gross,

and flares must be carried in case of an emergency by all travel trailers, motorhomes or disabled drivers traveling on highways. One to be displayed in front of the vehicle, and one behind. As an alternative, a red emergency reflector, lighted fuse or electric red lantern may be used.

A licence plate light is necessary.

A braking system, either hand operated or electric must be used with trailers with a gross weight of 1600 kg/4000 lb.

Mounted seats, riding in a towed vehicle is prohibited, it is permitted in a truck camper if equipped with permanent mounted seats.

Automatic safety valve No gas or oil appliance may be used when a trailer is in motion unless equipped with an automatic safety valve capable of shutting off gas or oil.

Mirrors If the trailer obscures the driver's rear vision, towing mirrors must be attached to the driver's car.

ACCOMMODATIONS

Hotels/Motels There is no shortage of hotel accommodations in Eastern Canada, the most densely populated part of Canada and standards are very high. The choice in price and style is particularly evident in major cities like Ottawa, Montréal and Toronto where large establishments cater to business guests and conference delegates as well as holiday-makers. In the cities, you will find big chain names like Hilton, Sheraton, Holiday Inn and Canada's own top notch hotel company names: Four Seasons, CN Hotels and CP Hotels.

A number of the CP Hotels are old landmark hotels with the appearance of a château, *eg:* the Château Frontenac in Québec City and the Royal York in Toronto. Most of the chains have UK representation or maintain their own European reservations offices as well as those in the US.

Several holiday companies and hotel groups operate their own voucher schemes whereby you can pre-pay for your accommodation but do not necessarily have to specify dates. Canadapass is another example — purchased with any Air Canada ticket, it entitles the user to stay at designated accommodation on the day of his choice. If the hotel is full, other accommodation at a similar hotel accepting the voucher, will be offered.

Rates at large hotels are more likely to be on a room-only basis than anything else, though some will include breakfast. In resort or country areas, they may be half board or M.A.P. as it is called (breakfast and dinner). These days it is difficult to find full board or American Plan rates. Tax and services vary with the province.

Motels are abundant along Eastern Canada's highways and in some cases may be referred to as 'motor hotels'. Generally speaking, rates are lower than those of hotels.

There is no national classification of hotels in Canada but some provinces, including Ontario, Québec and Nova Scotia, operate their own rating. For instance, Ontario gives all its members a special 'Recommended' logo sign and awards a star grade from one to five. Basically, wherever there is star grading you can expect the following standards.

* Clean and comfortable but only designed to meet basic requirements with no or only limited guest services.
** Better than minimum requirements with limited range of services.
*** Reasonable accommodation and services.
**** Superior accommodation and amenities.
***** Deluxe accommodation and a full, complete range of services and facilities.

Inns What Canada calls an inn bears little relation to an English inn; instead, it is more like the American variety, and therefore larger than expected. Most inns are located in resort regions like Ontario's Muskoka Lakes and can be quite plush.

Bed & Breakfast has become increasingly popular though the British-style guest house is hard to find in the cities. There are guest houses in Ontario and Québec's resort areas and the Maritimes. There is also farmhouse accommodation, primarily in Ontario and those Atlantic provinces, such as Prince Edward Island, where farming is very strong.

Self-Catering Cities like Toronto do have some executive apartments available for short or long-term rental, mostly for the business market. The Canadian term for 'self-catering' is a 'housekeeping cottage', but they are few and far between for holiday rentals. You will find some in the resort areas, especially in Ontario. Log cabins cannot be rented.

Youth Hostels are to be found in Canada. They are listed in the International Youth Hostellers Handbook, published annually each spring, or are listed in each province's accommodation booklet.

Camping Outdoor living is very much an element of Canadian life and there are literally hundreds of campsites in and out of National and Provincial parks. A list of campgrounds may be obtained from each province's tourist office or from tourist information offices within Canada. While campground maintenance standards are high, camping in Canada is more geared to wilderness lovers than to campers expecting luxury touches.

FOOD AND DRINK

I suppose if there were three foodstuffs associated worldwide with Canada, they would be salmon, bacon and maple syrup. And how right the world would be. A proper Canadian breakfast is very likely to comprise pancakes with bacon (or sausages) and authentic maple syrup.

As for salmon, it comes fresh or smoked but in such a country where fishing is a major sport, seafood of all kinds makes for a splendid feast. The inland rivers, lakes

Pancake breakfast, Québec City

and streams provide good trout and the Atlantic coast has always been known for its excellent cod and lobster.

In the Maritime Provinces especially, you can expect top quality seafood, and plenty of fish stews and brews. Lobster dinners are a big attraction in Prince Edward Island especially and that does not mean skipping the steamed clams and seafood chowder! P.E.I. is also noted for its potatoes. Lobster was so plentiful in this part of Eastern Canada that it used to be considered a staple foodstuff for the poor and some of today's adults still remember when it was a little humiliating to have to take a *lobster* roll to school for their lunch!

Each center has its own culinary specialties. No famous New Brunswick menu would be without fiddleheads, a local fern often incorporated into a soup or cooked in butter and served as a vegetable. Acadian cuisine has left its influence as well with *frictos* (meat stews), *poutines* and clam pies. In Acadian restaurants you can try hominy, corn which has been soaked for hours first in lye and then in water, or *rapure* which is generally made from shredded potatoes mixed with pork and chicken bits.

There are two major influences on food, French and American. Acadian is the old French, as is the Québecois cuisine which offers hearty pea soup, *tourtières* (meat pies) which are delicious, and *cipaille* (game pie). French cooking and the French love of food have given Québec City and Montréal (both in the province of Québec) a reputation for fine restaurants. Until recently when Toronto acquired a better image for restaurants, visitors who wanted to eat well went to Québec Province.

The US influence is obvious in the size of the portions, the ubiquitous fast food outlets and the first-rate beef. National dishes like buckwheat cakes, pumpkin pie and blueberry desserts almost sound American though I reckon maple sugar pie is Canadian through and through. Game is first class but tends to be cooked American style rather than British (*ie:* it is not hung first for some time).

An influx of European immigrants after the Second World War and more recently from the Orient have added a cosmopolitan flavor to the cities and Toronto in particular, which nowadays has ethnic pockets including a tiny Chinatown and Greek quarter. In such cities dining hours are later than in rural areas and Atlantic Canada. No longer do the sidewalks roll up at 10 pm. No longer is it just Montréal for the night owls.

For choice of restaurant, Montréal and Toronto are the best. These days, both have bistros and brasseries, elegent eating places which can be found in old town

houses, atop skyscrapers or in courtyards. Both cities also have cafés in the European style, as does Québec City, where lighter meals, a glass of wine or a special coffee or ice cream dessert are available and many are located outdoors. Favorite cafés are found in Québec's Old Quarter, Montréal's Place Jacques Cartier and Toronto's Yorkville.

Restaurants may or may not include a service charge, if so, it is usually 15 per cent; the better ones may have a cover charge besides. There are no specific licensing laws though the drinking age is 19 in Ontario, New Brunswick, Newfoundland and Nova Scotia, 18 in Québec and Prince Edward Island. Throughout Eastern Canada, you will find taverns, bars, cocktail lounges and pubs. *NB* women are excluded by law from taverns in Québec.

Canadian beer tends to be stronger than US beer — among the most popular brands are Molson's and Labatt's. Wine has always been favoured in Québec province but in recent years its popularity has increased throughout the country. Local wines have been improved to meet demands — one of the best known is Inniskillen.

Because of its soil and climatic conditions, most vineyards are situated in Ontario, especially in the Niagara Peninsula where the Niagara Escarpment affords wind protection and Lakes Erie and Ontario modify temperatures. The traditional Labrusca grapes are nowadays less favored due to the fashion for drinking a dryer wine.

Although wine making can be traced back to the Indians, a German, Johann Schiller who started making wine in the 1800s, is recognized as the province's first commercial winemaker. Canadian wines were recognized abroad shortly after Canada became a nation in 1867 but the oldest existing wine company in Ontario is Barnes, dating to 1873.

Perhaps I should just mention the 'oddities' in Newfoundland and Labrador. After all, it is not so surprising that in a province which gives its towns names like Jerry's Nose and Come-by-Chance, the food might comprise Squid Delight, Cod Tongues and Seal Flipper Pie! A few years ago, hotels and restaurants in this province were asked to include at least one typically Newfoundland meal on their menus. So do ask for Fish and Brewis, Rabbit soup, and Screech Marinated Chicken. Many dishes cannot be copied elsewhere because the ingredients are not available, so also keep an eye out for moose meat soup, fried cod tongues and partridgeberry pudding!

Canoeing in Algonquin Park

ENJOY YOURSELF

Beaches It goes without saying there are lakeside and island beaches in Eastern Canada — Torontarians, for example, spend summer days on the Toronto Islands in Lake Ontario and on the lakeshore in The Beaches. But the best beaches without a doubt, are those surrounding the Atlantic Provinces. Nowhere in Nova Scotia is further than 56 km/35 mi from the sea and there is a whole coastal region of secluded beaches and coves. New Brunswick's beaches tend to be underused but there are some good ones. Best of all, are Prince Edward Island's 800 km/ 500 mi of beaches which curve round the island and include white and red sand.

Boating is a popular pastime throughout this area of Canada. Rentals run the range from sailboats to houseboats and Ontario publishes its own booklet on boating whys and wherefores. (*See Useful Addresses.*) In many resort areas, there are also sightseeing cruises.

Canoeing is possible in a variety of areas. A list of outfitters may be obtained from any of the travel centers in each province. Northern Ontario, Newfoundland and Labrador are especially good canoeing destinations. Canoe trips are often packaged with wilderness camp trips and most of the national and provincial parks have canoe trails, *eg:* in Ontario the Pukaskwa River in Pukaskwa National Park; the Kejimkujik National Park in Nova Scotia and Kouchibouguac National Park in New Brunswick.

Climbing is possible in most of the national and provincial parks.

Cycling Bike rentals are available in most of the parks. You do not need a special licence to ride a bike but the bike must be equipped with an audible bell and the same regulations for motorists apply to cyclists — *eg:* keep to the right, signal your intentions and observe the 'stop' and 'yield' signs.

Fishing can be as diverse as you like, and the unspoilt parks are ideal for this sport. In the rivers and lakes you might angle for Atlanic salmon, perch, doré, bass or trout. Deep sea fishing is an exciting alternative with perhaps a catch of bluefin tuna though cod and mackerel are more likely. All of Atlantic Canada is excellent for fishing with a special mention for Conception Bay in Newfoundland. In the far north of Ontario and Québec there are fly-in fishing camps. A license is required for angling and is obtainable from most sporting goods stores, fly-in camps and offices of the Ministry of Natural Resources. A license is not necessary for deep sea fishing when you are part of a charter boat party.

Golf Nowhere will you find so many golf courses with a water view (without the water traps) than Prince Edward Island which boasts seven 18-hole and three 9-hole courses. Best are Green Gables and Brudenell. In Nova Scotia, golfing is best at the resorts, notably Liscombe Lodge, The Pines at Digby and Keltic Lodge. Ontario and Québec both have a plethora of golf courses — a list may be obtained from tourist centers.

Hiking There are countless hiking trails signposted in the parks. In Algonquin National Park alone, the Highland Hiking Trail feaures 19 km/11.8 mi and 35 km/ 21.8 mi of loops while the Western Uplands Hiking Trail has 32 km/20 mi, 55 km/34.3 mi and 71 km/44.3 mi of loops. There are unlimited hiking opportunities in Fundy National Park and one of the best ways to explore Terra Nova National Park is on foot. Some of the hiking trails in Cape Breton Highlands National Park lead to the beaches, and some to good fishing areas and in Kejimkujik National Park there are more than 100 km/62.5 mi of trails. Pukaskwa, too, is hiking country with a 68 km/42.5 mi coastal trail and Forillon National Park is another one for hikers.

Hockey Ice hockey is the Canadian national sport, and it is played almost literally everywhere in winter. The best places to watch the game are at The Forum in Montréal and Maple Leaf Gardens in Toronto.

Hunting A license is required for hunting but this is a sport which may be enjoyed in many of the wilderness regions in Eastern Canada. Each province has its own licensing requirements and the hunting of migratory birds is restricted by the federal government. Bag limits for small game and birds are generous but larger game is strictly limited. Game hunting is possible in Prince Edward Island which has an open season from early October to mid-December. In Labrador there is an open season for hunting moose, caribou and bears. There are fly-in camps for hunting in northern Ontario and Québec. New Brunswick is popular for hunting woodcock and deer. Each province publishes a list of outfittters. Provincial fish and game offices, such as Québec's Department of Recreation, Fish and Game, should be contacted for further information. Provincial tourist offices will also supply details of hunting restrictions and practices.

Riding/Racing There are riding trails in many of the parks and resorts plus stables where you can rent horses. For harness racing, Montréal's Blue Bonnets track operates year-round. The stables here, by the way, are an attraction in themselves, housing over 1000 horses — tours by appointment may be made in spring and summer. For a list of stables in any particular area, look at tourist publications and check the local yellow pages.

Swimming In addition to salt water swimming, you will find pools and lakes in the parks for a refreshing dip. Top hotels also have their own swimming pools and health clubs.

Tennis Resort hotels usually have their own tennis courts and quite often there are public courts in the parks. But as with the US, where enthusiasm for tennis has increased recently, most tennis facilities are 'clubs'. Some will welcome visitors as temporary members — ask at your hotel.

Winter Sports Ontario is big on cross-country skiing. For instance, when Georgian Bay freezes over in winter, cross-country skiers, snowshoers and snowmobilers may reach their favorite winter camping spot this way. Forillon and La Mauricie National Parks have snowshoe and cross-country ski trails. For alpine skiing, Québec is the province. The Laurentians region (where there are many first class lodges) is one of the most popular areas. For information, contact the Conseil Québecois du Ski, 4545 Ave. Pierre-de-Coubertin, C.P. 1000, Station 'M', Montréal, Québec H1V 3R2, tel: (514) 252 3089. For a snow report, call 873 2015 from Montréal or 1 800 361 5405 from anywhere else in Québec.

ENTERTAINMENT

Canada is not exactly the world's hot spot when it comes to entertainment. Gambling is illegal and you will not find many Follies-style showgirls or sequin-studded revues. In rural areas, there is little nightlife but in the last decade city sparkle has become evident. It is most notable in Montréal and Toronto, where there are clubs for jazz, discos, bars with music and first class cultural programs.

Clubs and Discos are not located in any distinct area other than in major hotels. Well known Toronto discos include Jacqui's at the Harbour Castle Hotel and Misty's at the Toronto Airport Hilton. The plus factor at Sparkles is its location atop the CN Tower but other recommendations include Copa in Yorkville. Toronto has several jazz clubs and in Montréal there are several around Place Jacques Cartier and on Crescent St as well as in the immense shopping malls and luxury hotels.

In Halifax, Nova Scotia, Misty Moon and The Palace are both large cabaret clubs and Argyle St is the place for 'Singles' bars. Outside of the capital cities in the Maritime provinces, late night hours are not kept.

Cinemas are to be found in all the cities, most especially in the shopping malls like Toronto's Eaton Centre and Montréal's Place Bonaventure. In some parts of Québec films will be in French. Toronto is Canada's film centre, there is also an annual film festival in Montréal.

Dinner Theater is popular throughout

Canada. You either eat first then watch an amusing musical cabaret, as in Toronto's Old Firehall — a city landmark, or actors improvise on a theme during dinner as happens at Brothers Two Restaurant in Charlottetown, P.E.I. A fixed price pays for the meal and entertainment but drinks are extra.

Music can be heard in all its forms. Piano bars are very much in evidence in and out of city hotels; other bars have jazz combos. Usually there is no cover charge or minimum. Both Montréal and Toronto have a Symphony Orchestra — the home for Toronto's orchestra is the magnificent Roy Thomson Hall. Opera and ballet may also be enjoyed in season and Toronto's O'Keefe Centre is one of the best venues for both.

Theater The main cities for good theater are Ottawa, Montréal and Toronto. Remember that many productions in French Canada will be given in French. Pre-Broadway tryouts tend to take place in Toronto's O'Keefe Centre and that city's most outstanding theater is the Alexandra, rescued from the bulldozers by discount tycoon Ed Mirvish and restored to its former grandeur. Place des Arts is Montréal's prime cultural complex.

Summer theatre is most successful at Niagara-on-the-Lake and Charlottetown P.E.I. where Anne of Green Gables is presented annually in the Confederation Centre of the Arts. There is also, of course, the world famous Stratford Festival every summer in Ontario.

Folk Festivals are prevalent in country areas, and often include square dancing, fiddle playing and singing. They frequently revolve around a seasonal food — strawberries or blueberries, the collection of maple syrup or oyster shucking and in the Maritimes have an added Scotttish flavor.

SHOPPING

It is the shopping malls rather than what you can buy that makes Eastern Canada unique, for many of them are underground and linked so that whatever the weather you do not have to know about it. Montréal, with its subterranean world of shops, offices *etc* has always been called 'The City Below', an answer both to ground-level congestion and the winter freeze. Since the metro connects giant underground complexes, you have easy access to thousands of stores, restaurants, bars, cinemas, hotels, railway stations, the main bus terminal, art galleries, theaters and the Olympic Park complex. Thanks to high ceilings, pleasing and

Eaton Centre

colorful decorations, greenery and masses of lights, the whole thing is bright and airy — not at all claustrophobic and depressing. *The* complexes to head for are **Place Ville-Marie, Place Bonaventure** and **Complexe Desjardins** but do not forget to visit **Les Terrasses.**

Toronto is also weather-proof when it comes to shopping. For the most part, this 'underground city' is located through and underneath four skyscrapers: the Bank of Montréal, Toronto-Dominion Bank, Canadian Imperial Bank of Commerce and the Royal Bank. (You have to come up for air on only a couple of occasions.) The most famous complex is Eaton Centre, home to the major department store Eaton's, and linked to Simpsons. The 860 ft Galleria, which was patterned after Milan's celebrated showplace, houses over 300 stores, restaurants and boutiques on several levels.

The Lanes is a mall that runs under the Sheraton Centre Hotel, northwards to New City Hall and south to Adelaide St. Inside the Bank of Montréal (First Canadian Place), there are more shops and a protective route to the Royal York Hotel and Union Station. The TD Centre has a variety of boutiques and an underground walkway leads south to the Royal Bank whose lower mall takes you to a sunken garden encircled by more stores. Alongside the TD Centre, the Canadian Imperial Bank of Commerce houses its own Commerce Court shopping mall. Ottawa has the famous Sparks Street pedestrian mall and in Halifax there is the Historic Properties area, also pedestrianised.

Furs, sheepskins and leathers are probably the best Canadian buy but crafts are also a fun souvenir. Look out for carvings and in Atlantic Canada, Acadian handmade items. Travellers from the US may well find savings on British china and crystal and other British-made goods.

ALL YOU NEED TO KNOW

Chemists/Drugstores may be called pharmacies in French Canada. Hours of opening vary depending upon whether the area is urban or rural. In major cities you will find at least one drugstore open until 2 am.

Churches For attendance check the local paper within each province for the nearest church. *NB* in Québec the main religion is RC.

Climate Given the land mass of both Québec and Ontario, temperatures can vary by district. Generally it is pleasantly hot though humid in summer in both Toronto and Montréal, up to around 26°C/78°F and bitterly cold in winter, down to around −6°C/21°F. Atlantic Canada tends to be more temperate year-round.

Consulates/Embassies There are consulates in Toronto and Montréal. Embassies are located in Ottawa. (*See Useful Addresses* p. 19.)

Drinking age is 19 years old in Ontario, 18 in Québec. In Ontario the licensing hours are commonly 1100-0100 Mon.-Sat. and noon-2300, Sun. Cocktail lounges are generally closed on Sun. Licensing is less strict in Québec.

Health insurance is strongly recommended. Tourism centers and hotels will help find you a doctor, or dentist. Each center has its own emergency number for police, fire or ambulance which should be listed on all public booths. However it is just as simple to dial 'O' for the operator, wherever you are and request which emergency service you require.

Newspapers and magazines can be purchased from newsagents and kiosks in hotels and throughout cities. It is difficult to acquire a British newspaper but American ones are flown in daily. One of the biggest English-language dailies in Canada is the *Globe & Mail*. French language dailies include *la Presse*.

Postage Post office hours vary between cities and provinces. In Toronto, Postal Station A at 17 Front St., is open 0800-1100 on weekdays and 1000-1400 Sat. The main office in Montréal is at 715 Peel St, and is open 0800-1800 Mon.-Fri., 0900-1200 Sat.

Public Holidays are basically the same throughout Eastern Canada though in some cases some American public holidays are recognized, and in some cases, additional French ones. The following should be a guide: New Year's Day, Jan. 1, Jan. 2 (Q), Lincoln's Birthday (US), Washington's Birthday (US), Good Friday, Easter Sunday, Easter Monday, Victoria Day and Dollard des Ormeaux Day, 3rd Monday in May, Memorial Day (US), St-Jean Baptiste Day, June 24 (Q), Canada Day, July 1, Independence Day, July 4 (US), Labor Day, Thanksgiving, Oct., Columbus Day (US), Remembrance Day, Nov., Thanksgiving, Nov. (US), Christmas Eve, Christmas Day, Boxing Day, New Year's Eve.

Shops Shopping hours vary so much from town to town and province to province that it is best to check local papers, tourist publications *etc* for opening times.

Tax Each province has its own sales tax which is added to the price of certain goods and services.

Telephone Most public telephone booths are the kiosk variety. Bear in mind that more and more telephone booths in North America are operated by credit card. Each province has at least one facility for 24-hour telegrams and cables.

Tipping Most restaurants do not include a service charge so tipping anything from 12 per cent to 20 per cent is standard practice.

Visitor Services There are posted information centres throughout Eastern Canada which will provide information on every aspect of the area. In Toronto, additionally, visitors can use Teleguide terminals for free information on where to shop, eat, stay and what to do. They are located in hotel lobbies, shopping malls and in the information centres themselves.

FESTIVALS AND EVENTS

In Eastern Canada, any excuse is used for a party and there's no shortage of events

Winter Carnival Ice Palace, Québec City

which visitors can join in. Many revolve around sporting events though other annual festivals are set around the potato, lobster and other seafood, fruits *etc*. Most cities hold an annual winter carnival — of particular note are the Québec *Carnival* and Ottawa's *Winterlude*. Spring is the time for Nova Scotia's *Apple Blossom Festival*, Québec's *Maple Festival* in Plessisville and Ottawa's *Tulip Festival*. Summer is of course the busiest season with features like *Charlottetown Festival* (P.E.I.), the *Shaw Festival* at Niagara-on-the-Lake and the *Stratford Festival* in Ontario. In the autumn, there are schooner races off Halifax (N.S.) and the *Royal Horse Show* in Toronto.

Exact dates change with the year but major annual events include the following:

Ontario Winterlude Ottawa (Feb.), Shaw Festival (May-Oct.), Stratford Festival (June-Oct.), Canadian National Exhibition, Toronto (Aug./Sept.) Oktoberfest, Kitchener/Waterloo (Oct.).

Québec Québec City Winter Carnival (Feb.), Montréal International Jazz Festival (June/July), Québec City Summer Festival (July), Festival of the Snow Geese, Montmagny (Oct.).

New Brunswick Loyalist Days, Saint John (July), Acadian Festival, Caraquet (Aug.).

Prince Edward Island Charlottetown Festival (June-Sept.), Oyster Festival, Tyne Valley (Aug.).

Nova Scotia Annapolis Valley Apple Blossom Festival (May), Gathering of the Clans, Pugwash (June/July), Nova Scotia Gaelic Mod, St Ann's Cape Breton (Aug.).

Newfoundland Conception Bay Folk Festival (June), Signal Hill Tattoo, St John's (July/Aug.).

USEFUL ADDRESSES

Canada

Amex Canada Inc., 101 McNabb Street, Markham, Toronto (416-474-8000).

Bank of America Canada, 120 Adelaide Street, Toronto (416-360-8022).

British High Commission, 80 Elgin Street, Ottawa (613-237-1530).

Canadian Automobile Association, 1775 Courtwood Crescent, Ottawa, Ontario.

Canadian Govt., Office of Tourism, 235 Queen Street, Ottawa (613-996-4610).

Dept. of Tourism, Nova Scotia, PO Box 130, Halifax, N.S. (902-424 4247).

Ontario Travel, 900 Bay Street, Queen's Park, Toronto (800-268-3735).

P.E.I. Visitor Services, PO Box 940, Charlottetown, P.E.I. (902-892-2457).

Tourism New Brunswick, PO Box 12345, Fredericton, N.B. (506-453-2377).

Tourism Newfoundland, Dept. of Development, Box 2016, St. John's, Newfoundland (709-576-2830).

Tourism Québec, PO Box 20,000, Québec City (514-873-2015).

Tourist Information:

Montréal, 2 Place Ville-Marie (514-873-2308).

Québec City, 12 Rue Ste. Anne (418-643-2280).

Toronto, 220 Yonge Street (416-979-3143).

VIA Rail Canada, Box 8116, 2 Place Ville-Marie, Montréal PQ H3C 3N3.

USA

American Automobile Association (AAA), 8111 Gatehouse Road, Falls Church, Virginia 22047 (703-222-6000).

Amtrak, 400 North Capital Street, Washington DC 20001.

Canadian Consulates, Tourism Section:.

Chicago: 310 South Michigan Ave, 12th Floor, Chicago, Illinois 60604 (312-782-3760).

Dallas: Suite 1600, 2001 Bryan Tower, Dallas, Texas 75201 (214-742-8031).

Los Angeles: 510 West Sixth Street, L.A., California 90014 (213-622-1029).

New York: Exxon Building, Room 1030, 1251 Ave of The Americas, N.Y. New York 10020 (212-257-4917).

Washington DC: NAB Building, Suite 200, 1771 North Street, W. Washington DC 20036 (312-782-3760).

Greyhound Lines Inc., Greyhound Tower, Phoenix, Arizona 85077.

UK
Air Canada, 140/144 Regent Street, London W1 (01-759 2636).
British Airways, Speedbird House, Heathrow Airport (01-759 5511).
C.P. Air, 62/65 Trafalgar Square, London (01-930 5664).
Greyhound Bus Lines, 14/16 Cockspur Street, London (01-839 5591).
Tourism Canada, Canada House, Trafalgar Square, London (01-629 9492).
Tourism Nova Scotia, 14 Pall Mall, London (01-930 6864).
Tourism Ontario, Ontario House, 13 Charles II Street, London (01-930 4400).
Tourism Québec, 59 Pall Mall, London (01-930 8314).
Wardair, Rothschild House, Whitgift Centre, Croydon, Surrey (01-680 4281).

NATIONAL PARKS

Throughout Eastern Canada there are numerous recreational parks (provincial and otherwise), forests and preserves. The following, however, are designated National Parks:

Ontario
Georgian Bay Islands National Park can be reached northwest of Toronto via Highways 400, 69 and Muskoka Road 5. Basically the park comprises some 50 islands, which in summer can only be reached by water taxi, and in winter on skis. A noted beauty spot is Flowerpot Island but the largest island is Beausoleil where there are several campsites, an outdoor theater and self-guiding nature trails. This is also the center for interpretive programs.
Point Pelee National Park is not too far from Windsor and may be reached to the southeast on Highway 3. It is one of Canada's smallest and busiest National Parks and has no individual campsites, though accommodation is possible nearby in the Leamington vicinity. It is best known to bird watchers for the thousands of birds which arrive here in spring and autumn. A 1.5 km/0.9 mi boardwalk winds through marshland where you can see aquatic life and there are 25 km/15.6 mi of sandy beaches.
Pukaskwa National Park is situated on the northern shore of Lake Superior protecting a vast area of Canadian Shield wilderness. Within the rugged terrain there is a multitude of lakes and rivers and abundant wildlife. The Lake Superior coastline is its most notable feature. The only access to this park is by foot or boat and campsites are primitive. For adventurous canoeists and kayakers, the Pukaskwa River and White River are both challenging.
St Lawrence Islands National Park is situated between Kingston and Brockville on Highway 2. It is Canada's smallest national park and is located in the heart of the famed Thousand Islands region. (Until the area was flooded by the St Lawrence, these islands were hilltops.)

The park comprises some 17 islands and 80 rocky islets scattered along a scenic 80 km/50 mi stretch of the river, particularly beautiful in spring. The islands are only accessible by water taxi and some have primitive campgrounds, but most accommodation is along the river on the mainland.

For information on all Ontario Parks, contact Parks Canada, P.O.B. 1359, Cornwall, Ontario K6H 5V4 (613) 933 7951.

Québec
Forillon National Park, northeast of Québec City, can be reached on Highway 132. Lying at the eastern tip of the Gaspé Peninsula, this park's northern coast features limestone cliffs while the south coast is indented by small coves with pebbled beaches. This is a marvelous area for nature lovers, with its own camping facilities.
La Mauricie National Park is a heavily wooded region between Montréal and Québec, reached via Highway 55 northeast of Montréal and Highway 351 south. It contains dozens of lakes and is popular with campers and canoeists. Guided nature walks are given from a good interpretive centre and there are winter campgrounds.

For information on Québec parks, contact Parks Canada, P.O.B. 10275, Ste Foy, Québec G1V 4H5 (418) 694 4042.

Atlantic Canada
Fundy National Park, N.B., north of Saint John, can be reached via Highways 1, 2 and 114. This is the place for some of the world's highest tides and the wooded interior provides the hiker with splendid opportunities. It is considered one of Atlantic Canada's most dramatic and beautiful natural areas with a full range of sports facilities and accommodations.
Kouchibouguac National Park, N.B. is not too far north of Moncton, via Highways 11 and 17. One of this park's notable features is its sandy sweep of beaches

Gros Morne N.P. (top), Georgian Bay N.P. (bottom)

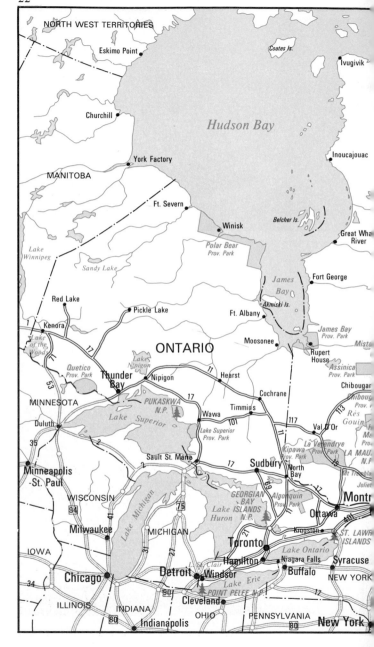

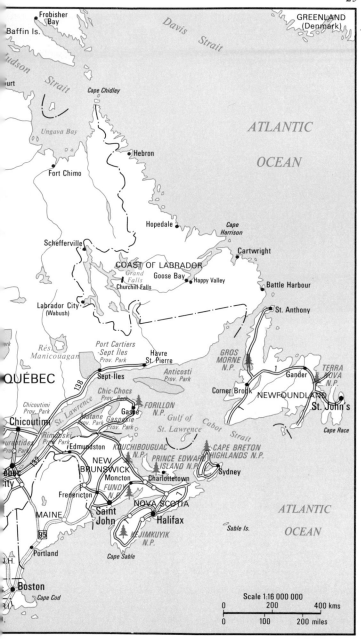

Waterfall, Forillon N.P.

along the Northumberland Strait, sheltered by offshore sand bars. You can frequently see seals frisking offshore and the interior's rivers and lagoons may be discovered by canoe, rowboat or kayak. (Rentals May to Sept.) The main campsite here is well equipped.

Gros Morne National Park, Newfoundland, north of Corner Brook on Highways 1 and 430, this park contains the most spectacular section of the Long Range Mountains plus lakes and bays. You can fly in to Gros Morne, climb the James Callaghan Trail, charter a fishing boat around Bonne Bay and the Gulf of St Lawrence, or rest on the sandy beaches at Shallow Bay and Western Brook. Good camping.

Terra Nova National Park, Newfoundland, not far southeast of Gander via the Trans-Canada Highway. A good bet for fishermen, canoeists and hikers though cycles may also be rented here. Guided nature walks are available and evening talks are given in the outdoor theatre. Open year-round with good facilities.

Cape Breton Highlands National Park, N.S. is on the Cabot Trail and is one of the most attractive areas of Nova Scotia. The trail itself (named for John Cabot who came to the island in 1497) is the park's main route stretching for 303 km/189.3 mi. An ideal park for hiking, fishing and golfing — with camping and hotel accommodations.

Kejimkujik National Park, N.S., southwest of Halifax via Highways 103 and 8, is a superb example of inland Nova Scotia terrain. There are a number of established canoe routes in this park — many of which were once used by the Micmac Indians. (You can also see Indian rock carvings.) Primitive campsites are located along the canoe and hiking trails but there are also better equipped sites including one winter campsite. Guided nature walks and interpretive programs are other features.

Prince Edward Island National Park is only a few miles north of Charlottetown on Highways 6 or 15. This park's red sandstone cliffs and dunes provide the backdrop to some of Canada's best saltwater beaches. A family-oriented park, this one offers tennis, golf, picnic grounds, playgrounds, a lawn-bowling green and wintersports.

For information on Atlantic Region parks, contact Parks Canada, Historic Properties, Upper Water St., Halifax, N.S. B3J 1S9 (902) 426 3457.

ONTARIO

Ontario has a lot to boast about. The Indians called this province 'Shining Waters' and it is not hard to see why with 400,000 sq mi of water to its credit. Niagara Falls is here, so are the greatest of the Great Lakes, along with thousands of other lakes and waterways. If those are not unlimited enough, northern Ontario is a mecca for canoeists and fishermen and lovers of wildlife — a wilderness quite often only accessible by foot, canoe or plane.

Yet for all that great expanse of outdoors, Ontario has both the sophisticated push-button luxury of an ever-growing city like Toronto and the national capital of Ottawa, proving that not only is it the most populous of Canada's provinces, but in many respects, it is also the most varied. It is both an industrial heartland and an outdoors dream. Within an hour's drive of Toronto or Ottawa, another world awaits you — lakes and farmland, resorts and country inns.

Travelers through Ontario can follow distinctive routes taking them across several of the province's regions. **The Heritage Highway** leads from Windsor to Québec's Gaspé peninsula. It runs for 1895 km/1184 mi along a historic path lined with forts, battle sites and museums which tell Eastern Canada's story.

From Windsor to Fort Erie, **The Talbot Trail** follows quiet highways and country roads for 400 km/245 mi on its way through three historic and scenic counties and two regions.

Keeping close to lake and river shores, **The Bluewater Route** stretches for 1120 km/700 mi from Windsor to Manitoulin Island. The most famous waterway is the **Rideau-Trent-Severn Route** — 680 km/425 mi of locks, parks, canals and open water linking Ottawa with Lake Ontario and Georgian Bay.

Route of the Voyageurs was once just that — an early traders' route. It now extends for 2080 km/1300 mi. It will take you through wilderness areas and parks and past wildlife reserves. Similarly, **The Frontier Route** stretches for 1600 km/1000 mi through the north's lumber and mining towns.

Perhaps a more pleasurable route is the **Algonquin**, a circular tour of the best of the lake country where country stores and small resorts lie scattered. **The Great River Road Route** means taking the scenic Lake of the Woods Parkway on its way to northwest Ontario for 600 km/365 mi.

The province of Ontario is split into 12 tourist regions as follows: **Southwestern Ontario** often called 'The Garden of Ontario'. Between two great lakes, this rolling farmland is decidedly pastoral, just right you might think to act as stage for an annual Shakespeare festival held in a town called — yes — Stratford. It is in this corner of the province that most of the vegetables and fruit are grown, in some places visitors can pick their own.

They call the area around Niagara **Festival Country** because fairs and festivals take place right through the year — anything from a beer fest to tossing the caber and including the *Shaw Festival* in summer. The side roads will lead you to the best of Canada's vineyards and tobacco fields. One of the man-made wonders in this area is the Welland Canal which allows ocean-going vessels to bypass the obstruction that Niagara Falls causes in navigating the lakes and thus allows travel from Lake Ontario to Lake Erie.

The **Georgian Lakelands** are a southern playground whatever the season. In summer, it is sailboats and scuba diving; in winter it is skis and snowmobiles. Considered part of this area are the lovely Muskoka Lakes, bounded by Georgian Bay to the west and the Severn River on the south. Resorts and holiday homes galore surround the Muskokas, largest of which are Lake Muskoka itself and Lakes Rosseau and Joseph. **Algonquin Park** is also here — set aside as a wildlife preserve back in 1893.

Metro Toronto is an area in itself. Framing the main part of the city are four major highways — The 401, Gardiner, Highway 427 and Don Valley Parkway. Beyond them are the suburbs of Scarborough, Agincourt, Willowdale, North York, Rexdale and Mississauga.

Central Ontario mainly consists of an intensely cultivated farm belt that hugs

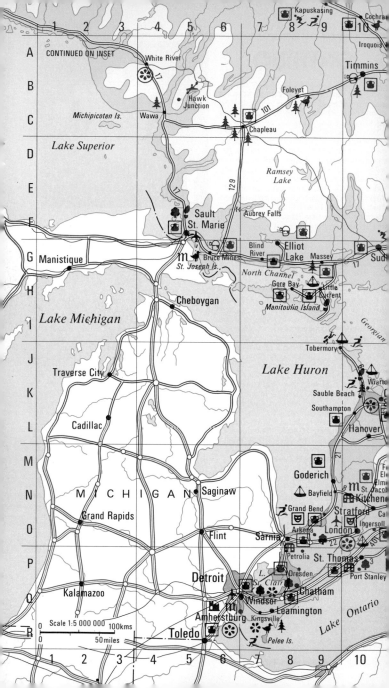

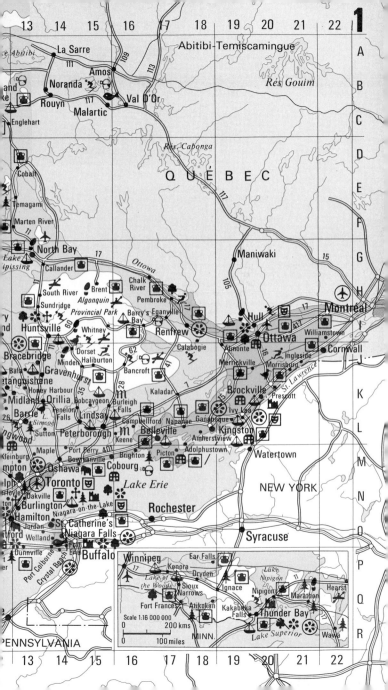

the shores of Lake Ontario, some of whose shoreside dunes rise 100 ft. To the north the region includes highlands with more lakes and resorts.

Ontario East starts at the St Lawrence yacht basins and extends north to the forests of the Ottawa Valley. This part of the province is full of classic historical buildings and stone battlements. The capital of Ottawa is located here at the confluence of the Gatineau, Ottawa and Rideau rivers. Just across the way is Québec and up in the Gatineau Hills there is winter skiing.

For those who do not need urban pleasure, the **Near North** is a densely forested portion of the province laced with trails symbolic of the past when pioneer cabins and trading posts for fur trappers were scattered in these parts.

What Ontario calls **Rainbow Country** is full of crashing rivers and foaming streams which, along with quiet lakes and islands, constitute this section much favored by boaters and anglers. Among the islands here is Manitoulin.

One of Canada's largest game reserves is situated in the **Algoma-Kinniwabi** section where it is just as possible to waterski and play tennis as it is to take on a wilderness adventure by canoe or rent a houseboat. Many day trippers take the Algoma Central train from Sault Ste Marie to Agawa Canyon where the only sign of civilization is the railway.

For those who have the call of the wild foremost in their mind, the **James Bay Frontier** can offer a great deal. This is where the true Ontario wilderness lies. **North of Superior** is also for the adventurous with its towering granite lookouts, its mineral wealth and abundant nature trails. Thunder bay, noted for its ski jump is located in this section. Canada's downhill champions practice around here but there are also plenty of cross-country ski trails.

Sunset Country is where the fly-in hunters and fishermen go, where the backpackers go. Camping and cookouts are the main feature.

Aberfoyle   N12
(pop. 100). A small village with 19th-century buildings and an antique market. *Guelph 12 km/75 mi.*

Adolphustown   L18
Location of the **United Empire Loyalist Museum** with exhibits relating to the Loyalist emigration to Ontario and their contributions to the province's development. *Kingston 53 km/33 mi.*

Algonquin Provincial Park   I15
A wilderness park that cover 7500 sq km/

Canoeing on a forest lake

2900 sq mi and is ideal for the sportsman, criss-crossed as it is with canoe routes and hiking trails. *The* through road is Hwy 60 which runs for 60 km/37 mi. Along it you will find accommodations, picnic areas and outfitters. In the *Park Museum* presentations show the park's history, geology and wildlife. There is also a *Pioneer Logging Exhibit. Toronto 125 km/78 mi.*

Almonte   J19
(pop. 3693). A small town on the Mississippi River in eastern Ontario, one of the first to be settled in the Ottawa Valley. See the *Mill of Kintail*, an 1830s stone mill converted into a summer home for Robert Tait McKenzie, world-famous surgeon and sculptor. Today it is a museum displaying his artistic work and pioneer artefacts. (Open daily mid May-mid Oct.) *Ottawa 48 km/30 mi.*

Amherstburg   R7
(pop. 5566). One of the oldest settlements in southwestern Ontario. It was here that General Brock plotted with Shawnee chief Tecumseh in the 1812 War to capture Detroit. See **Fort Malden National Historic Park.** The British established this fort in 1796 on the Detroit River — it became a major base for operations on the Detroit frontier during the War of 1812. Today you can see part of the early British earthworks and visit several buildings which contain mementoes of all those who controlled the area at various times. *North American Black Historical Museum* on King St. is somewhat unique. It illustrates black heritage from African origins, through slavery to emancipation and settlement in Essex County.

For fun, try the *Bob-Lo Island Amusement Park*, an island in the Detroit River. Open May-Labour Day, it features rides, an arts and crafts center, an old blockhouse plus picnic facilities. Good place for boat watching. *Windsor 32 km/20 mi.*

Amherstview   L18
(pop. 2000). A riverside village opposite Amherst Island reached via the Heritage

Route up the St Lawrence. Ferries operate to the island. See The Fairfield White House as an example of a 1793 mansion built by a wealthy Loyalist. *Kingston 15 km/9 mi.*

Arkona   O9
(pop. 44). Southwest Ontario site of *Rock Glen Park* where fossils have been found dating back millions of years. A particular attraction for geologists. The *Indian Artefacts Museum* is housed in the Arkona Public School on Hwy 7, open afternoons only, year round, Tues.-Thurs. and weekends. *London 54 km/35 mi.*

Atikokan   Q18
(pop. 5668). A modern town close to **Quetico Provincial Park** with good tourist facilities. Some of its prosperity is due to its large iron mines. In the downtown Civic Centre visit the *Centennial Museum* which shows mining and pioneer exhibits as well as changing art displays. Outside there is a restored logging engine. Atikokan is a good base for visiting Quetico Park which connects with Superior Park, Minnesota. At the lakeside park campsite, the *Quetico Park Museum* illustrates the area's history. *Thunder Bay 210 km/131 mi.*

Aubrey Falls   F7
Beauty Spot on the Mississagi River with falls that drop 128 ft.

Bala   J13
(pop. 536). A summer resort on Lake Muskoka with attractive places to stay and shops in and around town. Bala Bay is one of Ontario's most scenic areas. *Gravenhurst 28 km/17.5 mi.*

Bancroft   J16
(pop. 2300). A pleasing community in central Ontario and a major center for the Highlands of Hastings, notable for summer fishing, swimming and canoeing and in winter, cross-country skiing and snowmobiling. Most of Bancroft's fame stems from its minerals — the majority of Canada's minerals come from this region at the edge of the Precambrian Shield. Recommended for rockhounds. A gathering of rockhounds, *The Bancroft Gemboree*, takes place in Bancroft late July/early Aug for 4 days of selling, swapping and learning. Demonstrations of gem cutting are given and visits made to prospect sites. The festival also includes square dancing and corn roasts. The best view of the countryside is from *Eagle's Nest Lookout* on a 183 m/600 ft hill that overlooks Bancroft. In the village itself, visit the *Bancroft Museum*, a two-storey log house with

19th-century furnishings. *Peterborough 97 km/60 mi.*

Barrie   L13
(pop. 34,398). A vivacious city on Lake Simcoe's Kempenfelt Bay, offering accommodations and entertainment, including summer theater and all-year, evening harness racing at the *Fairgrounds* where there is a heated, enclosed grandstand. Visitors are welcome at the *Midhurst Forest Tree Nursery* (open weekdays April-Oct) and at the **Springwater Provincial Park** where beavers, raccoons and deer may all be viewed in their natural surroundings. Also see *Simcoe County Museum and Archives*, a complex that traces man's development in this area from 5000 BC to the present time, and includes among other things an 1840s shopping street. An array of military hardware and memorabilia is displayed at the *Base Borden Military Museum*. Molson *Park* has a series of annual attractions including the Renaissance Festival. *Toronto 90 km/51 mi.*

Barry's Bay   I16
(pop. 1266). Main centre for shops and outfitters serving the Kaminiskeg Lake holiday region. Basically, this is a lumber town — visits can be arranged to logging operations in the nearby forests. River rafting trips are available some 5 km/3 mi from *Madawaska Kanu camp*, mid June-Aug. *Mt. Madawaska*, just south of town, is a ski center in winter for downhill and cross-country. At Barry's Bay, see the *Madonna House Pioneer Museum* which features items used by early settlers (open daily except Wed. late May-mid Oct.). *Pembroke 87 km/54 mi.*

Bayfield   N9
(pop. 549). Peaceful village on Lake Huron with one of the lake's best harbors boasting a modern marina. Many of the old buildings lining the main street have been restored and converted into craft shops. *Goderich 21 km/13 mi.*

Belleville   L17
(pop. 35,311). A lovely town at the mouth of the Moira River on the Bay of Quinte. It obtained its name in 1816 when Lieut. Gov. Gore visited with his wife, Anna Bella. The town acts as a gateway to the Highlands of Hastings and Quinte Isle, both superb holiday regions. The town itself has one of the province's finest yacht harbors and can offer golf, swimming and flying. The Victorian mansion, Glanmore is now the *Hastings County Museum*, designed like a French château and containing Victorian artworks and furnishings. *Kingston 80 km/50 mi.*

Blind River   G7

(pop. 3142). Resort area on Lake Huron. See the *Timber Village Museum* which is filled with relics of pioneer agriculture and lumber days. Among featured items are steam engines and a late 1800s operating press. *Sault Ste Marie 140 km/87.5 mi.*

Bobcaygeon   K15

(pop. 1562). A town on three islands in central Ontario. Its Indian name means 'shallow rapids' and rapids do still surround it, though they are kept under control by the *Trent Canal Lock No. 32* built in 1883. It is a major pleasure center on the Kawartha Lakes. Step dancing and fiddle playing are part of the annual late July Kawartha Lakes celebration held in Bobcaygeon. One of North America's best preserved examples of log architecture is *The Beehive* built as a retreat in 1838. *Peterborough 53 km/33 mi.*

Bowmanville   M15

(pop. 9500). Former milling center utilizing its fine harbor on Lake Ontario. Only the Vanstone Flour and Feed Mill at the western end of town remains these days. The town features a large private zoo, open mid April-Thanksgiving, and the *Bowmanville Museum*, an 1860s home with period rooms. *Oshawa 27 km/16 mi.*

Bracebridge   J13

(pop. 8428). A charming resort center on a series of cascades that run into Lake Muskoka. Best known attraction is *Santa's Village*, a children's entertainment complex on the Muskoka River with rides, river boat, animals and Santa himself in his 'summer home'. (Open daily mid May-mid June and Sept.-Thanksgiving, weekends.) See also the *Woodchester Villa and Museum* (1882). *Gravenhurst 16 km/10 mi.*

Brampton   M12

(pop. 103,459). The 'Flower City', established in the 1820s and noted for its numerous flower nurseries. Tours are possible through the American Motors plant. Also see the *Peel Region Museum and Art Gallery* which shows the district's pioneer history, and *The Great War Flying Museum* where displays include World War I linen maps and aircraft. *Toronto 37 km/23 mi.*

Brantford   O12

(pop. 66,950). City on the Grand River named for Indian Chief Joseph Brant who led the Six Nations Indians from their New York State territory to this site. This is also the city where Alexander Graham Bell invented the telephone and made that first long distance phone call from his home here to the town of Paris, Ontario in 1876.

The Bell Homestead is furnished as it was when he lived there and contains some of his inventions (open daily year round except Mon.).

There are many Indian associations with this city: a good collection of Six Nations Indian artefacts can be found in the *Brant County Museum* on Charlotte St. *Chiefswood*, birthplace of Indian poetess Pauline Johnson, was the home that Chief George Henry Martin Johnson built for his English bride, on the Six Nations Reserve (open daily Victoria Day to Labour Day). *Her Majesty's Chapel of the Mohawks* is the world's only Royal Indian

Chapel of the Mohawks, Brantford

Chapel and, also on Mohawk St., the *Woodland Indian Cultural Educational Centre and Museum* explores the culture and history of Eastern Canada's native peoples. Indian history and culture is re-enacted every August in a forest amphitheater on the Six Nations Indian Reserve.

Also see the *Art Gallery of Brant* where paintings, sculptures and photographs by Canadian artists are displayed. The *Octagon House* (1840) is now a country restaurant called the Heritage Inn. In Glenhyrst Gardens estate overlooking Grand River, the main house has gallery shows and in the grounds there is a nature trail. (Open Tues.-Fri., weekend afternoons only.) All the points of interest in historic Brantford may be covered on a special sightseeing train tour. *Toronto 90 km/56 mi.*

Brighton   M16

(pop. 3199). A small community named after the English resort town and situated among apple orchards at the entrance to **Presqu'ile Provincial Park.** The park is ideal for birdwatching and has extensive camping facilities as well as swimming beaches. In the natural history museum here there is a theater and an aquarium. Also visit *Proctor House Museum*, a restored merchant's home on a hilly point overlooking the town (open daily late June-early Sept.). *Belleville 32 km/20 mi.*

Petroglyphs near Peterborough

Brockville K20
(pop. 19,903). Eastern gateway to the Thousand Islands boating and resort area. This Loyalist center was named for the hero of the 1812 War, Gen. Sir Isaac Brock. The District Court House and Jail is one of the buildings dating to Loyalist times and is still performing its original function. *Kingston 79 km/49 mi.*

Bruce Mines G6
(pop. 517). A mining town that has since become a holiday center. See *Bruce Mines Museum* the history of the area with particular emphasis on mining (open daily May-Oct.). *Sault Ste Marie 67 km/42 mi.*

Burleigh Falls K15
Fishing and boating center on a series of rapids between Lovesick and Stoney Lakes. Every August there is kayak racing. From here visit **Petroglyphs Provincial Park** where figures and symbols are carved in the flat white marble and are still well preserved. They are thought to have been carved between 500 to 1000 years ago. *Peterborough 33 km/20 mi.*

Burlington N13
(pop. 104,314). A lakefront residential city on Burlington Bay. You will find some interesting boutiques and restaurants around Village Square, converted from older homes. See *St Luke's Anglican Church* (1834), the *Burlington Culture Centre's* art exhibits, and the *Joseph Brant Museum*, a replica of the famous Mohawk Chief's last home. *Toronto 62 km/40 mi.*

Calabogie I18
(pop. 300). A year round tourist center. In winter Calabogie Peaks offers downhill and cross-country skiing for intermediates. *Ottawa 103 km/65 mi.*

Callander G14
(pop. 1058). A resort town on Lake Nipissing which hit the headlines in 1934 when the Dionne quintuplets were born here.

The Quints Museum is dedicated to them and is in the original Dionne farmhouse, open Victoria Day-Labour Day. Watch the sunset from Callander Lookout or at the town dock. *North Bay 19 km/12 mi.*

Cambridge O11
(pop. 72,383). A city only since 1973 when Galt, Preston and Hespeler amalgamated. Situated along the Grand and Speed rivers, all three started out as mill towns. Cambridge is still noted as a flour and woollen center. *The Cambridge Highland Games* are in July. *Toronto 92 km/57.5 mi.*

Campbellford L16
(pop. 3487). Situated on the Trent River at the heart of a dairy district. Old style cheese making may be watched at *Old Warkworth Cheese Factory* (Sat. mid May-Thanksgiving) and tours are possible through the *World's Finest Chocolate Canada* factory. Visitors are welcome at the *Codrington Trout Hatchery* on weekdays all year. Also see Healey Falls and *The Trent River Pioneer Museum* where early settlers' home and farm life is portrayed. *Peterborough 63 km/39 mi.*

Chalk River H16
(pop. 1070). Site of a nuclear research center. Get an insight by visiting the *Nuclear Laboratories* where plant tours are available weekdays, June-Labour Day. Also in the area is the *Petawawa National Forestry Institute* which gives informative half-hour walking tours for those interested in forest ecology. (Daily June-mid Sept.). *Pembroke 19 km/11 mi.*

Chapleau C7
(pop. 3253). A hunting and fishing center in the north of the province with fly-in services. A perfect base for enjoying four close provincial parks: *Five Mile Lake* 35 km/22 mi south with good swimming and fishing; *The Shoals* 52 km/32 mi west, for fishing and watersports; *Wakami Lake* 64 km/40 mi south; and *Missinaibi Lake* 80 km/50 mi north in the middle of the *Chapleau Game Reserve* for boating and fishing in a wilderness setting. In town, *Centennial Museum* on Monk St. shows pioneer items (open daily June-Sept.). *Sault Ste Marie 250 km/157 mi.*

Chatham Q8
(pop. 38,685). A city near the mouth of the River Thames which began as a naval dockyard in 1793. It was the northern terminus of the *'Underground Railroad'*, the secret route that brought slaves north to freedom prior to the American Civil War. Some 5000 slaves are thought to

have entered Canada around 1850/51. See the *Chatham-Kent Museum* in Tecumseh Park. The museum contains pioneer and Indian artefacts and the park is the setting for art shows and band concerts. *Windsor 75 km/47 mi.*

Cobalt   D13
(pop. 2056). A silver mining town with frontier charm. In summer mine tours may be made through Cobalt's *Northern Ontario Mining Museum* which has mining exhibits and fine native silver (open daily May-Oct.). *North Bay 144 km/90 mi.*

Cobourg   M15
(pop. 11,400). A handsome Upper Canadian town which served as a lake port for Lake Ontario's early steamers and a stagecoach stop on the Toronto-Montréal run. It is internationally recognized for its July *Highland Games.* See *Barnum House Museum* (1817) as an example of neoclassic Georgian architecture; *Marie Dressler Home* now a popular restaurant; *Cobourg Art Gallery* in Victoria Hall. *Peterborough 55 km/34 mi.*

Cochrane   A10
(pop. 4974). A tourist town built around Commando Lake. The biggest attraction is a ride on the **Polar Bear Express,** a day trip to the Arctic tidewater of **James Bay,** part of Hudson Bay. It takes you through untouched wilderness. Tours of the Plywood Plant on Railway St. are available July-Labour Day, Mon., Wed. and Fri. Take the self-guided *Muskeg Trail* west of town where a feature is the live beaver house and dam. In the *Railway Museum,* the history of the James Bay Frontier is traced. *North Bay 375 km/234 mi.*

Collingwood   L12
(pop. 11,114). A ski center at the base of the Blue Mountains, the highest part of the Niagara Escarpment. The place became wealthy as a Great Lakes port and its prosperity is reflected in many of its fine mansions and its Victorian main street. In summer, take the Blue Mountain chairlift ride, round trip or sled down. In winter, slopes on both sides of the mountain are used for skiing with runs for all levels of expertise plus cross-country trails. Near the top of the escarpment there are naturally formed scenic caves.

In an old railway station, *Collingwood Museum* deals with pioneer life and includes a courtroom display. *Kaufman House* has modern, period and traditional furniture. Candy making the old fashioned way may be seen at *The Candy Factory* west of town on Hwy 26. Also on Hwy 26 to the west of town is the *Blue Mountain Pottery* which offers guided tours all year round. *Barrie 54 km/34 mi.*

Cornwall   J22
(pop. 46,121). Ontario's most easterly city with a big French-speaking population. Pitt Street Mall is a good place for browsing boutiques — it's a pedestrianized zone where open air concerts are often given. The *Wood House Museum* features a variety of Canadiana and Indian items (open daily May-Oct.). *Inverarden Regency Cottage Museum* is a good example of 1816 architecture. Traditional Indian living can be found at the *Indian Village Museum,* where in summer, a family lives in 17th-century style. The village itself is open late May-Labour Day, Wed.-Sun., and the museum is open daily year round. Cornwall is also the headquarters for the St Lawrence Seaway. *Kingston 175 km/ 109 mi, Ottawa 100 km/62.5 mi.*

Crystal Beach   P14
(pop. 2618). A holiday resort on Lake Erie with a sandy beach. Family attraction is the *Crystal Beach Amusement Park* where rides include the Comet Coaster and water slide. *Niagara Falls 30 km/19 mi.*

Delhi   P11
(pop. 3929). Ontario's tobacco capital. The surrounding land of Norfolk County produces almost half of the province's tobacco crop. See the *Ontario Tobacco Museum* on Talbot Rd, which illustrates the history and technology of tobacco production. (Open April-Aug., Tues.-Sun.; Sept.-Nov., Tues.-Sun. afternoons.) *Brantford 61 km/38 mi.*

Doon   N11
(pop. 550). A small village in a picturesque setting. See *Doon Pioneer Village and Heritage Community,* a 60 acre complex that includes a museum, church, school, store and railway station. A number of festivals are held here during the warm months. (Open daily May-Oct., afternoons in April and Nov.) *Kitchener 11 km/7 mi.*

Dorset   J14
(pop. 400). Situated at the northwest corner of the Haliburton Highlands, this is a gateway to **Algonquin Provincial Park.** At *Leslie Frost Resources Centre* there are wildlife displays and guided tours of the local fauna and flora plus seasonal hiking, cross-country skiing, snowshoeing and snowmobiling. *Bracebridge 48 km/ 30 mi.*

Dresden   P8
(pop. 2450). A quiet town on the Sydenham River in southwest Ontario. It was here that Rev. Josiah Henson (whose early days in slavery inspired the novel 'Uncle Tom's Cabin') came and lived. Six build-

Canadian Fall

ings and two graveyards, including Henson's home and grave, comprise *Uncle Tom's Cabin Museum.* (Open May-Oct. daily.) *Chatham 45 km/28 mi.*

Dryden   P18
(pop. 6480). A prosperous town with good fishing and hunting. Paper making is one of its industries and tours are available through the *Great Lakes Forest Products* plant June-Aug., Mon-Fri. Look out for the *Agricultural Society Fall Fair* on Dryden's fairgrounds in late Aug. *Thunder Bay 355 km/222 mi.*

Dunnville   O13
(pop. 11,642). A farming town on the Grand River. Base for visiting **Rock Point Provincial Park** recommended for birdwatchers and those interested in fossils. *Hamilton 54 km/34 mi.*

Ear Falls   P18
(pop. 2035). The center for the Lac Seul holiday area with especially good fishing and moose hunting. See the log-built *Ear Falls Museum. Dryden 143 km/90 mi.*

Eganville   I17
(pop. 1328). A pretty village named for Irish immigrant John Egan who became a leading lumber merchant. Sportsmen choose Eganville to hunt white tail deer and to fish in the Bonnechere River. Guided tours are available of the *Bonnechere Caves* which are full of stalactites and fossils, Victoria Day-mid Sept. daily. *Pembroke 35 km/22 mi.*

Elliot Lake   G8
(pop. 16,723). A modern town founded when uranium was discovered nearby. The lake on which it is situated is one of 170 in the area, offering year round sporting facilities. At *Elliot Lake Mining and Nuclear Museum* there are exhibits relating to uranium mining. Arrangements may be made for visiting a mine. *Sault Ste Marie 200 km/125 mi.*

Elmira   N11
(pop. 7834). One of Upper Canada's earliest settlements, located in Ontario's Pennsylvania German country. It is a center for the area's Mennonite farmers and craftsmen. Typical crafts are quilts, rugs and hand-made dolls like those found in *The Sap Bucket,* a Church St. store. Also look at the shops in Brox's Olde Town Village. A unique collection of dolls is housed in *House of Dolls* on South St. On the first Saturday in April, Elmira celebrates the rising sap in the maple tree with the *Maple Syrup Festival.* Summer tours of the immediate area include the *Mennonite Museum* in St Jacobs. *Kitchener 19 km/12 mi.*

Elora   N11
(pop. 2500). A scenic village on the Grand River Falls with several turn-of-the-century buildings. Just below the village *Elora Gorge* is a notable limestone canyon with caves, waterfalls and rapids, believed by the Indians to be a haunt of spirits. The rock in the middle of the Grand River Falls is known locally as 'Tooth of Time'. The former 1859 grist mill here is now a country inn. *Guelph 24 km/15 mi.*

Englehart   C12
(pop. 1767). A lumber town surrounded by a wilderness area dotted with lakes with good hunting and fishing facilities. Also see the Historical Museum displaying the pioneer life style. *Cobalt 65 km/40 mi.*

Fenelon Falls   L14
(pop. 1637). This 'Jewel of the Kawarthas' is named for Father Fenelon, an early Canadian missionary. Cameron and Sturgeon Lakes meet on its main street — the 23 ft difference in their levels accounts for the falls, rapids and gorge below. The oldest house in town is now the *Fenelon Falls Museum*, containing pioneer and Indian artefacts. *Peterborough 6 km/38 mi.*

Fergus   M11
(pop. 6000). A pretty town on the Grand River which changed its name from Little Falls to honor Scottish immigrant Adam Fergusson. Among the 19th-century buildings here is Fergusson's home, now the Breadalbane Inn. On weekends you'll find a farmers' market in the 1834 flour mill and in mid Aug. the *Fergus Highland Games* take place. *Guelph 20 km/12.5 mi.*

Foleyet   B8
(pop. 538). A base for fishing and hunting moose and bear. To the west is the vast *Chapleau Game Reserve*. Also near is **Ivanhoe Lake Provincial Park.** *Timmins 102 km/64 mi.*

Fort Erie   O15
Entry point to Canada at the junction of Lake Erie and the Niagara River, connected to the US by the *Peace Bridge.* See **Old Fort Erie.** The original was built in 1764 — the restored structure here now is the third, containing relics of British and American armies. In summer the guard, in period uniform, perform military drills daily. *Niagara Falls 35 km/22 mi.*

Fort Frances   O15
(pop. 9325). Major fly-in center for the wilderness sports country to the north and east. Situated opposite International Falls in Minnesota. In *Pither's Point Park* on Rainy Lake is a reconstructed trading fort with a lookout tower and museum. (Open daily mid June-Labour Day.) *Fort Frances Museum* deals with the Indian and fur trade eras. *Thunder Bay 335 km/209 mi.*

Gananoque   L19
(pop. 5120). In the center of the **Thousand Islands** resort area, this is a boarding point for tours of that area by boat or plane. Cruises through the islands are possible mid May-mid Oct. See *Gananoque Historic Museum* in the old Victoria Hotel (1840) featuring military items. (Open Mon.-Sat. afternoons June-Sept.) For family fun, visit the *House of Haunts.* *Kingston 33 km/21 mi.*

Goderich   N9
(pop. 7340). An elegant city situated on a bluff overlooking Lake Huron. One of the most charming accommodations here is Benmiller Inn created from two old mills. Also see *Huron County Jail*, an octagonal stone building now a museum. *Huron County Pioneer Museum* houses an impressive collection of pioneer artefacts. (Open daily May-Oct., Mon.-Fri., Nov.-April.) *London 100 km/62.5 mi.*

Muskoka River

Gore Bay H8

(pop. 767). A quiet town on the north coast of Manitoulin Island that serves as a supply center for boaters. The old jail is now the *Gore Bay Museum* housing period furniture and curios. A few miles east is the beauty spot of *Bridal Veil Falls. Sudbury 196 km/122 mi.*

Grand Bend N9

(pop. 750). One of the main resorts on Lake Huron with a broad, soft sandy beach, a summer playhouse and plentiful accommodations. See the *Lambton Heritage Museum* which concentrates on county history and features a slaughterhouse, chapel and pioneer home. (Open daily year round.) *London 51 km/32 mi.*

Gravenhurst J14

(pop. 7900). Gateway to the Muskoka Lakes and a tourist center since last century. From here summer cruises on '*Lady Muskoka*' travel down one of the province's most beautiful lakes whose shores are sprinkled with large old holiday homes, some of which have become hotels. From late June-late Sept. the restored *S.S. Segwun* steamship also cruises the Muskokas. Summer Sunday evening concerts are given free from a stage in Gull Lake. This is also the town where Dr Norman Bethune, doctor with the Chinese Communist Army during the Revolution, was born. The *Bethune Memorial House* is open daily, year-round. *Orillia 43 km/26 mi.*

Guelph N12

(pop. 67,538). A major manufacturing center built on several hills, this town is a treasure house of early Canadian architecture. See the *Colonel John McCrae Home*, birthplace of the Canadian poet best known for '*In Flanders Field*'. (Open Tues.-Sun. mid May-mid Oct.; mid Oct.-mid May, Sun. afternoons.) The *Guelph Civic Museum*, in a former 1840s inn, presents the city's story. On the city's highest hill, *Church of Our Lady* was modeled after Cologne Cathedral. In *Riverside Park*, the mechanical floral clock contains thousands of flowers and measures 44 ft in diameter. *Kortright Waterfowl Park* features over 70 species of ducks, swans, geese and other wild birds in their natural habitat. Also see *Halton County Radial Railway*, an operating electric railway museum with a variety of historic streetcars. On weekends from Victoria Day-Oct., you can ride through this 'bygone era'. *Kitchener 25 km/16 mi.*

Haliburton J15

(pop. 1124). A lakeland village in the middle of the Haliburton Highlands that is now a year-round resort center. Over 600 lakes are scattered through the surrounding countryside. Arts and crafts are displayed in the turn-of-the-century railway station and visitors are welcome at the *Haliburton School of Fine Arts*. Highlands pioneer life is on view at the *Haliburton Highlands Museum* in Glebe Park. (Open June-Thanksgiving.) *Peterborough 92 km/57.5 mi.*

Hamilton-Wentworth O13

(pop. 453,000). Located half-way between Toronto and Niagara Falls, this area's theme parks and entertainment hold special appeal for the day-tripper. At *African Lion Safari*, the animals roam free and you stay in your car as you drive through some 500 acres. (Open March-Nov.) *Wentworth Heritage Village*'s costumed guides will take you through 30 historic properties. (Open Tues.-Sun., April-Dec.) Not to be missed are the *Royal Botanical Gardens* which cover 2000 acres of flower displays, natural parkland and a wildlife sanctuary. Most spectacular is the *Lila Garden* in the Arboretum in May to early June. A two week Sugaring-off Festival to celebrate maple syrup making takes place in the gardens each March.

Football fans can visit the *Canadian Football Hall of Fame* at City Hall Plaza. Flying fans may note that all 35 aircraft at the *Canadian Warplane Heritage Museum*, Hamilton Airport, are still operational. The 19th-century *Dundurn Castle* contains a military museum. It was the home of Sir Allan Napier McNab, Prime Minister for Canada 1854-56. In summer the garden courtyard and adjacent *Cockpit Theatre* are used for performing arts events. During July and August, a *son et lumière* presentation is given twice weekly.

A less impressive but nevertheless handsome Georgian mansion is *Whitehorn House*, open all year. What was a settler's home in 1795 is now *Hamilton Battlefield Museum and Monument* devoted to 'The Battle of Stony Creek', a significant encounter in the War of 1812. Guides dressed in period costume give tours during July and August.

Arrangements may be made to tour Dofasco and Stelco Steel works; also day and evening escorted tours through Andres Winery. In downtown Dundas, visit *Ben Veldhuis Greenhouses* where there are huge numbers of cacti and other succulents. On Old Dundas Rd, guided tours are given May-Oct. of an 1863 operating grist mill.

For shopping, Hess Village is pleasant: these restored homes have been converted to specialty stores, art galleries and restaurants. On Tues., Thurs. and Sat., you will find a farmers' market on the ground floor of a complex at James St. N and York St. For a musical evening, book for Hamilton Place, home of Hamilton Philharmonic Orchestra and Opera. *Toronto 70 km/44 mi; Niagara Falls 80 km/50 mi.*

Hawk Junction   B5

(pop. 400). Starting point for canoeists and hunters heading to the Whitefish and Manitowik Lake areas. *Sault Ste Marie 247 km/154 mi.*

Hearst   Q22

(pop. 5195). Starting point for canoe trips to the north and known for good moose hunting. Agawa Canyon on the Algoma railway is nearby. *Sault Ste Marie 590 km/368 mi; Timmins 320 km/200 mi.*

Honey Harbour   K13

A small resort town on Georgian Bay with good swimming and fishing. Accessible by boat from here is the **Georgian Bay Islands National Park.** Take a water taxi to Beausoleil, the largest island, or to Tobermory. *Orillia 42 km/26 mi.*

Huntsville   I13

(pop. 11,100). A holiday town that is the center of Bays Resort Region and located at the western entrance to **Algonquin Park**. In summer there are cruises along the Muskoka River to Peninsula Lake and in autumn the towns of Muskoka celebrate the turning of the leaves with street dances and turkey dinners. There is more celebrating at carnival time in mid Feb., with cookouts, snowmobile races and other events in the *Winter Carnival.* The second Sun. in Jan. sees Canada's largest single day cross-country ski event — the *Muskoka Loppet.*

See *Muskoka Pioneer Village* comprising several pioneer buildings on a wooded hill site. (Open late May-Labour Day daily, Labour Day-Thanksgiving, weekends.) *Modill Church,* one of the few surviving square-timbered log churches. *Dyer Memorial,* a ten-acre botanical garden around a 43 ft memorial built by Detroit Corp. lawyer Clifton G. Dyer in memory of his wife. For a view of Huntsville, Fairy Lake and the Muskoka River, go to *Lion's Lookout Park. Gravenhurst 51 km/31 mi.*

Ignace   Q19

(pop. 2130). Major fly-in base and start of Hwy 599, *The Road North,* leading to Hudson Bay, passing through the tourist centers of Savant, Pickle and Central Patricia Lakes. Antiques and early settlers' belongings are displayed at the Ignace Museum. In **Sandbar Lake Provincial Park** there is superb fishing and

in the neighbouring lakes there are Indian pictographs. *Thunder Bay 250 km/156 mi.*

Ingersoll   O11

(pop. 8198). A town famous for its cheese. Near the site of Canada's first cheese factory, the *Cheese Factory Museum* shows tools and machinery used in bygone days. In mid Sept. a nine day wine and cheese festival takes place at Ingersoll. *London 32 km/20 mi.*

Ingleside   J21

(pop. 1106). A village on the St Lawrence with good accommodations and recreational facilities. The St Lawrence Seaway dam at Cornwall has created *Long Sault Parkway's* 11 islands, connected by causeways and bridges. Good places for fishing, picnicking and swimming. *Cornwall 19 km/11.8 mi.*

Ivy Lea   L19

Turnoff point for the *Thousand Islands Bridge* which connects Ontario with New York State. From the observation tower at *Skytown* entertainment complex, there's a panoramic view of the islands. Within the complex is a wax museum, aquarium, arctic display and shops. Boat tours are possible from here. *Gananoque 16 km/10 mi.*

Jordan   O13

(pop. 120). A village on the Twenty Mile Creek and center of Canada's wine industry. See *Jordan Historical Museum of the Twenty,* consisting of three buildings and a churchyard. There are displays concerned with the early settlers and of interest is the large fruit press in the grounds of Vintage House. *St Catherines 10 km/6 mi.*

Kakabeka Falls   Q19

Impressive waterfalls in the northwest. A great volume of water cascades over a 128 ft drop. Next to the falls is a provincial park with camping and beach facilities. *Thunder Bay 26 km/16 mi.*

Kapuskasing   A9

(pop. 12,676). The 'Model Town of the North' was designed in the early 1800s with the streets radiating from a central point like spokes from a wheel. *Memorial Museum* is located in an old steam train. A good area for fishing, hunting, swimming, cross-country skiing and snowmobiling. *Timmins 220 km/137 mi.*

Keene   L16

(pop. 334). A peaceful village on the Indian River north of Rice Lake. Just to the south is *Serpent Mounds Provincial Park* where there are Indian burial mounds dating from 2000 years ago. You can see nine earth mounds, the largest of which is 190 ft long. Rice Lake used to produce wild rice, at one time a valuable food for the Indians. *Century Village* is an interesting pioneer museum with more than 20 restored buildings including a shingle mill, inn and cider barn. Arts and crafts are demonstrated here in summer. (Open mid May-mid Oct., weekend afternoons; mid June-Labour Day, daily afternoons.) *Peterborough 17 km/10.8 mi.*

Kenora   P17
(pop. 10,565). Tourist center for the Lake of the Woods to the south and the northern wilderness territory. First class accommodations can be found in this town which offers excellent fishing, boating, sailing and hunting. Cruises are available from late May-mid Sept. through the islands of Lake of the Woods. Kenora is the start and finishing point for the *International Sailing Regatta* through the islands, one of many festivities which take place here. *Thunder Bay 475 km/ 296 mi.*

Kingston   L18
(pop. 56,032). A city located where the St Lawrence River flows out of Lake Ontario, at the southern end of the Rideau Canal. Rich in history, Kingston started as a fur trading post and developed into a military stronghold and at one time was national capital. Today it is a flourishing industrial and agricultural center with many tourist amenities including theaters, an Olympic sailing course and an open air market every Tues., Thurs. and Sat.

Its numerous 19th-century buildings, built from local limestone, give the city a distinctive appearance. The City Hall (1843/44) was built when Kingston was capital and is one of the country's greatest classical structures. *Bellevue House* (1840) used to be home to Canada's first Prime

Kingston Legislative Building

Minister, Sir John A. Macdoland, and is now a museum, open year round. Brock Street was Kingston's center in the 1800s and even now has retained many shops of that era like Cooke's Old World Shop, a gourmet grocery.

Old Fort Henry was Canada's most powerful fort at one time. Today it is a living museum with soldiers, cannon and military ceremonies in summer. (Open mid May-mid Oct. daily). A remnant of Kingston's 1846 defenses is *Murney Tower Museum*, a stone Martello Tower with historic exhibits. (Open Victoria Day weekend-June, weekends; July-Sept. daily.) The largest Martello Tower is in the grounds of the *Royal Military College* and contains a small arms collection. (Open daily mid June-Labour Day.) The city's 1849 Pumping Station has also become a museum. All the main pumps, engines and scale models on view here run on steam. (Open daily mid June-Labour Day.)

Kingston has museums of all kinds. See also the *Canadian Forces Communications and Electronic Museum* (open Mon. Fri. afternoons). The *Marine Museum* covering the history of Great Lakes shipping since 1678 (open daily June-Oct.). *Maclachlan Woodworking Museum* which displays carpentry tools and equipment for making maple sugar, butter, barrels etc. The city was also the birthplace of organized hockey as you will discover in the *International Hockey Hall of Fame* which traces the game's development. (Open mid June-mid Sept. daily, mid Sept.-mid June weekends.) *Bell Rock Mill* is a working museum featuring a saw mill, planning mill, shingle mill, veneer mill and flour and grist mill.

In summer, a special tour trail runs a 16 km/ 10 mi ride through Kingston. *Toronto 255 km/159 mi.*

Kingsville   Q7
(pop. 4790). Canada's most southerly town, on the migratory path of the Canadian goose. See *Jack Miner's Bird Sanctuary* — best times for visits are late March, late Oct., early Nov. Exotic birds can be seen in Colasanti's Tropical Gardens. *Windsor 52 km/33 mi.*

Kirkland Lake   B12
(pop. 13,567). A modern town built on gold-bearing rock. This is a vacation center with first class facilities for visitors. Nearby Lake Kenogami is a popular boating and fishing area. In summer, mine tours are available. Native animals and birds can be seen year round in *Harman's Wildlife Park*. The development of mining is traced at the *Museum of Northern History*, open year round. *Toronto 585 km/365 mi.*

Kitchener-Waterloo   N11

(pop. 178,500). Twin cities with a common heritage. Early German settlers, Amish and Mennonite farmers, came here from south of the border and their descendants continue to give the city a unique air. North America's biggest and brightest **Oktoberfest** takes place here every October. The famous *Kitchener Farmers' Market*, featuring local produce and handicrafts, is located in the city center — a smaller one is in Waterloo. On the last Sat. in May, an internationally recognized *Mennonite Relief Sale* is held at New Hamburg Arena a few miles out of town.

Oktoberfest, Kitchener

See **Woodside National Historic Park**, boyhood home of William Lyon Mackenzie King, Canada's tenth Prime Minister. It has been restored and refurnished in 1890s style, open daily year round. *Joseph Schneider House* is a Pennsylvania German Mennonite home restored and refurnished in the 1850s fashion. (Open daily Victoria Day-Labour Day, rest of year, Wed.-Sun.) *Toronto 110 km/69 mi.*

Kleinburg   M13

(pop. 300). An attractive village within easy reach of Toronto. The **McMichael Collection** is the most important collection of the Group of Seven Canadian artists in the world. It is housed in log buildings in the Humber valley. (Open daily all year — closed Mondays in winter.) At *The Doctor's House* restaurant you can sample Canadian dishes of the 1800s and at *Puck's Farm* there are weekend events and year round hayrides. This scenic riverside park with nature trail, vegetable plots and barnyard animals is ideal for children. *Toronto 40 km/25 mi.*

Leamington   Q8

(pop. 11,090). Colloquially known as 'Tomato Capital of the World', this is a major canning center. Buy fresh fruit and vegetables from wayside stands. This is also a base for **Point Pelee National Park** which covers 4000 acres and features interpretive centers, tour trains, nature trails, picnic grounds and 23 km/ 14 mi of beaches. A special feature is the mile-long boardwalk through the marsh with observation towers at each end. *Windsor 60 km/37.5 mi.*

Lindsay   L14

(pop. 13,000). Gateway to the Kawartha Lakes area and part of the Trent Canal System. A tourist center with Kawarth Summer Theater, an art gallery and the *Victoria County Historical Museum*. *Peterborough 40 km/25 mi.*

Little Current   H9

(pop. 1440). A town on the northeastern tip of Manitoulin Island that grew from a tiny Hudson's Bay post. It is a rendezvous point for Great Lakes pleasure craft. For good views, go to *McLeans Mountain*. A hiking trail takes you to the island's highest lookout, called the Cup and Saucer Bluff. Another vantage point is Ten Mile Point looking across Georgian Bay, the Bay of Islands and Killarney. See the *Howland Centennial Museum* for its pioneer and Indian artefacts. *Sault Ste Marie 293 km/183 mi.*

London   O10

(pop. 240,392). Known as 'Forest City' due to the 1000s of trees from the tree planting programme begun last century and still continuing today. An important city on the River Thames, which like its namesake, supports a university, many museums, theaters etc. The oldest house, *Eldon House* (1834) is a period-furnished historical museum, open afternoons March-Nov. The region's history is displayed in the *Centennial Museum*, open afternoons year round. *Fanshawe Park and Pioneer Village* is a conservation area where pioneer crafts are demonstrated and a lake can be used for sailing or fishing. *Labatt Pioneer Brewery* on Simcoe St. is open afternoons, May-Labour Day. *Lawson Museum* (1853) contains memorabilia of the Lawson family. Children are encouraged to learn in the *Regional Children's Museum* on Riverview Ave.

Also see the *Ska-Nah-Doht Indian Village*, a re-created Iroquois village that includes long-houses and a palisade. Special events are often held here. (Open Victoria Day-Labour Day.) The *Museum of Indian Archaeology* displays the prehistory of southwest Ontario. (Open year round Tues.-Sun.) The Royal Canadian Regiment Museum is located in historic Wolseley Hall, open year-round Mon.-Fri.

London holds many exhibitions and fairs throughout the year. It is also a city with numerous parks. Of particular interest to youngsters is *Storybook Gardens* in

Springbank Park, reached either by car or paddlewheeler. *Sifton Bog* is also of interest being a 15,000-year-old black spruce bog which contains rare specimens of orchids and medicinal plants. *Toronto 190 km/118 mi.*

Manitoulin Island　　　H9
A large freshwater island with a scenic coastline, sandy beaches, many lakes and holiday towns.

Maple　　　M13
(pop. 1747). Location of one of Ontario's major attractions — **Canada's Wonderland,** Canada's answer to Disneyland. It is a 370 acre theme park with shops, restaurants, rides and shows, designed to please all the family. As with Disneyland and Disney World, cartoon characters mix with visitors and the themed 'lands' vary from medieval to international. Rides include flumes and roller coasters. (Open daily May-Labour Day, then weekends to the end of Sept.) *Toronto 30 km/19 mi.*

Marathon　　　Q21
(pop. 2258). New town on Lake Superior harbor with plenty of accommodation. A base for visiting *Neys Provincial Park* which boasts one of the best beaches on the North Shore. Especially recommended for fishing and hiking. Also not far from town is **Pukaskwa National Park,** good for hiking. *Thunder Bay 289 km/181 mi.*

Marten River　　　F13
A tourist center for hunting and fishing. See the *Trappers' Museum* with displays of pelts and an original trapper's cabin, open late May-mid Oct. *North Bay 58 km/36 mi.*

Massey　　　G9
(pop. 1320). A town at the junction of Sauble and Spanish Rivers, near *Chutes Provincial Park,* popular with summer campers. See *Massey Pioneer Museum* depicting the area's history from the Indian era through the 1790s trading post times to the timber period. *Sudbury 103 km/64 mi.*

Canada's Wonderland

Merrickville　　　J19
(pop. 900). Named for the first settler, millwright William Merrick. From a mill village it grew to become a Port on the Rideau Canal. See the *Blockhouse Museum,* built as a fort to protect the canal (1826-32). (Open mid June-mid Sept.) *Ottawa 68 km/42.5 mi.*

Midland　　　K13
(pop. 11,568). A busy metropolis whose history dates to 1639 when the Jesuits erected a fortified mission here. From the town you can take a cruise that follows the route of explorers Brulé, Champlain and La Salle up through the inside passage to Georgian Bay. Midland is located in what used to be Huron Indian land. There are many interesting exhibits on the area in *Huronia Museum* and *Gallery of Historic Huronia* (open Victoria Day-Thanks-

Ste. Marie among the Hurons

giving). An authentic replica of a Huron vilage can be found in *Little Lake Park* (open late May-Thanksgiving). **Sainte-Marie among the Hurons** is a reconstruction of the 17th-century Jesuit Mission which once stood here (open late May-Thanksgiving). Some of those missionaries were murdered by the Iroquois on the site where the *Martyrs' Shrine* now stands. Also see *Wye Marsh Wildlife Centre* whose boardwalk trails, observation tower and underwater window reveal many a marshland secret. (Open Victoria Day-Thanksgiving.) *Barrie 49 km/31 mi.*

Milton　　　N12
(pop. 20,800). A bustling city on Hwy 401. Pioneer memorabilia Indian artefacts and a light collection can be seen at *Halton Regional Museum,* open daily May-Thanksgiving, rest of year Mon.-Fri. The extensive *Ontario Agricultural Museum* is particularly worth a visit, open mid May-Oct. Outside of town, many seasonal events take place at the *Mountsberg Wildlife Centre. Toronto 40 km/25 mi.*

Minden　　　J14
(pop. 590). The entrance to the Highlands

of Haliburton, this town is at its most beautiful in autumn when the leaves turn. A panoramic viewpoint can be had from *Panorama Park Lookout. Buttermilk Falls* is a nearby beauty spot with a 70 ft torrent from Halls Lake to Boshkung Lake. See *Kanawa International Museum of Canoes and Kayaks* — an international collection of 400 of the finest craft. Also here is the *Heritage Trail* which represents the first Haliburton settlement with sawmill, smithy and other replicas. (Open daily May-Oct.) *Peterborough 133 km/83 mi.*

Moosonee   *see map p. 22*

(pop. 1277). Not accessible by road but at the end of the line for the **Polar Bear Express.** There are many attractions, mostly concerned with the *Hudson's Bay Post,* established here in 1673. *Reveillon Frères Museum* tells the story of Hudson's Bay's French rivals (open afternoons late June-Labour Day). The original site of Hudson's Bay post was on *Moose Factory Island* which you can reach by a 15 minute boat trip. Several early 18th-century buildings remain here and there is an excellent museum to illustrate the fur trade. In *St Thomas Church* there are beaded moose hide altar cloths and Cree language prayer books. Note the floor plugs, pulled during floods to allow the water in so the church does not float away! Another summer boat trip takes you to *Fossil Island* to see Devonian fossils, 350 million years old. Expensive but unique is the fly-in trip to **Polar Bear Provincial Park** for which a permit is required from the Ministry of Natural Resources in Moosonee. *Timmins 353 km/221 mi.*

Morrisburg   J21

(pop. 2150). One of the earliest settled parts of Canada. See **Upper Canada Village,** a composite pre-1867 town recreating that period. Costumed guides lead you through a woolen mill, a sawmill, blacksmith's — all in working order. There are some 40 buildings, roads, canals and a fort. Touring may be done on foot, by ox-cart or boat. Recommended as a day's outing. (Open mid May-mid Oct.) Spring and autumn are the best seasons for bird viewing at the *Upper Canada Migratory Bird Sanctuary,* a 3500 acre refuge. Early vehicles displayed at *Auto Wonderland* include an 1890 McLaughlin Motorized Surrey and an 1898 Locomobile Steamer. *Ottawa 69 km/43 mi.*

Napanee   L17

(pop. 4844). Originally a Loyalist town built in 1786. A Scotsman, Allan McPherson, became wealthy from renting the grist mill here and his house is one of the

area's most impressive. Visitors are welcome daily late May-mid Oct. The former 1864 county jail is now the *Lennox and Addington County Museum,* open afternoons year round. *Kingston 35 km/22 mi.*

Niagara Falls   O14

(pop. 69,423). Probably Canada's greatest attraction and well known honeymoon destination. In addition to the Falls themselves, this tourist town has many manmade attractions, accommodations and restaurants. The Falls are spectacular whatever the time of year and are illuminated at night. A trip not to be missed is on the *'Maid of the Mist'* which carries you close under the Horseshoe Falls. Hooded rain gear is supplied — and necessary. (Available mid May-mid Oct.) If that is too wet, take a helicopter flight over the Falls, or the elevator to the Niagara River gorge below the falls where a walkway leads along the edge of the rapids to the famous *Whirlpool Rapids.* Another tour takes you to viewpoints behind the Falls.

Marineland aquarium is one of the popular family attractions with dolphin, sea lion and whale performances. The *Spanish AeroCar* will carry you high above the *Whirlpool Rapids* but for a high place with a meal too, head for the 520 ft high *Skylon Tower* which has a revolving restaurant at the top. There are also dining facilities at the top of *Panasonic Centre* (666 ft), an entertainment complex. Shops and restaurants are located in *Maple Leaf Village. Niagara Falls Museum* is North America's oldest with over 700,000 exhibits including the Daredevil Hall of Fame. A year round floral display is featured at *Parks Commission Conservatory.* The best place to listen to the free summer carillon concerts is *Rainbow Gardens.* Opposite Skylon Tower, *Pyramid Place* comprises a variety of things to do and see including presentations on the six-story Imax screen. *Toronto 130 km/81 mi.*

Niagara-on-the-Lake   O14

(pop. 12,500). Upper Canada's first capital. A beautifully preserved 19th-century town on Lake Ontario with several charming inns for overnighting or eating out. It is best known for its summer **Shaw Festival,** late May-Sept. The main street is Queen St. A stroll down it will take you past the 1866 *Niagara Apothecary Museum;* a shop where they make fudge while you watch; *McClellands Store* which has been operating since 1835; *Greaves Jam,* fourth generation jam makers, and the *Prince of Wales Hotel,* a well restored inn.

See **Fort George** (1797-1799), which replaced Fort Niagara. It has been

Niagara Falls

destroyed, rebuilt, abandoned and was finally restored in 1939. Open mid May-Oct. *McFarland House* furnished in the style of the 1800s, open late May-Sept., weekends; July-mid Sept., Sat.-Wed. *Niagara Historical Museum* with a collection of 20,000 items pertaining to Niagara's colorful history, open daily May-Oct., rest of the year, afternoons. *Niagara Fire Museum* houses equipment used from 1816-1926, open afternoons July-Labour Day. *Niagara Falls 20 km/13 mi.*

Nipigon   Q20
(pop. 2224). The first permanent white settlement located on Lake Superior's north shore. Exhibits in the *Nipigon Museum* relate to the area's history. A sweeping view of Lake Superior shore can be seen from *Kama Bay Lookout. Thunder Bay 120 km/75 mi.*

North Bay   G3
(pop. 51,639). A bustling northern tourist city popular for hunting and fishing. From here boat cruises follow the Voyageur Route across Lake Nipissing to the Upper French River. There are nature trails on *Canadore College* campus and *Golden Mile's* sandy beach also has parkland and picnic facilities. *North Bay Fish Hatchery* is one of Ontario's newest. Also see *North Bay Area Museum* which houses relics of the pioneer era. *Sudbury 130 km/82 mi.*

Oakville   N13
(pop. 68,950). A prosperous harbor-front city with many 19th-century buildings between Toronto and Hamilton on Lake Ontario. The *Thomas House* (1829) and the old *Post Office* (1835) are both located in *Lakeside Park* (open afternoon May-Oct.). A working turn-of-the-century farm is situated in *Bronte Provincial Park* which also offers a sports complex and wagon tours. *Gairloch Gallery* in a 1922 lakeside mansion features changing art displays as does *Centennial Gallery.* Tour trains of *Ford Motor Co.'s* plant are available Nov.-June, Mon.-Fri. *Toronto 33 km/21 mi.*

Orillia   K14
(pop. 24,480). A resort center on the narrows between Lake Couchiching and Lake Simcoe, a major link in the Trent-Severn Canal System. It was a center for Indian activity centuries before Champlain came through in 1615. There is a monument to that explorer in the lakeside park. The *Stephen Leacock Home* was the humorist's lakeshore mansion, open daily mid June-Labour Day. At the *L.B.K. Buffalo Ranch* you can see wild buffalo, moose, elk and deer. (Open July-Labour Day, daily,

Victoria Day-June and after Labour Day, weekends.) *Barrie 33 km/21 mi.*

Oshawa   M14
(pop. 107,000). Now a center for the car industry though many old lakefront buildings are evidence of its days as a lake port. An interesting collection of early autos may be found in the *Canadian Automotive Museum,* open year-round. McLaughlin's mansion, *Parkwood,* houses antiques and is open Tues.-Sun., June-Labour Day. Known as 'Mr. General Motors of Canada', Robert McLaughlin has also lent his name to an art gallery. *The Henry House* and *Robinson House Museums* are restored homes of the 1850-1880 period. (Open Victoria Day-Thanksgiving, Tues.-Sun.) *Toronto 36 km/22.5 mi.*

Ottawa   I20
(pop. 304,462). Canada's national capital. Situated on the border between Ontario and Québec, this is a sophisticated city with a wide choice of hotels and shops. The highest point is Parliament Hill with its cluster of **Parliament Buildings** guarded by scarlet-clad Mounties. Canada's seat of government is here, in three Gothic stone, green copper-roofed buildings. The center block is crowned by the 291 ft *Peace Tower* whose carillon has 53 bells. When Parliament is in session, a white light burns on top of this tower. Symbolizing Canada's nationhood, an eternal flame burns in front of the buildings. Free tours are available through the House of Commons, Speakers Chamber, Senate Chamber and Library. A summer attraction is the *Changing of the Guard* ceremony, similar to that in Britain. Every noon Mon.-Sat. and at 1000 on Sun., the great gun here is fired. Parliament Hill is also the site of the Supreme Court of Canada.

Equally famous is the *Rideau Canal* and Locks, completed in 1832. The canal was the Duke of Wellington's idea, built with the purpose of allowing British gunboats to avoid the American cannon on the St Lawrence. It was never actually used for military purposes and became a commercial waterway instead. Today boat tours cruise along it and in winter residents skate on it.

Ottawa has a number of open areas downtown: *Garden of the Provinces* is a handsome square with flagpoles and a fountain. Outdoor summer concerts are often given at *Nepean Point* and wagon tours will take you through the downtown *Central Experimental Farm* Mon.-Fri., May-Sept.

Among the capital's significant houses is *Laurier House* (1878) which was the

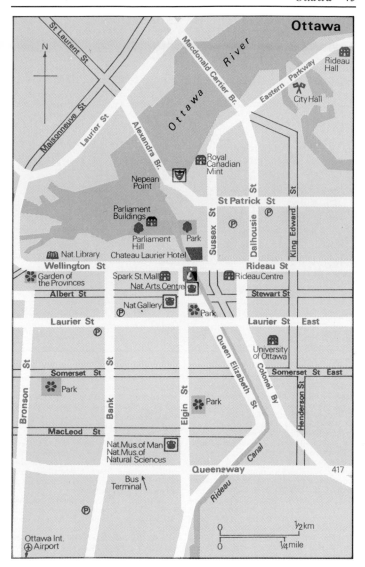

Ottawa

St Laurent St.

Macdonald Cartier Br.

Ottawa River

Eastern Parkway

Rideau Hall

N

City Hall

Maisonneuve St.

Laurier St.

St Laurent St.

Alexandra Br.

Royal Canadian Mint

Nepean Point

St Patrick St

Sussex St

Dalhousie St

King Edward St

Parliament Buildings

Parliament Hill

Park

Nat. Library

Chateau Laurier Hotel

Rideau St

Rideau Centre

Wellington St

Garden of the Provinces

Spark St. Mall

Nat. Arts. Centre

Stewart St

Albert St

Nat Gallery

Park

Laurier St

Laurier St East

Queen Elizabeth St

University of Ottawa

Colonel By

Somerset St

Somerset St East

Bronson St

Park

Bank St

Elgin St

Park

Henderson St

MacLeod St

Nat. Mus. of Man
Nat. Mus. of Natural Sciences

Queensway

417

Bus Terminal

Rideau Canal

Ottawa Int. Airport

0 .... ½km

0 .... ¼mile

Smallest of Eastern Canada's four main cities, Ottawa was chosen by Queen Victoria to be capital of the newly merged colonies of Upper and Lower Canada in 1858. At Confederation nine years later it became the national capital. What had once been a brawling lumber town became a city of ceremonies, gracious buildings, art galleries and museums, a lively modern city which combines business and pleasure.

Ottawa Parliament

home of two former Prime Ministers. Inside, memorabilia related to both Wilfrid Laurier and William Lyon Mackenzie King. (Open year round Tues.-Sun.) The official residence of Canada's Gov. Gen. is *Rideau Hall* whose extensive grounds are open to the public. Mackenzie King's summer estate is *Moorside* in **Gatineau Park,** open afternoons, May-mid Oct.

The city is a notable arts and museum center. See *Bytown Museum,* named for the man who built the Rideau Canal, Lieut. Col. John By (open Mon.-Sat. mid May-early Sept.). *Canadian War Museum* shows everything from Indian clubs to guided missiles and next door is the *Royal Canadian Mint* which can be visited. Canadian and British North American stamps are displayed at the *National Postal Museum.* Early ski equipment helps show the development of this sport at the *Canadian Ski Museum.*

One of the principal museums is the *National Museum of Science and Technology,* open year round. Man is related to his environment in the *National Museum of Man and Natural Sciences* with special emphasis on Canadians, open year round. The life story of Lord Baden-Powell and the history of scouting in Canada is the focus of *Museum of Canadian Scouting,* open year round.

The major cultural complex is the *National Arts Centre* on the banks of the Rideau Canal. In a series of inter-related hexagonal forms here is a combination of an opera house, theaters, restaurants, sculpture and flower-bordered terraces. The *National Gallery of Canada* is the city's prime art gallery.

Shopping is combined with outdoor cafes along the pedestrianized *Sparks St. Mall,* though Rideau St. is the main shopping street with two large department stores. *Byward Market* is the local York St. farmers' market, Mon.-Sat., May-Oct. and Fri. and Sat., Nov.-Dec. There is also the *Rideau Centre* built at a cost of 250 million dollars it boasts a convention centre, hotel, 200 stores, 18 restaurants and 3 cinemas. On top there is a 5 acre park with trails, benches and trees.

Spectator and participant sports include golf and boating, hockey and football and wooded country is not far away for hiking, canoeing, fishing or skiing. *Toronto 395 km/249 mi; Montréal 195 km/ 122 mi.*

Owen Sound K11

(pop. 19,525). A thriving city looking out over Owen Sound towards Georgian Bay. Local beauty spot is Inglis Falls. Two famous Canadians were born here: Tom Thomson (one of the Group of Seven) and Billy Bishop. Many of Tom Thomson's paintings are displayed in the *Memorial Art Gallery* named for him. The area's history can be reviewed in the *County of Grey & Owen Sound Museum. Storybook Park* speaks for itself — great for kids. *Toronto 185 km/103 mi.*

Parry Sound

Parry Sound I12

(pop. 5501). A summer resort town that is the main access point to the islands in Georgian Bay. The best view is from *Tower Hill Lookout.* A cruise on the *'Island Queen'* takes you through the biggest concentration of islands, operating June-mid Sept. *Barrie 150 km/94 mi.*

Pelee Island R7

A family resort for fishing and swimming, located half way between the Ontario and the Ohio shores of Lake Erie. There is frequent ferry service from Leamington and Kingsville.

Pembroke H17

(pop. 14,927). A town linked to the timber trade. *Riverside Park* here is the site of Ontario's largest totem pole. See the *Champlain Trail Museum,* so named for its location — close to the end of the trail of Champlain's first explorations. (Open daily June-Aug.) Pioneer artefacts are displayed at *Algonquin Indian History Museum* along with canoes made from birch bark. (Open May-Labour Day.) *Stone Hill Animal Farm* is a working farm, open daily Victoria Day-Labour Day. In the vicinity of Pembroke it is possible to try whitewater rafting on the Ottawa River. *Ottawa 150 km/94 mi.*

Penetanguishene K12

(pop. 5460). In 1817 this was the headquarters port for the British Navy on the Great Lakes. See the *Historic Naval and Military Establishments* where 17 buildings have been renovated or reconstructed. Tours are given by horse-drawn wagon and demonstrations of 19th-century musketry are given. (Open late May-Labour Day.) The garrison church for the military is St James-on-the-Lines (1836), made with an aisle wide enough for four men abreast. Exhibits relating to the town's early development are found in the *Centennial Museum,* open Victoria Day-Labour Day. From the town dock, boat cruises are available in July and Aug. *Barrie 56 km/35 mi.*

Peterborough L15

(pop. 59,600). Southeastern city gateway to the Kawartha Lakes holiday area and main link in the *Trent-Severn Waterway.* Cruises are available through the locking system and up the Otonabee River in summer. See *Centennial Fountain,* Canada's highest jet fountain. At the *Centennial Museum* and *Museum of the Trent-Severn Waterway,* the area's history is told through minerals, fossils and pioneer artefacts. Items include a working model of the waterway system. (Open daily year-round.) Hearth cooking and baking, spinning and quilting are all demonstrated in the 19th-century *Hutchison House,* open afternoons Tues.-Sun., March-Dec. There is the *Peterborough Summer Festival,* racing at *Kawartha Downs* and the modern architecture of *Trent University.* *Toronto 135 km/84 mi.*

Petrolia P8

(pop. 4393). Canada's first oil boom town which by 1890 was the hub of a refining empire. Visit *Petrolia Discovery* a working 60 acre oilfield, open daily May 8-Sept. 7. The *Oil Museum of Canada* houses actual drill rigs as well as working models. (Open daily late May-Sept., afternoons, Oct., weekends Nov.) *Victoria Hall* (1889) is a good example of Victorian architecture. *London 96 km/60 mi.*

Picton M17

(pop. 4600). Peaceful *Quinte Isle* town favored by artists. Along the western shore of the island there are miles of beaches and dunes. Several craft centers are located in nearby *Tyendinaga Indian Reserve* where a Mohawk landing is re-enacted each May. Also see the *District Courthouse and Jail,* an 1832 Greek revival building, and the *Ameliasburg Museum* comprising an 1868 church, a furnished log cabin and two pioneer barns. (Open daily July-

Labour Day, Labour Day-Thanksgiving, weekends.) *Belleville 37 km/23 mi.*

Port Colborne   O14
(pop. 20,536). Site of one of the largest single locks in the world, Canada's flour milling center and one of the biggest nickle refineries in the world. The *Historical and Marine Museum* is worth a visit. Each July there is *International Week. Toronto 160 km/100 mi.*

Port Dover   P12
(pop. 3300). A freshwater fishing port. Local hotels and restaurants specialize quite naturally in fish and fish fries are part of summer festivals. *Brantford 51 km/32 mi.*

Port Perry   M14
(pop. 3917). Lakeside town with marinas, swimming and fishing. See the *Scugog Shores Museum. Oshawa 35 km/21 mi.*

Prescott   K20
(pop. 4975). Trans-shipping point with a deep water port, connected to Ogdensburg, N.Y. via the *International Bridge.* Fort Wellington, the last military post to see action in the War of 1812, stands in a commanding position on the St Lawrence. You can see the barracks, armory, guardhouse and officers' quarters and in July there's a military pageant. (Open mid May-Oct.) *Kingston 104 km/65 mi.*

Renfrew   I17
(pop. 8617). Scottish pioneer founders gave this thriving town its name. Visit *McDougall Mill Museum* which was once a grist mill, open daily July-mid Sept. *Storyland* is a delightful theme park where animated characters are displayed in fairy tale settings. Also featured in Storyland is a wildlife museum, an Astro playground and Frontierland section. (Open daily mid May-Labour Day; Labour Day-Thanksgiving, weekends.) From Champlain Lookout, located at the end of Storyland, the view of the Ottawa River is magnificent. *Ottawa 87 km/54 mi.*

St Catherine's   O14
(pop. 123,351). Historic city in the middle of Niagara's fruit belt and wine country, often referred to as 'The Garden City'. Originally it was a Loyalist settlement which became a depot for the 'Underground Railroad' and site of the first *Welland Canal.* Displays showing the construction of that canal may be seen in *St Catherine's Historical Museum,* open year round. A fine place for ship watching is *Lock Three Observation Platform.* Remnants of the first three Welland Canals are preserved throughout the city.

Tours are possible of *Jordan Winery* all year Mon.-Fri. and a special wine festival takes place in St Catherine's in late Sept. Scale models of famous round-the-world landmarks can be seen at *Tivoli Miniature World,* open daily late May-late Sept. Also see *Mountain Mills Museum,* a waterpowered mill at De Cew Falls. *Niagara Falls 20 km/12.5 mi.*

St Jacobs   N11
(pop. 852). A charming Mennonite village with a restaurant specializing in Mennonite fare. *Waterloo 14 km/7 mi.*

St Joseph Island   G6
The most westerly island in the Manitoulin chain, situated in the channel between Lakes Huron and Superior. A rural island, fine for fishing and swimming. See **St Joseph National Historic Park.** Guided tours through the ruins of the original fort (1796-1812) are available. Also on this site is a large wilderness area and bird sanctuary. In *St Joseph Island Museum,* there are many finds from the fort. *Sault Ste Marie 50 km/31 mi.*

St Thomas   P10
(pop. 27,206). A town noted for its Victorian architecture. Look at City Hall, the Courthouse, Alma College and St Thomas Church. On weekends a narrow gauge steam train runs through *Pinafore Park* where there's a wildlife sanctuary and sport facilities. A superb collection of Canadiana is on view at the *Elgin Country Pioneer Museum,* open Tues.-Sun., Feb.-Dec. Only the earthworks remain of a nearby Neutral Indian fort but the site has atmosphere. *Hamilton 145 km/91 mi.*

Sauble Beach   K10
(pop. 350). Resort town with plenty of holiday accommodations including housekeeping cottages. Popular for watersports with a fine 11 km/7 mi sandy beach. Exceptional trout fishing at *Sauble Falls Provincial Park* to the north. *Owen Sound 25 km/16 mi.*

Sault Ste Marie   F5
(pop. 81,050). A city with a twin of the same name on the Michigan side of the St Mary's River, the link between Lakes Huron and Superior. The canal here is one of the most active in the whole of the St Lawrence Seaway system since lake freighters traveling to and from the Great Lakes, use the locks to bypass the rapids. French missionaries built the city in 1669. Take the *Algoma Central Railway* in order to see the **Agawa Canyon,** a scenic wilderness area. Special excursion trains make it a day's trip with a stop in the

canyon for climbing, rock hounding or fishing. Lock tours are offered June-Thanksgiving, through both the Canadian and American locks. The Canadian lock (1895) is the system's oldest. A tour of the waterfront includes the M.S. *'Norgama'*, last passenger ship built for the Great Lakes. The *Abitibi-Price* tour of a paper making plant is available on Tues. and Thurs., June-mid Oct.

See the *Algoma Art Gallery, Bellevue Park*, the *Tarentorus Fish Hatchery* and *Ermatinger House* (1814). The latter was built by a wealthy fur trader for his Indian princess wife. *Toronto 715 km/448 mi; Thunder Bay 715 km/448 mi.*

Sioux Narrows   Q17
(pop. 410). Good vacation center on Lake of the Woods where there are facilities for hunting, fishing and boating. *Kenora 88 km/55 mi.*

Southampton   K10
(pop. 2700). A charming Lake Huron resort on the Saugeen River with good fishing, sandy beaches, campsites and a museum. *Owen Sound 32 km/20 mi.*

South River   H13
(pop. 1100). An access point to Algonquin Park for canoeists and a horse ranch area. Guided horseback trips are available from Base Lodge through the Almaguin Highlands. *North Bay 62 km/39 mi.*

Stratford   N10
(pop. 25,657). Purposely resembles England's Stratford, complete with a River Avon and world famous **Shakespeare Festival** (June-Oct.). Also well known for its summer musical programs. *Toronto 155 km/97 mi.*

Sudbury   G11
(pop. 97,600). Plenty to do in this city set amid lakes and protected woodland. Take a mine tour. Visit *Copper Cliff Museum, Flour Mill Heritage Museum* or take in *Doran Planetarium and Art Gallery* at Laurentian University. In the summer, Sudbury can offer swimming and boating and in winter, skiing. Also notice the 30 ft-high 5 cent piece or 'nickel' which is actually made from stainless steel. *Toronto 395 km/249 mi.*

Sundridge   H14
(pop. 692). Tourist town on Lake Bernard that offers challenging deep-water trout fishing. You can learn all about maple syrup and its making at the *Maple Syrup Museum* where demonstrations are given in late March/early April. *North Bay 67 km/42 mi.*

Sutton   L14
(pop. 3655). Established in 1820 on the Black River near Lake Simcoe, this town is a center for winter ice fishing in the lake. See the *Eildon Hall* museum and estate in *Sibbald Point Provincial Park. Toronto 82 km/51 mi.*

Temagami   E13
(pop. 1350). Fishing center located on the northeast arm of Lake Temagami. Winter sports here include ice fishing for the great grey trout. It is a base for visiting *Finlayson Point Provincial Park* or taking a guided mine tour. *North Bay 96 km/60 mi.*

Thunder Bay   R20
(pop. 111,476). A large thriving northern port. Years ago canoes were the transporters and fur the cargo, on the Kaministikwia River which then was 'the highway west'. Turn back the clock when you visit **Old Fort William** on the Kaministikwia river banks. It is an impressive reconstruction of the original fort where in 1803 the North West Co. held its first annual 'rendezvous' for fur traders and agents. Costumed guides are here to answer questions and show you around, besides demonstrating craft skills. The historic restaurant here specializes in home-baked, brick-oven bread and hearty voyageur stew. At *Thunder Bay Museum*, there are Indian artefacts, pioneer, marine and military materials. (Open daily mid June-mid Sept., Tues.-Sun. rest of the year.) In summer, cruises take in the shipping areas and offshore islands, or cruise up to old Fort William. *Great Lakes Forest Products* offers summer tours of its plant.

Thunder Bay

For the best view of the town and the area, go to *Mt McKay*, a 183 m /600 ft ledge located in an Ojibwa Reservation. See also the 1910 logging camp and museum in *Centennial Park* which has 19 km / 12 mi of nature and cross-country ski trails. There's a beach and fun fair in *Chippewa Park* and tropical plants in the *Centennial Conservatory*. The *International Friendship Garden* represents nine nations in separate floral beds. A lookout point in *Hillcrest Park* shows the harbor and *'Sleeping Giant'* rock formation. The *Dorian Fish Hatchery* contains speckled and lake trout fingerlings and adults. There are five amethyst mines 72 km/ 35 mi east of Thunder Bay where you can pick your own stone in open pit mines or buy one.

Winter skiing is possible in five areas in the immediate vicinity of town. The tow and lodge facilities are all first class and uncrowded. There are also good cross-country trails and plenty of *apres ski* life. *Big Thunder Ski Jump* is a major facility. *Toronto 1415 km/884 mi; Winnipeg 665 km/416 mi.*

Timmins   B10
(pop. 44,747). The largest city in area in Canada and center of the Porcupine mining area which was once the largest gold producer in the Western Hemisphere. Nowadays it is rich in silver-zinc. In summer, mine tours are possible and at the *Porcupine Outdoor Mining Museum*, there is a collection of mining machinery. The first Ukrainian immigrants arrived in Canada in 1891, soon followed by thousands more escaping tyranny. Their culture and contributions are featured through art and crafts in the *Ukrainian Museum*, open June-Sept. daily, Oct.-May weekends. Changing exhibits are featured at the *National Exhibition Centre*. *Kettle Lakes Provincial Park*, 32 km/20 mi away offers sporting opportunities. *Toronto 690 km/431 mi.*

Tobermory   J9
(pop. 340). An enchanting village on the top of the *Bruce Peninsula*. Although it is a busy resort, it looks like a quiet fishing village with its twin harbors and frame houses. Water taxis leave from here to *Flower Pot Island*, part of the off-shore **Georgian Bay Islands National Park.** It takes its name from water-worn rocks that resemble giant flower pots. The island also has caves and water trails. In the waters around Tobermory, there are many wrecked vessels, a treat for scuba divers. *Toronto 300 km/187 mi.*

Toronto   N13
(pop. 2,137,725, metro area). In just over 150 years, Toronto has become Canada's most dynamic city, a center for the performing arts and film and a communications center. One third of all Canada's buying power lies within a 100 miles radius. About 170 types of industry are represented here and Toronto is head office to more companies with over C$1 million in assets than any other Canadian city. Located on the northwest shore of Lake Ontario, it covers 244 sq mi and is in the Eastern Standard Time Zone.

The name 'Toronto' is an Indian one, meaning 'a meeting place', though when it was a mere fur trading post back in the 1600s and 1700s, it was known as Fort Rouillé since it had been built by the French. It became predominantly British after they burnt it down in 1759.

The site was bought from the Mississauga Tribe in 1787 and the original town was laid out by Gov. John Simcoe in 1793 and was named York in honor of George III's son, Frederick, Duke of York. It became a strategic garrison town and later, in 1796, capital of Upper Canada. Despite its reputation for being staid, Toronto has always been innovative and inventive — insulin and Pablum were both invented here. A Torontonian invented the paint roller and Standard Time originated here in 1884. North America's first commercial jet was built and designed in Toronto; a young entrepreneur initiated five-pin bowling in 1904; and the battery-less radio was pioneered here in the 1920s.

Toronto and the Lakeshore

Today's Toronto is safe, clean and lively and its lakefront setting gives it a 'seaside' atmosphere that few other metropolises can claim. What better place for an overview than from the observation level of the **CN Tower.** Almost twice as high as the Eiffel Tower, its revolving restaurant allows almost a 360° view over the city and the lake. It is the world's tallest freestanding structure and since its opening in 1976

Cinesphere at Ontario Place

has become Toronto's most visible and famous landmark, containing a popular disco and a newly opened attraction in its base. It is located on Front Street West.

Harbourfront seems to continually grow, stretching from almost the foot of York St. to past Bathurst St. It is a 92 acre complex which combines culture and entertainment with office and residential accommodation. There are shops and boutiques here and in summer an outdoor antique market. There are places to eat and drink, free entertainment, exhibitions and activities throughout the year. Especially worth visiting is the Queen's Quay Terminal. (Located at Queen's Quay West.)

Somewhat further along the lakefront, on Lakeshore Blvd. W. is **Ontario Place,** another leisure complex built on three man-made islands in the lake. Some of the designers of Montréal's Expo '67 had a hand in the design. It contains fast food outlets and elegant restaurants, an outdoor concert hall, computer games and water rides and a particularly good playground for young children. A key feature is the Cinesphere Theatre used for multi-screen presentations. There is also a marina; HMCS *Haida,* a World War II destroyer; an amphitheatre and winter activities too, including *Winter Magic.*

Across from Ontario Place is **Exhibition Place** which hosts some of the city's most prestigious shows, concerts and sports events. It is where the annual *Canadian National Exhibition* takes place each summer which includes an air show, a horse show, an agricultural show — and entertainment for all the family.

Joggers can enjoy the waterfront and do themselves some good by covering the 20 km/12.5 mi Martin Goodman Trail, but the less energetic can take a boat tour. There are several cruises available operating between May and Sept.

Not far from the waterfront on Front St. is Toronto's newest hotel, L'Hotel, next to the city's brand new convention center. From the waterfront, practically next door to the Harbour Castle Hotel, ferries leave for the **Toronto Islands** in warm weather — to *Centre Island* which has recreational activities of all kinds including a children's amusement park, formal gardens and puppet theater. Also to less crowded *Ward's Island* or to *Hanlan's Point* which has the best beaches. In the winter you can cross-country ski on the islands.

Getting around central Toronto is incredibly easy since it is laid out on a grid system. All you really need to do to get your bearings is remember the two main streets of Yonge and Bloor. Yonge runs north to south through the center (the CN Tower is to the south). Bloor runs east to west. Take a taxi if you must but the

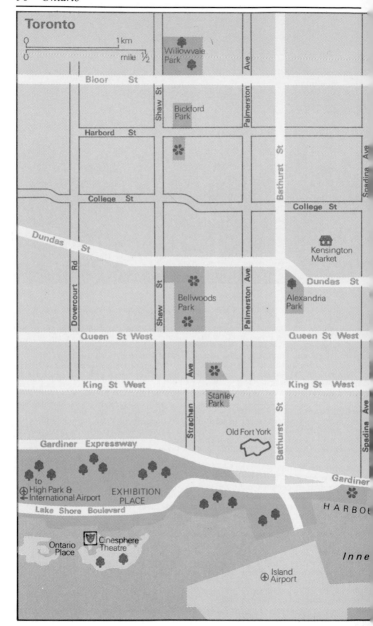

Toronto

0 _____ 1 km
0 _____ mile ½

Willowvale Park

Bloor   St

Shaw St

Palmerston

Ave

Bickford Park

Harbord   St

Bathurst   St

Spadina   Ave

College   St

College   St

Dundas   St

Dovercourt   Rd

Kensington Market

Shaw St

Bellwoods Park

Palmerston Ave

Dundas   St

Alexandria Park

Queen   St   West

Queen   St   West

Ave

King   St   West

King   St   West

Strachan

Stanley Park

Bathurst   St

St

Spadina   Ave

Old Fort York

Gardiner   Expressway

to
High Park &
International Airport

EXHIBITION PLACE

Gardiner

HARBOU

Lake Shore   Boulevard

Ontario Place

Cinesphere Theatre

Inne

Island Airport

Avenue Rd

YORKTOWN

Bloor St   Bloor St East

Rosedale Valley Rd

to Zoo &
Ontario Science
Centre

Royal Ontario
Museum
Mc Laughlin
Planetarium

Sherborne St

skin Ave

Queen's
Park

University
of Toronto

Parliament
Buildings

Wellesley   St

Wellesley St

Yonge St

Maple Leaf Gardens

College   St

Carlton   St

Jarvis St

Allan
Gardens

Art Gallery
and Museum

University Ave

Bus Terminal

CHINATOWN

Dundas St

Eaton
Centre

Grange Park

City Hall
Nathan Phillips
Sq.

St Michael's
Cathedral

Queen St   East

St James
Cathedral

King St East

King St East

Roy
Thomson Hall

University Ave

Railway Station
(Union)

Yonge St

O'Keefe
Centre

St Lawrence
Market

Jarvis St

Sherborne St

Tower

Gardiner   Expressway

xpressway

RONT

Harbour

N

Exhibition
Centre

Island
Airport

Hanlan's
Point

Inner Harbour

Centre   Island

TORONTO
ISLANDS

subway, bus and streetcar system is efficient and inexpensive. The streetcars operate regularly from east to west; buses and subway cover the whole city. There is one flat fare with free transfers available from one mode of transport to another.

Providing the weather is good, a walk around downtown will be most enjoyable and nowhere is better for strolling than **Yorkville,** a village within a city. These days, this section just north of Bloor, bounded by Avenue Rd and Yonge St. is one of the most elegant and fashionable areas of town where renovated townhouses have become boutiques, galleries and restaurants, and doors open onto courtyard cafes. Yorkville was incorporated in 1853 and has a coat-of-arms depicting the professions of the five original council members — brewer, smith, brickmaker, carpenter and farmer. It is displayed on the old *Firehall* on Yorkville Ave.

Look in on the **Royal Ontario Museum** on the corner of Bloor and Avenue Rd. It houses millions of treasures relating to science and evolution. The adjoining **McLaughlin Planetarium** is also certainly worth extra time.

In the same area, **Queen's Park** was named for Queen Victoria, and here, on the site of a former lunatic asylum, stands the Romanesque **Ontario Parliament Buildings.** You can visit the Legislative Chamber and the Assembly when it's in session, and view exhibits of Canadian art and minerals. Among the statues outside, stands Victoria herself with son Edward VII beside her.

One of Toronto's widest and most handsome streets, University Avenue, sweeps south from the steps of Parliament. Cutting across it is Dundas St., traditionally the heart of **Chinatown.** It is not large but it is lively with the Oriental signs you'd expect to find in a Far East community. The area now stretches west to Spadina.

If you walk west on Dundas to McCaul St. you will find the **Art Gallery of Ontario,** the city's most celebrated gallery with collections that range from Old Masters to contemporary Canadian. It is also noted for its extensive public collection of Henry Moore sculptures. In the Gallery's gardens, *The Grange* was built in 1818 as an elegant home for one of Toronto's leading citizens.

If you walk east on Dundas to Yonge St., you will come to the **Eaton Centre,** a spectacular shopping complex filled with fountains and greenery in an airy, glass-encased Galleria. The Centre was built around *Holy Trinity Church* and *Scadding House,* two old landmarks, now half hidden. There are 300 stores and services on

four levels and 21 theatres for film shows. An overhead glass-covered walkway connects the Eaton Centre with *Simpsons,* the store described as 'the finest building of its kind' when it opened in 1894.

Nearby stands the *Old City Hall* with its gargoyles and clock tower, alongside **New City Hall** at the corner of Bay and Queen Sts. Designed by Finnish architect, Viljo Revell, its centerpiece is a white dome housing the council chambers. In front, *Nathan Phillips Square* is a rendezvous point for relaxing or listening to concerts and in winter the pool here becomes a popular ice rink. Also in the square is a Henry Moore piece which most people refer to as 'The Archer' — better than its real name, 'Three Way Piece Number Two'!

City Hall, Toronto

The old building to the west on Queen St. is *Osgoode Hall,* home of the Law Society of Upper Canada which established itself here in 1830 at a time when it needed a fence to keep the cows out. *Campbell House,* a fine example of Georgian architecture, is also on Queen St. It is the restored residence of Sir William Campbell who was Chief Justice for Upper Canada from 1825 to 1829.

When you are exploring on foot, do not forget that Toronto is a city of neighbourhoods. Some, like Chinatown are ethnic, they include: *Roncesvalles,* Roncesvalles Ave, between Howard Park Ave and Queen St W. is the Polish district while the *St Clair/Dufferin area* is reckoned to be 'Little Italy' and *The Danforth,* Danforth Ave, between Broadview and Pape, is strongly Greek.

'Old' communities have taken on 'new' appeal, like *The Annex,* on Bloor St W. between Bathurst and Spadina, a village area where handsome houses line narrow streets. Similarly *Cabbagetown* in the Parliament/Carlton area where many homes have been renovated by young families. *Old York*, in the heart of downtown, bounded by Adelaide, George, Front and Parliament Sts., has acquired fashionability with new buildings like *Market Place*, housing shops and restaurants, but it still has the bustling *St Lawrence Market*, the city's own farmers' market.

Whatever the weather, *shopping* in Toronto is a pleasure. There are fine department and speciality shops, up-to-the-minute boutiques and craft centers. There are also several underground concentrations of shops, largely under buildings such as the Toronto-Dominion Bank headquarters. Among the most well known underground malls are the Richmond-Adelaide Centre (connected underground to the Sheraton Centre), The Toronto-Dominion Centre, which has over 50 stores the Royal Bank Plaza and Commerce Court. Currently the underground malls are connected continuously by passageways from Union Station to New City Hall but will link up with the Eaton Centre via Simpsons. There are similar though smaller malls at Yonge and College and on Bloor St. between Church St. and Bellair.

20th Century Toronto

This underground system is reputed to be the biggest such pedestrian network in the world. *Bloor St.* itself is well known for fashions and high class goods along its 'Mink Mile'. You'll find plenty of book shops and antique stores behind Honest Ed's department store in *Mirvish Village*, Bathurst/Bloor area; discount clothing on Spadina Ave, between College and King and all kinds of food and bric-a-brac at *Kensington Market*, Dundas/Spadina. Finally, like all North American cities,

Toronto has suburban shopping malls. They are air-conditioned, have plenty of parking and always have 2 out of the big 3 stores (Eatons, The Bay, Simpsons). Among these malls are Yorkdale, Fairview and Sherway Gardens.

Night life centers around Bloor and Yonge Sts., or The Esplanade for 'Singles' bars. The Canadian Opera Co.'s season at *O'Keefe Centre* is Sept.-June. The O'Keefe is Toronto's largest theater and also plays host to the National Ballet and Broadway musicals. The Toronto Symphony Orchestra's home is *Roy Thomson Hall* and the other big musical center is *Massey Hall*. Rock concerts and ice hockey games are played often in *Maple Leaf Gardens* on Carlton St.

There are also special events which take place annually with the *Metro International Caravan*, a celebration of Toronto's varied ethnic backgrounds, being the best known. *Caribana* is the giant West Indian festival which starts with a parade on University Avenue. The *Canadian National Exhibition* and the *Royal Agricultural Winter Fair* both take place at the Exhibition Grounds on Lakeshore Boulevard. On Victoria Day weekend in late May the *International Children's Festival* is held and early June on Centre Island is the time and the place for the *International Picnic*.

Black Creek Pioneer Village

Other Attractions

Allan Gardens, Carlton and Sherbourne St. blossom year round in the heart of downtown under a large domed greenhouse.

Black Creek Pioneer Village, Steeles Ave and Jane St. It used to take a day's journey to reach Daniel Stong's farm — now it takes half an hour. The farm and other pioneer buildings re-create rural life in Ontario around 1793-1867 with costumed guides to do the explaining. Open most of the year Mon.-Fri. 0930-1700, weekends 1000-1800.

Canada's Wonderland, Hwy 400 and Rutherford Rd. Canada's best theme park with distinct theme areas such as Medieval Faire, International Street and plenty of thrills and rides like 'SkyRider', a stand-up, looping roller coaster. The park covers 370 acres, has eating and entertainment facilities and lies ten minutes north of Metro Toronto. Open daily in summer 1000-2000; hours vary for rest of year.

Canadiana Building, 14 Queen's Park Cres. Displays early Canadian room settings and furnishings. Changing exhibitions of maps, prints and paintings are featured in the South Gallery.

Casa Loma, Austin Terrace. Sir Henry Pellatt wanted a dream castle and this is it, a concoction of castle features borrowed from elsewhere. Take yourself on tour of its 98 rooms. Open daily 1000-1600, in summer to 1700.

Colborne Lodge, Colborne Lodge Dr and The Queensway. A restored 19th-century Regency house named for one of Upper Canada's former governors. Daily craft demonstrations. Open Mon.-Sat. 0930-1700, Sun. 1200-1700.

Ecology House, 12 Madison Ave. Demonstrations of solar heating and energy conservation are given in this Victorian mansion at the heart of The Annex. Open Wed.-Sun. 1200-1700.

Fort York, Garrison Rd, off Fleet St. John Graves Simcoe established this fort in 1793 which was to become the site of one of the bloodiest battles of the War of 1812. Eight of the original buildings are still here and during summer a guard dressed in British uniforms of the period re-enacts its former military life with battle drills, cannon firings and parades. Open year round, in summer daily from 0930-1700.

George R. Gardiner Museum of Ceramic Art, 11 Queen's Park, is a new museum with a significant collection of ceramics including pre-Columbian art, Italian majolica and 18th-century European porcelain. Open Tues.-Sun. 1000-1700.

Gibson House, 5172 Yonge St. A restored 1850 home that once belonged to local politician, David Gibson. Tours and craft demonstrations are given daily and the house also contains exhibitions of art and local history. Open Mon.-Fri. 0930-1700, weekends 1200-1700.

The Grange, 317 Dundas St. W. Toronto's oldest surviving brick house was built in 1817 by D'Arcy Boulton Jr., and was the original home of the Art Gallery of Ontario.

High Park, Bloor St. W. and Keele St. is Toronto's answer to Hyde Park, being the largest wooded green belt in the city. There is a small zoo here and several recreational facilities.

Hockey Hall of Fame, Exhibition Place, honors the best of hockey players and displays the Stanley Cup. Open most of year Tues.-Sun. 1000-1700.

Mackenzie House, 82 Bond St. Toronto's first mayor and leader of the 1837 rebellion, William Lyon Mackenzie, once owned this Victorian townhouse, and died here in 1861. All the furnishings are authentic 1850s and include a pre-Confederation print shop with a working Washington flatbed press. Open Mon.-Sat. 0930-1700, Sun. 1200-1700.

Marine Museum of Upper Canada, Exhibition Place. Housed in the officers' quarters of Stanley Barracks, built in 1841, this museum depicts the influences of the waterways. Among the exhibits are a ship's wireless room, a fur trading post, diving equipment and a steam whistle collection. Open Mon.-Sat. 0930-1700, Sun. 1200-1700, later in the summer.

Metro Zoo, Hwy 401 Eat Meadowvale Rd. With over 700 acres divided into regions, this zoo features animals in their natural habitats. Weather permitting, you can take the Domain Ride and in season, the Zoomobile travels along the trails. Special trails are used for cross-country skiing in winter. Open daily.from 0930.

Metropolitan Toronto Police Museum, 590 Jarvis St. has a replica of a police station from the turn of the century plus displays of Metro Toronto's more famous crimes. Open Mon.-Fri. 1800-2100; weekends 1300-1700.

Montgomery's Inn, 4709 Dundas St. W. A restored Georgian inn of the 1847-1850 period and a prime example of Loyalist style. Costumed staff give guided tours and demonstrations. Open Mon.-Fri. 0930-1630, weekends 1300-1700.

Museum of the History of Medicine, 288 Bloor St. Permanent and changing exhibitions give 5000 years worth of medical history. Open Mon.-Fri. 0930-1600.

Ontario Science Centre, 770 Don Mills Rd is one of the most popular city attractions. It occupies 20 acres and has many elaborate exhibits, often the try/touch sort. Film presentations are shown in mini theaters, there's a new Hall of Technology, a simulated moon landing and much more besides. Open daily 1000-1800.

Puppet Centre, 171 Avondale Ave shows 400 puppets from around the world. Canada's only one, open Mon.-Fri.

Redpath Sugar Museum, 95 Queen's Quay E. Everything you wanted to know about the sugar industry is displayed here. Open year round.

Riverdale Farm, River and Garrard Sts. is a working farm where visitors can see a number of farm animals. Special festivals are held here throughout the year.

Royal Alexandra Theatre, 260 King St. was rescued from the bulldozer and restored to its red plush grandeur. Never mind the show — concentrate on the theater!

Spadina House, 285 Spadina Rd was the magnificent estate of prominent business-man, James Austin. It was built on Daven-port Hill in 1866 on six acres of landscaped grounds. Today its furnishings show life here through three generations. Open Mon.-Sat. 0930-1700, Sun. 1200-1700.

Todmorden Mills, 67 Pottery Rd. A com-munity museum on a 19th-century mill site on the Don River. It contains two res-tored pre-Confederation houses and a for-mer brewery. Open May-Dec., Tues.-Fri. 1000-1700; weekends 1100-1730.

Toronto Stock Exchange, Exchange Tower, 2 Canadian Place. Canada's largest secu-rities market located in the city's financial district. Displays in the Visitors Centre and a tour shows how the market works and all the trading being done. Open Mon.-Fri. 1000-1600.

Wasaga Beach K12

(pop. 4985). Resort center on a sand spit between Georgian Bay and the Nottawa-saga River, whose main attraction is its 14 km/9 mi sandy beach. *Wasaga Beach Pro-vincial Park* may be enjoyed year round. Visit *Nancy Island Historic Site* on the island. It is formed around British schooner *'Nancy'* which sank in 1814. The events of those days are electronically depicted in the museum and theater while displays include everything from the *'Nancy's'* charred hull to the wheelhouse of a Great Lakes steamer. (Open Victoria Day-Labour Day.) In *Dinosaur Valley,* life-size prehistoric creatures are the key feature. *Water World* is also a family attraction. *Barrie 40 km/25 mi.*

Wawa C4

(pop. 4722). During migration, thousands of geese take a break on Lake Wawa whose Ojibwa Indian name means 'wild goose'. Before 1700 this town was a fur trading post and later the site of three gold rushes. A landmark sculpture, in steel, of the *Wawa Goose* here is one of the largest sym-bols of its kind. Nature walks are con-ducted in *Lake Superior Provincial Park* and local scenic spot is *High Falls. Thunder Bay 485 km/303 mi.*

Welland O14

(pop. 45,047). Though essentially an industrial steel center, Welland is also known for its roses. A two week June fes-tival celebrates these famous flowers. Items that relate to the city and the *Welland Ship Canal* are well displayed at the *Historical Museum* on S. Pelham St., open afternoons late May-Thanksgiving. *Niagara Falls 20 km/12.5 mi.*

Whitney I15

(pop. 767). The town is the access point for main canoe routes through **Algon-quin Park,** hiking trails and fishing trips into the wild interior. Other sport possibi-lities in the area include hunting, horse-back trips and cross-country skiing. *Pembroke 129 km/81 mi.*

Wiarton K10

(pop. 2144). Pleasant sport oriented town on Colpoy Bay at the base of the Bruce Peninsula. Sailing is particularly good. Visitors are welcome at the *Cape Croker Indian Reserve* with its large Ojibwa settle-ment. Here there are craft shops and pic-nic areas, areas for boating and fishing and hiking trails along the shoreline. *Owen Sound 33 km/21 mi.*

Williamstown I22

(pop. 300). A picturesque village settled in 1784 by Sir John Johnson and his Loyal-ists. See *The Nor'western and Loyalist Museum* where displays tell the story of the North West Co. and the fur trade. (Open daily Victoria Day-Labour Day, weekends Labour Day-Thanksgiving.) The *Glen-garry Pioneer Museum* is housed in a log inn, barn and cheese factory and shows a large collection of Loyalist memorabilia and equipment. *Cornwall 26 km/16 mi.*

Windsor Q7

(pop. 196,526). Strategically located on the Detroit River, this city was a bone of contention between the British, French and Americans from the arrival of the first missionaries in 1640. Today, it is heavily industrialized and closely associated with the auto industry across the river in Detroit. Nevertheless, it boasts several attractive parks like *Dieppe Gardens* at the riverfront and *Jackson Park Sunken Gar-den.* There are also the *Memorial Rose Test Gardens* laid out in the form of a compass and with 12,000 rose bushes of 500 varieties. These gardens give Windsor its name — 'City of Roses'. The *Art Gallery* of Windsor is in a beautifully converted old waterfront brewery warehouse and offers constantly changing exhibits. *Hiram Walker Historical Museum,* in a well pre-served neoclassic 1812 house, illustrates human life in the region. The house was built by Col. François Bâby and used as headquarters by invading US forces in 1812. (Open Jan.-mid Dec., Tues.-Sun.)

The floating *International Peace Foun-tain* in the Detroit River is a much photo-graphed and admired attraction for its changing colored water patterns. The *Farm Fun Park* is a children's park with a country theme. (Open daily June-Labour Day.) Tours are available of both *Bell Telephone* and *Hiram Walker* plants. *Toronto 380 km/237 mi.*

QUÉBEC

The province of Québec is enormous, the largest of Canada's provinces, it is twice the size of France, with room for the UK as well. Equally, it is one of the most historic regions of the country (see History) and its history explains why it is still predominantly French speaking. These days, though, most people also speak English and most signs are international.

The province straddles the St Lawrence River, a strategic water route linking the Atlantic with the Great Lakes, a route which did so much for the development of America itself. Little did Jacques Cartier realize what the future held when he first sailed up the St Lawrence centuries ago. Nor did those early settlers along the river quite envision how the country would eventually grow. It is interesting to note, though, that the majority of Québec's population of six million plus still live in the vicinity of the river and those first two established settlements — Québec City and Montréal.

With such vast expanses of undeveloped countryside it is not surprising that this province pleases the outdoor sports enthusiast. All in all, there are 750,000 lakes and 300 million acres of untouched forests within the province. Some of it is quite desolate, like the frozen tundra around Ungava Bay. Some is richly foliaged as along the northern shores of the St Lawrence, some is mountainous. Each season offers something special, autumnal colors, especially of the maples, are superb.

Québec's woodlands are one of its biggest assests, well equipped with camping and picnic sites and well marked. Several of the parks stay open through the winter for cross-country skiers to enjoy.

Québec has recently been divided into 18 different tourist regions each with its own attractions and special features. Each region has its own information service and is co-ordinated through the government of Québec by Information Tourisme Québec. **The Laurentians,** often referred to as 'little Switzerland'. Thousands of years ago, glaciers carved mountains, lakes and valleys in this year-round resort area where sports lovers have a wide choice of things to do. The Laurentians are on Montréal's doorstep, dotted with unspoiled villages, studded with top class hotels.

Southeast of Montréal lie the **Eastern Townships,** settled by Loyalists after the American Revolution and now a series of charming towns surrounded by rolling farmland.

Close to Montréal, the **Richelieu Valley** has seen many a battle fought on its turf. The Richelieu River links the St Lawrence to Lake Champlain and today this is a peaceful, rural area with farm-fresh produce readily available, quiet river-front communities, country churches and the only sound is the stir of pleasure craft.

From the east end of Montréal island and spreading out to the northwest is **De Lanaudiere** which once lay beneath water. It is a region, famed for its beauty, that abounds in lakes and rivers but now also has acres of tobacco fields.

In the northwest, the **Abitibi-Temiscamingue** district is most famous for its gold and copper mining, though this area also offers fine rewards for fishermen.

The **Gaspé** region, east of Québec City, is thought by many to be Québec's most spectacular region. Here mountains practically tumble into the ocean, the manor houses and covered bridges are as old as Canada itself and the tiny fishing villages remain unspoilt.

In the north central part of Québec, you'll find the fjord of the **Saguenay River** bordered by majestic cliffs, and around **Lac-Saint Jean,** some of the tastiest blueberries in Eastern Canada. Wilderness delights include white water kayaking and backpacking at Cap-Trinité.

In **Charlevoix,** you'll discover artist's colonies and picturesque bays; inns that were once stately summer homes and also peaceful resorts. Another discovery is the region called **Maple Country,** on the south shore of the St Lawrence where the Appalachian Mountains end. Named for its great forests of maples, it is a lovely rural area whose population prove convivial company.

The adventurous might well head for **Manicouagan,** a rugged, scarcely tamed area where one of the world's greatest hydro-electric complexes has been built and whose dense forests provide the wherewithal for a thriving paper industry. Today's explorers might also go where yesterday's explorers were — **Duplessis** along the northeast shore of the St Lawrence, where the Vikings are thought to have landed. It is an area rich in minerals and of great interest to hunters and fishermen. One of the last frontiers is **Nouveau Québec,** a huge northern region that encompasses the east shore of James and Hudson's Bays, an area that covers over 50 per cent of the whole province but with the smallest population. This is the land of the Cree and the Inuit, of Arctic char and northern lights, polar bears and caribou.

By way of contrast, the **Îles-de-la-Madeleine** are warmed by the Gulf Stream. The archipelago lies off the Gaspé Peninsula and can be reached by air or sea. Some of the original settlers were probably shipwreck victims and many of the islanders today are their descendants. With miles of white sand beaches and traditional fishing villages, these isles are a unique attraction. **Bas-St-Laurent** is the beautiful south coast of the St Lawrence which extends from Lévis, opposite Québec City, to the Gaspé. Here there are 300 year old towns, islands and many bird reserves. **Maurice/Bois Francs** lies along the St Maurice river valley and includes the untamed wilderness of the St Maurice Reserve, plenty of small farms and a great deal of logging. The **Ottawa Valley** contains an estimated 20,000 lakes and 24 rivers making it a good area for hunting and fishing. But it also includes the cities of Hull and Ottawa itself plus of course the scenic Gatineau Park.

Finally there are the cities of **Montréal** and **Québec** with their environs and all the attractions which can be found there.

Abitibi-Temiscamingue   E2
see map p. 27

The northwest region of Québec, a vast area that was virgin wilderness until around the 1920s. When the Le Moyne brothers decided to attack the British on James Bay in 1686, they chose an overland route along Lake Temiscamingue and erected Fort Abitib at the mouth of the Duparquet River. The same expedition also investigated a silver and lead deposit near Saint-Bruno-de-Guigues but it took two more centuries before mining was developed. Until the 1929 depression, only a trickle of people had moved up here but the movement gathered momentum and the rural communities spread. Most Abitibi townships are named to honor

units and officers in Montcalm's army at the time of the Battle of the Plains of Abraham. It is an area of large game, 'moose crossing' signs are often seen along the highways, and an anglers' haven. There is also skiing in the winter. Principal towns are: *Rouyn, Val-d'Or, Noranda, Chibougamau, Amos, Malartic, La Sarre.*

Arthabaska   O5
(pop. 5907). Sits in a pleasant site at the foot of Mont St Michel in the Bois-Francs. This was the home of Sir Wilfred Laurier for many years and the **Musée Laurier** is open daily, except Mon., Feb.-Nov. *Québec City 91 km/56 mi.*

Bic   I11
(pop. 2670). An exceptionally beautiful town on the Lower St Lawrence. It sits in a rocky bay surrounded by a series of islands. There are two camping grounds in the area. *Québec City 292 km/182 mi.*

Golf at Bic

Cap-de-la-Madeleine   N4
(pop. 32,126). The sister city to Trois-Rivières, lying on the opposite bank of the St Maurice River. Due to a series of miracles associated with the building of the church and with the statue of the Virgin it has become a place of pilgrimage. *Montréal 142 km/89 mi.*

Chambly   P3
(pop. 11,815). Situated in the Richelieu Valley, about half an hour's drive south of Montréal, Chambly is most famous for its fort which you can see in the **Fort Chambly National Historic Park,** open year round. In 1665, four French companies led by Jacques de Chambly sailed up the Iroquois River and built a fort on this site, to safeguard the garrison from Indian attack. After an accidental fire in 1702, a second log fort was erected and in 1709 replaced by the stone fortification you see today. Displays and audio-visual presentations describe its history. *Montréal 35 km/20 mi.*

Charlevoix   K8
A fertile region stretching from Ste-Anne-de-Beaupré, not far from Québec City and

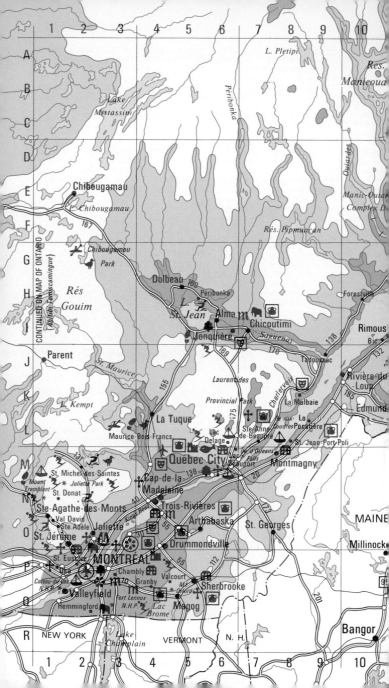

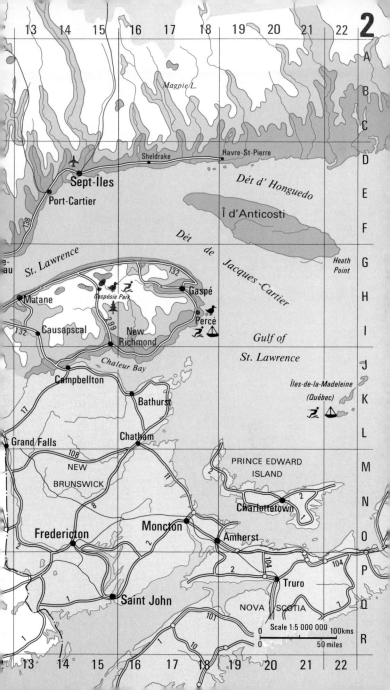

running up the north shore to Tadoussac. It is noted for its inns, often converted from bygone mansions, and its art colonies. In summer there are many art exhibitions and theater shows. Recommended places to stay include the *Manoir Richelieu* at Pointe-au-Pic (Murray Bay), *Hotel Cap-aux-Pierres, Auberge de la Roche Pleureuse* and *Auberge les Voitures d'Eau* — all at Île-aux-Coudres. (NB for touring, this region is often combined with Beaupré.)

Chibougamau Park   G3

This area, covering 11,025 sq km/4257 sq mi in central Québec, is excellent for fishing, hunting and camping. The Montagnais Indians prospered in the fur trade by hunting in this region. The park's highest peaks are du Sorcier, du Jongleur and Vermillon and most of the waters flow into Lac-Saint-Jean. The main rivers are the Chamouchouane, the Chigoubiche and the Vermillon and lakes include the Chigoubiche where you can canoe and swim. *Québec 307 km/192 mi.*

Chicoutimi   I7

(pop. 57,737). A major city in the central Saguenay-Lac Saint-Jean region of Québec. See the *Arthur Villeneuve Museum* for its paintings, the *Saguenay Museum*, one of the best regional ones of its kind and the *St-Félicien Zoo*. You can cruise down the Saguenay or fly over the region in a helicopter. *Québec 211 km/134 mi.*

Coteau-du-lac National Historic Park   Q1

Before modern technology created dams and canal systems, rapids were a great obstacle to moving ships and supplies along the St Lawrence. The first canal along the river was built in 1779-80 at the junction of the Delisle and St Lawrence to bypass one of those rough stretches of water. This park contains the remains of that first canal as well as a British military post dating from the War of 1812. *Montréal 58 km/36.25 mi.*

Drummondville   O5

(pop. 29,286). An industrial city on the banks of the St Francois River but nearby is the **Village Québecois D'Antan,** a collection of 19th-century buildings including a tavern, a school, a forge and various homes. It is open from late May-Sept., Wed.-Sun. *Montréal 111 km/70 mi.*

Fort Lennox National Historic Park   Q3

Situated on the Richelieu River at Île-au-Noix. Île-aux-Noix was fortified by the French in 1759 but was attacked and captured by the British the following year.

They destroyed the fort though during the American Revolutionary War, an American army used the island for its base to advance down river. After the island was recaptured in 1776, new fortifications were built, the remains of which can be seen today. *Montréal 48 km/30 mi.*

Gaspé   H18

(pop. 16,842). An industrial and commercial center on the Gaspé Peninsula. It was here in 1534 that Cartier took possession of Canada in the name of France and erected a wooden cross. This is a good base for visiting the typical, tiny fishing villages along the peninsula. *Québec 700 km/425 mi.*

Gaspésie Park   H15

Created in 1937 to preserve some of the rugged terrain that 17th-century travellers would have viewed. It covers 1289 sq km/498 sq mi of land formed by valleys and peaks as high as 4160 ft, part of the Appalachian chain. Fishing for salmon as well as trout is one major attraction, another is climbing. Naturalists and outdoor enthusiasts tend to rendezvous at Mont Albert though a scenic 88 km/55 mi route encircles the area. *Québec 580 km/362 mi.*

Granby   P4

(pop. 37,132). A town of great scenic beauty in the Eastern Townships nestled in the Appalachian foothills. See its zoo, its *Automobile Museum* which displays vintage cars; and its collection of antique European fountains. *Montréal 84 km/52 mi.*

Hemmingford   Q2

(pop. 763). Lies on what some term the 'Cider Road'. The town itself is most noted for its **African Safari Park,** a 9 km/5.5 mi area with lions and elephants besides smaller, less ferocious species. Close to town are the *Saint-Bernard* cider-making cellars and the roads run past orchards and through villages with English names. At Havelock, there are camping and riding facilities; at *Franklin Centre* a cider making station and from here a small road leads to the famous center at Saint-Antoine-Abbe. *Montréal 50 km/32 mi.*

Île-aux-Coudres   L8

(pop. 1600). Named for the hazel trees Cartier found here on his first visit in 1535 when he landed here to celebrate mass. Now it is inhabited by farmers, fishermen and boat-builders. *Québec 107 km/67 mi.*

Îles de la Madeleine   K22

(pop. 21,000). These islands lie in the gulf

of the St Lawrence nearer to P.E.I. and Cape Breton than to Gaspé. There are some twelve islands in a string about 100 km/60 mi long. Although the islands are often no more than rocky outcrops there are some fine beaches and red sandstone cliffs. You can fly to the islands from Montréal or Québec City or sail from P.E.I.

Île D'Orléans   M7

Lies just downriver from Québec City. When Jacques Cartier discovered it, he named it 'Isle of Bacchus' because so many wild grapes grew there. Later it was re-christened, taking its name from the Duke of Orleans. The soil is particularly rich and fertile, encouraging the first European settlers to farm and even today, the island is well known for its fruit and vegetables. In season, you can buy them from wayside stands.

Île d'Orléans

The island is only 34 km/21 mi long and 9 km/5.5 mi wide, with the estuary of the St Lawrence beginning at its eastern end and the roadstead of Québec Harbor at its western. In the north channel, the river is shallow, with broad tidal flats. The St Lawrence's main stream, south of the island, is that through which almost all the maritime traffic passes, including Great Lakes and transatlantic ships.

It is classified as a historic region as you will see when you tour around. Gardened farmhouses, old stone churches, tiny wayside chapels and windmills take you back to the early years of New France. An island tour starts by striking right after leaving the bridge (Pont de l'Île d'Orléans). This route (368) leads to the village of *Sainte-Pétronille*, known locally as Bout-de-L'île. (It is worth finding the side roads to reach this point and the wharf.) From here you'll get a spectacular view back to Québec City. General Wolfe had his first view of the City from Bout-de-l'île before he went to capture it in 1759.

Joliette   O2

(pop. 18,118). An industrial, commercial, farming town and the regional capital of De Lanaudiere. It takes its name from its founder, Barthelemi Joliette (who established the town in 1841) a descendant of the famous Joliette who discovered the Mississippi. See the *Saint-Paul Church* (1803-1804) designed by curé Pierre Conefroy and decorated by Perreault and Guiboard. You can browse for handicrafts and pottery and sample spa water at the Esplanade fountains. There are several resort areas close to this town including *Lakes Cloutier, des Francais, Pierre, Vert, Rouge des Pins*, all ideal for summer sporting activities. *Montréal 48 km/30 mi.*

Joliette Park   N2

Also takes its name from the town's founder, and forms part of the Laurentian plateau. The rivers L'Assomption, Ouareau and Noire all flow through it. You can come here for a day's fishing or hunting for small game and in winter snowmobiling is popular. *Montréal 146 km/83 mi.*

Jonquière   I6

(pop. 60,691). One of the principal cities in the Seguenay region, with several good places to stay and conference facilities. At the cultural center on *Mt Jacob*, events and exhibitions take place and Mt Jacob itself provides a magnificent lookout point over the city with wintersports available in season. See the *Aluminium Bridge*, the first of its type in the world, and the famous **Alcan Factory** which makes aluminium products and gives guided tours of its factory in summer. Visit also the *Price and Kraft Factories*, the *Shipshaw Hydroelectric Station. Mt Fortin* offers playgrounds and walking paths for outdoor enthusiasts; *Kenogami Park*, sandy beaches and rustic camping sites, and the *Prevert Race Track*, saddle horse racing. *Québec 215 km/134 mi.*

King's Road   N4

When New France was indeed very new, the easiest way to get to and from Québec City and Ville-Marie (Montréal) was by canoe or other water craft. Gradually, towns sprang up along the St Lawrence, connected by trails. In 1743 a highway was opened between these points which became known as 'Chemin du Roi' or King's Road. It is now known as Highway 138 and, if you travel along it, you will have a picture of both old and new Québec. It winds through several historic villages like Pointe-aux-Trembles, Repentigny, Saint-Sulpice, Lavaltrie, Lanoraie — all ancient seigniories. Also Berthierville where Canada's first protestant church was built, Maskinonge, an 18th-century postal relay station, and Louiseville where Champlain stopped in 1609. Yamachiche is part of a fief granted in 1656 to Pierre Boucher, first governor of Trois-Rivières. And, just before Trois Rivières itself, is pleasant resort area, Pointé-du-Lac. Past Trois-Rivières King's Road closely follows the north shore of the St Lawrence passing through villages such as Sainte-Marthe, Champlain, Batiscan, and Grendines. At Deschambault there is an agricultural research station and a ferry to Lotbinière on the south bank. In Portneuf a restored mill, the *Moulin Marceux* is now an art gallery; at Neuville the *Eglise Saint-Francois-de-Sales* contains several works of art and the village also has a mix of architectural styles — French, Québec, Victorian and American. The architecture of the church at *SaintAugustine*, before the King's Road finally reaches Québec City, is also worth looking at.

La Malbaie   K8
(pop. 4069). Named by Champlain whose ships were beached here by a low tide in 1608. At the resort centre of Pointe-au-Pic is the famous **Manoir Richelieu** hotel. *Québec 120 km/75 mi.*

La Pocatière   L9
(pop. 4319). A cathedral town in a pleasant location. The *Musée Francois Pilote* has displays on agricultural, social and wildlife history. Open daily. *Québec 135 km/86 mi.*

Lac Beauport   M6
A resort gateway only a 15 minute drive from Québec City and just a few miles from **Laurentides Park**. You will find

Sleigh ride at Lac Beauport

good accommodations and fine French cuisine along with sports activities that include an 18-hole golf course set among mountains and lakes.

Lac-Delage   L6
A famous four seasons resort town close to Québec City. Set in the Laurentian valley, it is a perfect place for relaxation. For the more active, sports include yachting, swimming, water skiing, tennis and golf on a nearby course. The Québec style inn, **Manoir de Lac-Delage,** is open to everyone. *Québec 32 km/20 mi.*

Lac Brome   Q4
In the Eastern Townships and among beautiful scenery, Lac Brome offers a Saturday market and a good historical museum. Winter sport enthusiasts come to the area to practice at the popular *Mont-Sutton* downhill ski center or on the ski runs at Glen and Shefford Mountains. *Montréal 117 km/70 mi.*

Lac St Jean   I5
A 971 sq km / 375 sq mi saucer-shaped lake drained by the Saguenay River. It is surrounded by a strip of fertile land which supports wheat and dairy farming. It is also well known for its blueberry harvest and for the *ouananiche* or land-locked salmon. *Québec 230 km/143 mi.*

Laurentians   N1
The mountain resort area which starts 32 km / 20 mi north of Montréal. It is considered by many to be one of Québec's most beautiful regions with over 150 resorts within the region's 90 mile sweep. Accommodation varies from small guest houses to luxury hotels, many of which are open year-round to cater for the winter sports visitors. For summer views and winter skiing, there are chair-lifts to the peaks of **Sainte-Agathe, Saint-Donat, Mont-Tremblant** and **Mont Sainte-Marie.** Summer excursions include river cruises while in autumn the colors are magnificent. Autumn is a popular time of year with fishermen and outfitters to help you organize whatever type of trip you are after are plentiful in the Laurentians. The winter slopes are among the best equipped in North America with a five month ski season starting from the end of November. Slopes are also floodlit until about 2200. Winter is also a time of carnival celebrations and international ski competitions. *Montréal 48 km/30 mi to 128 km/80 mi.*

Magog   Q5
(pop. 13,290). This is an attractive resort in a lovely setting at the northern end of Lake Memphremagog. **Mount Orford**

lies to the north of the town and the Appalachian Mountain's most northerly peaks also lie along the lake. *Sherbrooke 16 km/ 10 mi; Montréal 210 km/130 mi.*

Manic-Outardes E11

A series of seven dams and power plants along the Manic-ouagan and Outardes Rivers. Visits can be made to the **Manic 5** and the **Daniel Johnson** dams. The latter is the biggest multiple arch dam in the world. *Baie-Comeau 432 km/268 mi.*

Montmorency Falls M7

These falls happen when the Montmorency River drops 83.5 m/270 ft just before its mouth on the St Lawrence. In the winter the spray from the falls freezes and builds up a cone which can reach 20 m/ 70 ft in height. *Québec City 6 km/3.75 mi.*

Mont Orford Provincial Park Q5

Lying in the Eastern Townships this park includes Mount Orford itself and a small area around it. The mountain has a summit height of 876 m/2890 ft and there is a stunning view from the top. In the summer a chair lift operates to the top and in winter there is good skiing. The *Jeunesse Musicales du Canada* also takes place here every summer. *Sherbrooke 13 km/8 mi.*

Montréal P2

(pop. 1,177,796). Montréal is the second largest French-language city after Paris and it has a cosmopolitan and international reputation. It is in fact an island set in the St Lawrence River with a busy port that has helped make it into a commercial and industrial center to be reckoned with.

When Jacques Cartier first saw the settlement in 1535 it was called Hochelaga and it was not until 1642 that the city was founded by Paul de Chomedey, sieur de Maisonneuve. From a fur trading capital in the 18th century, Montréal became a financial capital in the 19th century, and a major metropolis in the 20th century.

Montréal's first name was Ville-Marie, though the current name is taken from the hill rising from its center — Mount Royal, a long extinct volcano complete with panoramic views, lake trails and picnic areas that has become Montréalers' favorite park.

International status came to Montréal in 1967 with Expo '67, one of the most memorable world fairs, and in 1976 when the city hosted the Olympics. The city has made its mark in the world of fashion, art, entertainment as well as sport and business, and above all, food!

There are literally thousands of restaurants in every price bracket with French cuisine, of course, but also food from other

rue St. Denis

countries around the globe. You will find lots of eating places on and around *Crescent St.* and bars and cafés in profusion on Prince-Arthur, Duluth and Saint-Denis Sts. (an area good for night life, too). There are even more bars and cafés in the underground complexes and the Old Quarter of Montréal.

Old Montréal is a very good place to start sightseeing. Montréal is easy to get around — streets and boulevards are on a grid system. Saint-Laurent Boulevard is the dividing line between east and west. One fare pays for use of bus and/or metro and the metro connects many of the city's major attractions and shops. But here, where Ville-Marie began, getting around the cobbled streets is best on foot — or at the very most, by horse-drawn carriage *(calèche)*.

The Old City lies southeast of the financial district on the north shore of the St Lawrence and in summer several of its streets are pedestrian. The best place to start is *Place Jacques Cartier*, which was once the main marketplace. You may well be tempted to linger in this square, filled with flower sellers in summer and lined with pretty cafés and bistros. The *Nelson Column*, by the way, was erected in 1809 to honor Britain's victory at Trafalgar. It is the City's oldest monument. The southern portion of the square opens onto the old port where an annual summer festival is a highlight.

Stand in the middle of the square and look northeast and you will see the historic *Château Ramezay*, now a museum. It was built in 1705 as home for Montréal's governor, Claude de Ramezay, and during the invasion of 1775, became the headquarters of the American army. To the east of the Château, Bonsecours St. takes its name from *Notre-Dame-de-Bonsecours Chapel* which lies at the end of the street. This is one of Montréal's oldest streets with beautiful examples of period houses. The chapel itself was the old sailors' church built in 1657 by the founder of the

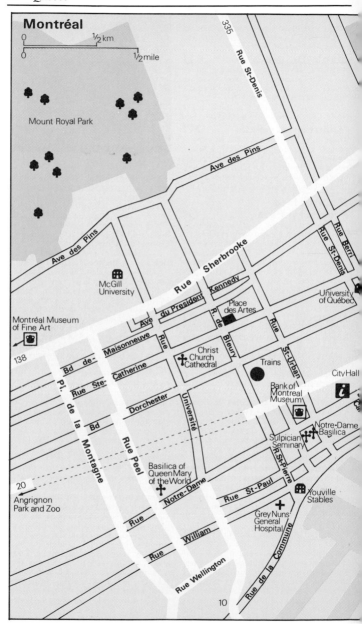

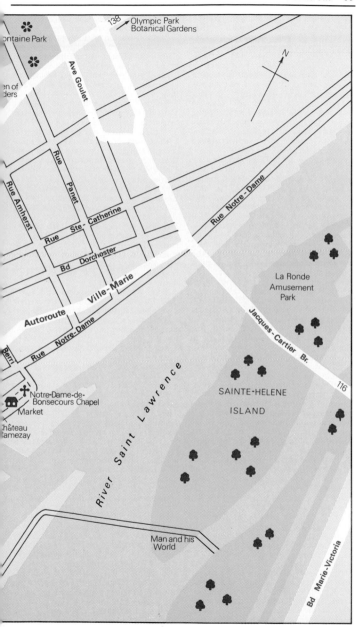

138 → Olympic Park
Botanical Gardens

ontaine Park

en of
ders

Ave Goulet

Rue Penet

Rue Amherst

Rue Ste - Catherine

Bd Dorchester

Ville-Marie

Autoroute

Rue Notre - Dame

Berri

Rue Notre - Dame

Notre-Dame-de-
Bonsecours Chapel

Market

hâteau
amezay

River Saint Lawrence

Man and his
World

La Ronde
Amusement
Park

Jacques - Cartier Br.

116

SAINTE-HELENE

ISLAND

Bd Marie-Victoria

Congregation of Notre-Dame, Marguerite Bourgeoys. Twice destroyed by fire, the present structure dates from 1771. Many of the sailors who worshiped here left model ships as a token of their faith. The Statue of Mary on the roof gazes towards the river with outstretched arms to welcome sailors. It is well worthwhile entering the chapel whose lovely interior contains many works of art. Also on Bonsecours is the *Maison Calvet*, one of the best remaining examples of architecture from the French regime. It contains pieces of Québec furniture and art taken from the Museum of Fine Arts.

You could return to Place Jacques Cartier via *Saint-Paul St. East*, Montréal's fourth street opened in 1674 and named for founder, Paul de Chomedey. It is now a fashionable street where many buildings have been restored, though the old Bonsecours market has given way to municipal offices. Another old city street lies just west of Place Jacques Cartier — *Saint-Vincent St.*, which during the 19th century was the legal and journalistic centre of the city. *The Beaudoin House* (1690) here is a historic monument.

From Saint-Vincent St., it is a mere stroll past the Old Courthouse to *Place Vauquelin* with its statue and fountain and view north of Champ-de-Mars which was woodland when Maisonneuve ceded it to Lambert Closse in 1658. East of this square (named for Jean Vaugelin who defended New France at Louisbourg in 1758) stands the *City Hall* which dates from 1872.

Another favorite starting point for a tour of the Old Quarter is *Place d'Armes*, which commemorates the city's founding and has a statue of Maisonneuve at its center. Many battles with the Indians took place nearby, but today major bank buildings and offices flank the area. To the south of the square you will see the Sulpician Seminary and *Notre-Dame Basilica* (1829). The Basilica, designed in a neo-Gothic style, is one of the largest and most beautiful in Canada, and its western tower contains the famous 12 ton Gros Bourdon church bell. Inside, of particular interest, is the powerful organ, built by Casavant; a striking main altar; the stained glass windows; and the side chapel of St Amable which contains the altar from the older original church on this site. The overall design of the interior was the work of Victor Bourgeau.

The *Sulpician Seminary* is still a Sulpician residence and is Montréal's oldest building (1685), constructed by Dollier de Casson. The clock over its façade is reputedly North America's oldest, though these days an electric mechanism has replaced the wooden one which marked out the time for over a century.

Notre-Dame St. was Montréal's first street (1672), but a year later came *Saint-Joseph St.*, which was the birthplace of many famous soldiers and explorers. Today, you will find luxury shops and apartments, converted from old warehouses.

Another tour starting point could be *Place Royale*, a military square which later became a public marketplace, in 1706. The current name was given in the mid 19th century. It was also the site of pillories and hangings. Just south of the square is *the* very spot at the mouth of the Saint-Pierre River where Maisonneuve built his Fort of Montréal on May 17, 1642. This is *Pointe-a-Callières* at what is now *De La Commune St.*, a street that marks the line of docks which served European sailing ships. Where De La Commune St. meets Youville, you can see the 19th-century docks of Montréal's port. Round the corner is Normand St., a tiny street that connected the *Grey Nuns' General Hospital* with the river. This hospital was Ville-Marie's second hospital, built in 1694 on drained marshland.

Walk north on Normand and you'll come to *Place d'Youville*, an early civic center built in the 19th century and now surrounded by monuments from different eras. Do not miss looking in at the *Youville Stables*, one of the most photographed courtyard complexes in the area and with a good restaurant.

To reach Old Montréal by metro, get off at Champs-de-Mars, Place d'Armes or Square-Victoria.

They call Montréal 'The Underground City' and for good reason. *Shoppers* won't even have to bother with coats and umbrellas. Thanks to miles of underground passages, pedestrians have access to railway stations, a bus terminal, car parks, major hotels, the University, countless offices and stores, restaurants, banks, theaters and cinemas, exhibition halls and metro stations. Wherever you are in downtown, it is easy to get below. The best known complexes are *Place Ville-Marie*, *Place Bonaventure* (for guided tours call (514) 395 2221), *Complexe Desjardins* (guided tours available), and *Les Terrasses*.

Whether or not you shop above or below ground, St Catherine St. is the city's busiest street with major department stores like *The Bay* and *Eaton's, Simpson's* and *Ogilvy's*. Art galleries and antique stores can be found on classy Sherbrooke St., while other fashionable streets meeting up with Sherbrooke are MacKay, Bishop, Crescent and Mountain Sts. This area is also full of nightclubs and restaur

Botanic Gardens, Montréal

ants. Laurier St., near the Greek district also has many entertainment hot-spots as does Saint-Denis St.

Montréal also has its markets: *Jean-Talon* on rue Casgrain, near Jean-Talon St., is outdoor in summer, but operates year round by using small indoor stalls in winter. You will find fresh produce and handicrafts in this Italian district market but it is usually closed on weekends. Fridays and Saturdays are the days to visit *Atwater Market* on the avenue of the same name. Fruit and vegetables are sold outdoors, other foods indoors. Not far away is an area of second hand stores. The city's largest market is *Greater Montréal Central Market* at the corner of Cremazie and L'Acadie Blvds, though it caters in the main to the wholesale trade. (Closed Sun.) From April to December, the *Maisonneuve Market* is open weekdays on rue Ontario East.

Montréal keeps late *night life hours* and visitors may find every kind of entertainment from the saucy to the sublime, in and

out of the luxury hotels. Hear poetry readings and jazz in the small cafés or reserve tickets for a concert, play or variety show at Québec's largest center for the performing arts — *Place des Arts*.

Other Attractions:

Alcan Aquarium presents marine shows. Open daily 1000-1700.

Botanical Gardens, 4101 rue Sherbrooke E. rank third largest in the world after London's and Berlin's. A mini-train ride gives a brief overall view, but there are some 20,000 species of plant life displayed here in outdoor gardens and greenhouses. Of special interest are the bonsai and orchid collections, open year round 0900-1800.

Basilica of Mary Queen of the World, 1085 avenue Cathédrale. The heart of the Montréal Catholic Archdiocese. Built in 1878 it resembles St Peter's in Rome. Open Mon.-Sun. 0700-2030 in summer, to 0700-1930 in winter.

Bank of Montréal Museum, 129 rue Saint-Jacques. Coins, documents and banking memorabilia bring Canada's financial history to light. Open Mon.-Fri. 1000-1600.

Canadian Guild of Crafts, 2025 avenue Peel. Here you can shop for crafts, but also enjoy exhibitions by promising as well as recognised artisans. Open Mon.-Fri. 0900-1700, Sat. 1200-1700.

Canadian Historic Wax Museum, 3715 chemin Reine-Marie. The scenes and wax figures are of early life and historic events in Canada. Open daily 0900-2130, in winter to 1700.

Christ Church Cathedral, 1440 avenue Union. Considered Montréal's best example of Gothic architecture. Inside, there are notable stained glass windows, interesting sculptures and other works of art. Concerts and organ recitals are frequent features. Open Mon.-Sun. 0800-1800.

Church of St Andrew and St Paul, corner of Sherbrooke and Redpath Sts. A handsome church built in 1932 as a Presbyterian church for the Royal Highland Regiment of Canada. Its choir is excellent. Open in summer 1000-1600.

Garden of Wonders, Lafontaine Park. Ideal for small children with 500 animals in a fairytale setting. Sea lion shows also. Open May-Sept. 1000-dusk.

Lachine Canal Trail runs along the Lachine Canal for about 12 km/7.5 mi, used by cyclists in summer, cross-country skiers in winter. It eventually joins up with Old Montréal's bike path. The Monk Pavilion houses a small interpretive center and on weekends, guided bike and walking tours (summer) leave from the corner of Berri and de la Commune Sts. Open year-round from sunrise to 2200.

La Ronde is the amusement park on the Île Sainte-Hélène with enough rides and games to suit most ages. A typical Québec village features craft workshops, places to eat and shop and a mini-rail offers a view of the river and the city. There is also entertainment in the evening and summer contests. Open in summer Mon.-Sat. 1200-0230, May/June weekends only.

Maison de Radio-Canada, 1400 Blvd Dorchester E., a vast radio and TV complex. From special observation galleries, visitors may watch studio operations, the master controls and projection rooms. Guided tours several times a day.

Marguerite Bourgeoys Museum, 3040 rue Sherbrooke W. Located behind Notre-Dame-de-Bonsecours, it uses miniature houses and figures to show the life of Mother Marguerite Bourgeoys and Québec's early history. Open Mon.-Sat. 0900-1130, 1330-1630, Sun. 1330-1630.

Marguerite d'Youville Museum, 1185 rue Saint-Mathieu. Often referred to as the Grey Nuns' Museum in memory of Mother d'Youville (1747). See the Motherhouse Chapel and memorabilia and religious artefacts from early colonial times. (Mother d'Youville was beatified by Pope John XXIII in 1959). Open daily 0900-1730.

Man and His World, on Sainte-Hélène Island. The pavilions used for Expo '67 are used annually for this permanent summer exhibition. It is a showplace for entertainment and cultural events on a site that sits

Montréal by night

in the St Lawrence River. La Ronde amusement park, gardens and restaurants are all located here. Open daily June-Sept. 1000-2400.

McCord Museum, 690 rue Sherbrooke W. Many valuable documents, prints and paintings are displayed in this handsome stone house. Exhibits also incude the William Notman photography collection and one of Canada's most extensive historic costume collections. Open Wed.-Sun. 1100-1700.

Montréal Museum of Fine Arts, 1379 rue Sherbrooke W. Founded in 1860, this museum hosts world-class exhibitions and features all categories of art from pre-Columbian to 20th-century work. In addition to 34 galleries of treasures, there are sculpture courts, film, concert and lecture programs and a 400-seat auditorium. Guided tours available. Open Tues.-Sun. 1100-1700.

Mont-Royal Art Centre, 1260 chemin Remembrance. Built in 1858 this stone farmhouse situated in Mount Royal Park houses attractive art exhibits. Open daily 1000-2000.

Mount Royal Park. Call it 'Mont-Royal' or Mount Royal, this hill offers splendid city views from the lookout points at its summit. The locals like to meet around Beaver Lake; visitors might like to take a carriage ride around the park. In summer, there are folk-dancing shows on the terrace near the lake and people are welcome to bike or walk the park trails. In winter, Montréalers come up here to ski, skate and toboggan.

Museum of Modern Art, Cité du Havre. Contemporary works on display here date from 1940 to the present. Special events to promote modern art are frequently staged by the museum. Open Tues.-Sun. 1000-1800, Thurs. to 2200.

Museum of Decorative Arts (Château Dufresne), corner of Pie-IX and Sherbrooke St. Highlights decorative arts from 1850 to present times. Open Thurs.-Sun. 1200-1700.

Museum of St Lawrence Art, 615 Blvd Sainte-Croix. The former Sainte-Croix college chapel now houses works to illustrate Québec's cultural heritage. Open Tues.-Fri. 1100-1700.

Olympic Park was built for the 21st Olympics and is now one of Montréal's main attractions. The architecture is space-age and there is activity year-round. The focal point is the Olympic Stadium which can hold up to 80,000 people. Its Astro Turf may be removed at any time to accommodate rock concerts as well as sporting events. The Vélodrome, built for Olympic cycling is also used for other sports, shows and conventions. Six different swimming

pools are located in the park. Guided tours of the complex are available daily. The park is open daily 0900-1700. Tickets for events can be purchased at the park's own box office (closed Sun.) or at Ticketron outlets throughout the city.

Planetarium, 1000 rue Saint-Jacques. The Dow Planetarium presents sky shows in its domed auditorium with several themes annually. A Zeiss projector realistically portrays the night sky and special effects are created by over 100 auxiliary projectors. Shows are presented Tues., Thurs. 1215-2130; Wed., Fri. 1415-2130; Sat. 1415-1630, 2130; Sun. 1300, 1530, 1630, 2130.

Saint-Gabriel House, 2146 rue Favard. Dating to 1688, this museum contains interesting Canadiana in the folklore and arts and crafts line. Open April-Dec., Tues.-Sun. 1330-1700.

Sainte-Hélène Island. The island play-

St. Joseph's Oratory

ground for Montréalers and visitors with sport all year round. Also located here: La Ronde amusement park, Aquarium, La Poudrière Theatre, The Old Fort.

Saint-Joseph's Oratory, 3800 chemin Reine-Marie. On the western slope of Mont Royal, this was founded by Brother André who was said to have cured many through his prayers. The Oratory dome is a city skyline landmark.

Sainte-Hélène Museum, Sainte Hélène Island. Canada's early history is well covered through artefacts, items from everyday life and military displays — all in

The Laurentians in winter

the Old Fort (1820-1824). In summer, historic drills are held here. Open daily in summer 1000-1700, in winter Tues.-Sun. *Museum of Cinema*, 335 Blvd de Maisonneuve E. A unique film centre housing film-making equipment since 1870. A different film is screened each day. Open Tues.-Sun. 1800-2100, Sun. 1500-2200. *Zoo*, Angrignon Park. Unusually, a winter season park where you will see species which thrive in a cooler climate and others cosily housed in their winter quarters. Open Oct.-April 1200-1800, Dec.-March 1000-2200.

Mont-Tremblant   M1

(pop. 1200). A famous winter sport resort, bordering on **Mont-Tremblant Park** and Lac Mercier, that is equally well known for its food. It is the location of one of the most spectacular motor racing circuits, some of the best skiing and exceptional snow — the peak rises 3150 ft. There are ten lakes in the vicinity, one of which is Lac Tremblant, ten miles long with a stocked fish hatchery. *Saint-Jovite 8 km/5 mi.*

Mont-Tremblant Park   M1

In the Laurentians, covers 2564 sq km/ 990 sq mi. Located on the southern edge of the Canadian Shield, this park was planned for the enjoyment of Québec's citizens, offering not only mountains, but almost 1000 lakes, rivers, streams and waterfalls. A winding touring road stretches for 160 km/100 mi between mountain and forest, dotted with good

vantage points. The major attractions in the park are fishing for trout and pike, swimming, boating and hiking along the numerous trails which have particularly scenic settings, such as *day du Diable, Croche, aux Rats Falls, de la Roche, de la Corniche.* Kayaking is another popular sport and in winter this is a wonderland of cross-country ski trails in the *Lac Monroe* area. There are several campsites and other more luxurious accommodations in the surrounding region. *Montréal 144 km/90 mi.*

Maurice-Bois-Francs   L4

A scenic region in the the heart of Québec, halfway between Montréal and Québec City, with the St Maurice River flowing through it. There is dairy and other farming in the south, the *Lac St-Jean swim* and the *St Maurice canoe race* in the north plus the famed *Notre-Dame-du-Cap* sanctuary.

Oka   P1

(pop. 1483). Situated at the foot of the two mountains from which Lac des Deux Montagnes takes its name. *The Trappist monastery* here is famous for the cheese it produces and there are also religious art works.

Percé   I18

(pop. 5198). A village which takes its name from the rock dominating its beach. In 1534 Cartier anchored his three ships just behind this odd formation in the Gaspé Peninsula, but today it is a resort center *par excellence*, surrounded as it is by cliffs and capes well worth several tours and noted for its comfortable lodging and fine cuisine. It is a first class base for deep sea fishing yet it is also noted for its artisan centers and craft boutiques. The nature trails and the wild bird refuge of **Bonaventure Island** which is a 1 hour boat trip away, all add up to a place with something to please everyone. During the summer, boats leave several times daily for tours of Bonaventure Island where thousands of seabirds of different species nest. *Québec 770 km/481 mi.*

Percé

Péribonka   H6
(pop. 6330). This village is located at the mouth of the Péribonka River which flows into Lac St-Jean. It is the setting for one of the most famous Canadian novels, *Maria Chapdelaine*. The author, Louis Hémon, lived in the village in 1912. *Tadoussac 190 km/119 mi.*

Québec City   M6
(pop. 570,000). The walled city of Québec is the provincial capital and clings to its French heritage. Built on cliffs overlooking the St Lawrence River, it owes its creation to Samuel de Champlain who made the first settlement here in 1608. Would he have thought then that this was to be the cornerstone of the French Empire in North America? Champlain's little colony was on the river banks but he also built a fort on the cliffs.

Thanks go to the British (after the Treaty of Paris) for strengthening the citadel and for enclosing the town with walls. Since then Québec City has grown well beyond the walls into a modern 20th-century city. The Plains of Abraham, which saw the death of both the British and the French general, have become well tended parkland.

Europeans will find the split-level city picturesque since shopkeepers and restaurateurs have taken over many of the buildings in the old quarter and have restored and converted them. Visitors from the US will think that they are in Europe. The Québecois are renowned for their hospitality and their *joie de vivre*. The Old City, though hilly, is compact and easy to get around.

Perhaps you might start at *Place d'Armes*, a beautiful square at the heart of Old Québec. It was once called 'Grande Place' and became 'Rond de Chaines' in 1824 when it was encircled by a belt of chains. The square has been used for military parades and public meetings. The gothic fountain in its center was erected in 1916 to commemorate the Récollet Fathers who had arrived three centuries earlier.

You'll find the *Musée du Fort*, which gives *son et lumière* performances, at one corner of the square, but there's a great deal more in the vicinity: The *Wolfe-Montcalm Monument* and below it *Dufferin Terrace*, a city landmark overlooked by the turreted *Château Frontenac Hotel* which was inaugurated in 1898 and finished in 1925. Lord Durham had the original terrace put here in 1838 and in 1878 it was extended to its present dimensions. It offers one of the best views down river to Île d'Orléans and across to Lévis, and is a favorite spot for strolling in the summer.

At the southwest end of the terrace, the *Promenade des Gouverneurs* follows the outer walls of the Citadel and brings you to the Plains of Abraham. A visit to the *Citadel* is, of course, a must. The large star-shaped fortress, completed in 1832, stands at the city's highest point — Cap Diamant. In summer a changing of the guard by the famous Royal 22nd Regiment takes place here daily. Guided tours are available and the military museum is included. These days the *Plains of Abraham* are also called Battlefields Park and form a 235 acre green belt along the cliff from the Citadel to Gilmour Hill. At the northern end of Dufferin Terrace is *Champlain's Monument*, sculpted by Paul Chevré in tandem with Paris architect Paul le Cardonnel.

Also on the upper level is *Montmorency Park*, named in honour of Quebec's first

Château Frontenac

bishop, François de Montmorency-Laval. There are several monuments in the park including one of the bishop. Down the hill are the colloquially named 'Break-neck' or Petit-Champlain stairs leading from

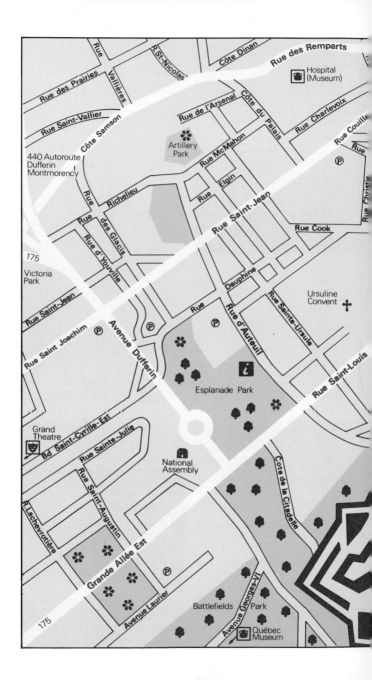

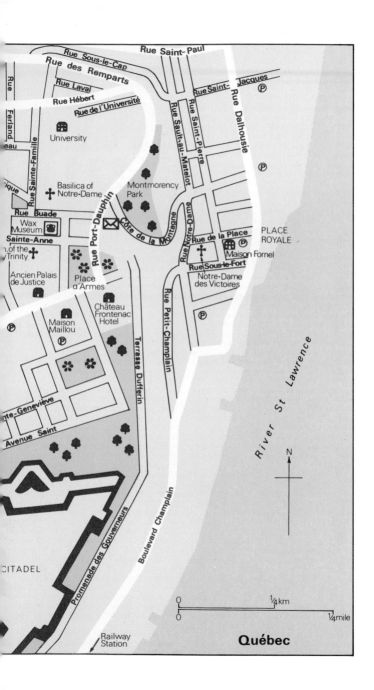

Rue Saint-Paul

Rue Sous-le-Cap

Rue des Remparts

Rue Laval

Rue Hébert

Rue Saint-Jacques

Rue de l'Université

Rue Ferland

University

Rue Sainte-Famille

Rue Sault-au-Matelot

Rue Saint-Pierre

Rue Dalhousie

Basilica of
Notre-Dame

Montmorency
Park

Rue Buade

Rue Port-Dauphin

Côte de la Montagne

Wax
Museum

PLACE
ROYALE

Sainte-Anne

Rue de la Place

Maison Fornel

.of the
Trinity

Rue Notre-Dame

Rue Sous-le-Fort

Ancien Palais
de Justice

Place
d'Armes

Notre-Dame
des Victoires

Château
Frontenac
Hotel

Maison
Maillou

Rue Petit-Champlain

Terrasse Dufferin

ante-Geneviève

Avenue Saint

River St Lawrence

N

Promenade des Gouverneurs

Boulevard Champlain

CITADEL

0   ¼ km
0   ¼ mile

Railway
Station

Québec

Côte de la Montagne to Sous-le-Fort St., and the lower level of town. (Non-walkers can take the funicular to the Lower Town and Place Royale.)

Notre Dame St., one of Québec's oldest streets, leads to Place Royale, center of the Lower Town. *Place Royale* is where this city was born. Under the French regime, wealthy merchants built homes and businesses round the square which became a market place and was called du Marché. It became Place Royale in 1686 when a bust of Louis XIV was put up in the square. Although fires destroyed much of the lower town in 1759, and the business community abandoned the Place in 1832 to establish businesses in the Upper Town, today the streets surrounding Place Royale still contain the greatest representation of 17th and 18th-century buildings in North America and the area continues to be carefully restored by the Provincial Government.

The focal point is *Notre-Dame-des-Victoires Church*, built in 1668 on the site where Champlain constructed his first 'Abitation' (1608). Inside the church there are several handsome paintings: a copy of Van Dyk's 'Christ on the Cross', a Van Loo and a Boyermans. Note the miniature boat in the nave and the main altar which is carved in the shape of a fort. Also on the square, you can visit the *Maison des Vins* in the Dumont House and the permanent exhibitions of a former era's lifestyle in the cellars of the *Maison Fornel* (1735).

From the end of Notre-Dame Street you can take a ferry across the river to Lévis. Alternatively, visit *Maison Chevalier*, now a museum. The house was built for Jean Baptiste Chevalier, one of the rich merchants. Another example of a bourgeois home is the *Maison Fargues* on Saint-Pierre St., a street which was once the financial district of Québec City.

The entrance to the funicular that makes the easy climb to Dufferin Terrace was the house built in 1684 for Louis Jolliet, who, together with Marquette, discovered the Mississippi River.

Back up top on Saint-Louis Street is the French Renaissance *Ancien Palais de Justice* and opposite, the *Maison Maillou*. It is said the capitulation of Québec was signed in the *Kent House* at No. 25 Saint-Louis St., which later was home for Prince Edward, Duke of Kent, governor of Canada 1791-94. One of Québec's smallest houses is the *Maison Jacquet* on Des Jardins St., dating from 1665. Legend has it this was Montcalm's headquarters, it is now a restaurant, the renowned *Aux Anciens Canadiens*. Round the corner at the end of du Parloir St, is the *Ursuline Convent*, founded in 1639 and the oldest

Maison Jacquet

school for young women in North America. Despite being burnt down twice some of the original convent walls still stand. You can see Montcalm's skull, preserved under glass, in the convent's museum. Also look at the *Cathedral of the Holy Trinity*, dedicated in 1804. This was the first English cathedral to be erected outside of the British Isles and its pews, doors and locks are made of English oak. Both the wall tablets and the stained glass are worth looking at.

Another religious edifice to see is the Roman Catholic *Basilica of Notre Dame*, part of which dates back to 1647. Treasures here include paintings and silver from the time of the French regime. An iron gate next to the Basilica marks the entrance to the *Québec Seminary*, founded in 1663 by Québec's first bishop, Laval, from which rose Laval University. The main chapel is interesting for its marble altar and also for Laval's sarcophagus. The museum has recently been renovated.

Rue de la Fabrique is an interesting little street: the first Bell Telephone office opened here in 1880 and the *Livernois pharmacy*, founded in 1854, is the oldest of its kind in Québec. Take Couillard St. through the so-called 'Latin Quarter', near the old Laval University. (The new University is now in the suburbs.) You can reach l'Université St. by turning onto Sainte-Famille St. and then turning left through the archway. At the end, turn right up Port Dauphin St. until you reach Buade St. Close by is one of the most popular streets in Québec, *du Trésor*. Tiny, but lined with the work of local artists. At the end of du Trésor you are back at Place d'Armes.

Other Attractions:

Artillery Park National Historic Park has been restored to its 19th-century appearance by the Provincial Government. On the site are barracks and buildings constructed gradually over the 18th and 19th centuries. In 1879 a munitions factory opened here which only closed down in 1964. You can view the scale model of Québec (1/300th scale and built between 1806-08), enter the restored fortress area called the Redoubte Dauphine and walk around the ramparts to the Citadel on a footpath.

Cartier-Brébeuf Park, contains a replica of Cartier's ship *La Grande Hermine.* On the St Charles River at de l'Espinay near Parc de l'Exposition.

National Assembly, the Québec government buildings which welcome visitors with guided tours.

Place Québec is a modern underground complex of offices, shops, restaurants and the Hilton hotel.

Québec Aquarium, 1675 avenue du Parc exhibits many marine species.

Québec Museum, Plains of Abraham. Collections include early Québec art and furnishings plus more contemporary works.

Wax Museum 22 rue Ste Anne.

Saguenay   I8
Although fed by several rivers Lac St-Jean is drained by only one — the mighty Seguenay. It is 160 km/100 mi long and has two distinctly different stretches. Dropping quite rapidly from the lake it is harnessed between Alma and Chicoutimi for industry. Then it enters the fjord which is about 1500 m/1 mi wide, 250 m/800 ft deep and lined by cliffs which rise to heights of 460 m/1500 ft in places. The fjord was formed when the glaciers of the last ice-age retreated and the sea invaded the trench they had gouged.

St-Jean-Port-Poli   L8
(pop. 1844). Has the largest number of sculptors and artisans of any place in Québec. The speciality here is wood carving, revived by the Bourgault brothers in the 1930s after it had almost died out. See the **Musee des Anciens Canadiens,** open daily, May-Oct. *Québec 93 km/58 mi.*

Ste-Anne-de-Beaupré   L7
(pop. 3284). Is one of Canada's most famous shrines, erected in the town of the same name on the north bank of the St Lawrence River east of Québec City. Back in 1658, the hamlet had but 25 families and was known as Petit-Cap. When the inhabitants decided to build a chapel dedicated to Saint Anne, local landowner Etienne de Lessard gave up part of his shoreside estate for it. The site proved too close to the river, however, and a second church was erected in 1662 in half timbered style. A third more stylish church

was built in stone in 1676. The reasons for so much dedication were the 'miracles'. Purported cures attracted more and more pilgrims over the years until finally a basilica was constructed in 1872. Saint Anne was recognized as the patron saint of Québec in 1876. The present shrine was built in 1926 after fire destroyed that first basilica.

The Shrine is not only a place for prayer, but worth seeing for its Romanesque architectural style and its artwork. For example the interior is unique in Canada. It has five naves, each of which has five bays. The stained glass windows are the work of August Labouret, assisted by master glassmaker Pierre Chaudière. One enormous piece of oak was used to create the statue of Saint Anne, crowned with solid gold ornamented by diamonds, pearls and rubies — all the work of Aurelio Hernandez.

Across from the *basilica* stands the *memorial chapel* constructed in 1878 with materials from the old church and built on to the transept of that original 1676 church. To the west is the *Scala Santa,* a re-creation of the holy stairway climbed by Christ.

There is a nearby inn with dining facilities and some rooms and there is a picnic site behind the basilica museum. Special ramps and other facilities have been specifically installed for the handicapped and the dark-shirted aides, wearing dark arm bands will assist those who need to be helped from one place to another. Guided tours available. Sightseeing tours from Montréal or Québec City in summer almost always include a stop here.

A number of annual religious events take place during the year. Indian Sunday in June sees the Amerindians (who have been visiting the shrine since 1707) come to pay homage to Saint Anne. On July 1 each year, the basilica is reconsecrated and from July 17-25, numerous pilgrims arrive for the celebrations leading up to the Feast of Saint Anne (July 26). Families are particularly welcome on the Sunday closest to the *Feast of the Nativity of the Blessed Virgin* when Saint Anne's motherhood is commemorated. Following the procession, the *Great Relic of Saint Anne* is venerated. *Québec City 35 km/21.8 mi.*

Sainte-Agathe-des-Monts   N1
(pop. 5435). The oldest of the Laurentian resorts, often called 'Metropolis of the Laurentians'. It encompasses Lac des Sables with 25.6 km/16 mi of beaches. From the chair-lift there are panoramic views year round. Summer sports include fishing, golf, water skiing and riding; win-

ter sports include skiing on several slopes and snowmobiling on marked trails. *Montréal 96 km/60 mi.*

Sainte-Adèle   O1

(pop. 4186). A popular Laurentian resort since 1852 with a pleasant setting on Lac Rond. One of the attractions is the re-created *Village de Seraphin* with several styles of French Canadian home. There are plenty of sporting opportunities including golf, riding, fishing, hunting, skiing, snowmobiling and curling. It is also a writers' and artists' colony. *Montréal 76.8 km/48 mi.*

Saint-Donat   N1

(pop. 1460). A Laurentian resort center situated between Lakes Ouareau and Archambault. This is the highest town in the Laurentians (1550 ft) with surrounding mountains rising to 2500 ft. Very popular with sports enthusiasts year round. *Montréal 132.8 km/83 mi.*

Saint-Eustache   P2

(pop. 21,248). This was the site of the worst fighting of the 1837 Rebellion when Doctor Chénier led 250 rebels against 2000 soldiers under the command of General Sir John Colborne. The resulting ransacking and burning of the village earned the General the name 'Old Firebrand'. Today, visitors may see several historic buildings including the *Legare Flour Mill* (1765), Chénier's restored home and the church, dating from 1840. *Montréal 30 km/18 mi.*

Saint-Jérôme   O2

(pop. 25,175). Gateway to the Laurentians, founded in 1830. Under the leadership of Curé Labelle, most of its development took place between 1868 and 1891. It is a Catholic bishopric and important hydroelectric center. There is a monument to Curé Labelle in the park opposite the cathedral. Tours of *Rolland Paper Co.* (Canada's oldest, operating since 1882) are available. Sports include golf, riding, fishing, hunting and snowmobiling. *Montréal 48 km/30 mi.*

Saint-Michel-des-Saints   M2

(pop. 1647). A neat and pretty town first settled by a priest, Abbé Théophile Provost in 1862. Still surrounded by forests, many visitors come here to hunt and fish. Along the Matawin River and nearby lakes are a number of resorts: Carmel, Anglais, Hetu, des Pins, Kiagama, Trefle, Bouteille, Tremblay and Taureau. *Montréal 153.6 km/96 mi.*

Sherbrooke   Q5

(pop. 76,804). Queen of the Eastern Townships with the charm of a rural community, and good accommodations. Various events are scheduled year round at the *University of Sherbrooke Cultural Centre.* See the museum at the Sherbrooke Seminary, Domaine Howard, the old Courthouse, St Peter's Church (1844) and the gothic style *Saint Michel Cathedral.* There is a panoramic view of the area from the *Beauvoir Shrine. Montréal 147 km/91 mi.*

Tadoussac   J9

(pop. 998). Is probably the oldest settlement in North America outside of Mexico. This site was visited by Cartier in 1535 and the first house, a trading post, was built here in 1599. The town's prime position at the mouth of the Saguenay has ensured its continued existence. *Québec 211 km/ 131 mi.*

Trois-Rivières   N4

(pop. 52,508). Principal town in the Saint-Maurice Valley, midway between Montréal and Québec City. Great Lakes and transatlantic vessels come through its inland seaport. The city was founded in 1634 by Laviolette on the site where Champlain had earlier established a fur trading post. Here today you will see many reminders of the past — monuments and 18th-century architecture plus the oldest house in the city, *de Tonnancour* (1690). The first heavy industry established in Canada was the **Forges de la Saint-Maurice,** a few miles north of town, now partially reconstructed for tourist interest as a National Historic Park and open to visitors in summer. The combination of bog iron deposits, an abundant water and fuel supply and nearby river transportation all contributed to the choice of this site for metal working in 1729. *Montréal 142 km/88 mi.*

Valcourt   P5

(pop. 2566). Was the birthplace of J. Armand Bombardier, the inventor of snowmobiles. It was here that Bombardier later developed the snowmobile into the ski-doo in 1958. A museum shows the history and development of both vehicles.

Val-David   O1

(pop. 2073). A well known tourist and sports center much loved by painters and crafts people. Noted for its high class restaurants and its outdoor activities such as hunting, fishing, mountain climbing at monts Condor and Cesaire, riding, cross-country skiing and snowshoeing. See *La Butte à Mathieu Museum* which has vintage cars and antique tools; *Santa Claus Village. Montréal 88 km/55 mi.*

NEW BRUNSWICK

New Brunswick is the closest Maritime province to the rest of Canada, it lies between Québec's Gaspé peninsula, and Nova Scotia. It is the most Acadian of all Atlantic Canada with some 35 per cent of its 696,000 inhabitants being French-speaking descendants of Acadian settlers. Both English and French are designated as official languages.

The largest cities are Saint John, Moncton and Fredericton, but large expanses of the province are densely forested and extremely rural. As with the rest of Atlantic Canada, crafts have flourished here and, just as with the other Atlantic Provinces, lobster along with other sea food is staple fare. Its colonial heritage has left it historic sites and numerous Scottish traditions.

New Brunswick's architecture also reveals its history. For instance, the Loyalists brought their New England homes from Maine, ferrying them over the river to St Andrews by barge during the American Revolution. In the older sections of the province you will note splendid Georgian style homes and in the coastal regions the fishermen's houses have balconies called 'widow's walks', so called because the wives would keep watch for the return of the boat from them.

Hikers and fishermen adore New Brunswick. The energy of the sea is best seen at the Bay of Fundy where towering tides can rise 50 ft. By way of contrast, the northeastern sandy bays are gentle and warm. This province is large enough to boast 57 provincial parks, ranging from Mt Carleton Provincial Park, which includes the highest point in the province, to Mactaquac which is available to nature lovers all year round. The sun tan brigade enjoy Parlee Beach; the skiers, Sugarloaf's slopes. There are also the National Parks of Kouchibouguac and Fundy. For its tourists New Brunswick is divided into six regions: The **Acadian Coast** extends from Nepisiguit Bay along the northeast coast to Miscou Island, then south along Northumberland Strait to the Miramichi Basin. It was the rewarding fishing grounds of this area that pleased the first European explorers so it is hardly surprising thousands of Acadians fleeing oppression settled here. The coast is also rich in mineral deposits. For the tourist, sea-fishing expeditions from here have set world records on tuna catches.

The **Fundy Tidal Coast** is a favored area if only for its tidal phenomenon, but it also lays claim to Canada's oldest city and the peaceful Fundy Isles. The area spreads across the southern shore of the province from Maine to Fundy National Park. It was Samuel de Champlain who established a winter settlement in 1604 on a small island in the St Croix River but it was an influx of Loyalists which prompted the incorporation of Canada's first city, Saint John, in 1785. The major highway is Route 1 but you might be better off taking side roads if you are looking for seaside views.

At the heart of New Brunswick is the **Miramichi Basin** — very peaceful and quite isolated. This is where the serious sportsman feels at home — fishing the countless rivers and streams, hunting and canoeing. Most of the province's outfitters are located in this area. This name, Miramichi, is undoubtedly Indian and probably the oldest name still in use in Eastern Canada. Because of its forests, the region was a base for shipbuilding. Major highways are Routes 8 and 11.

The **Restigouche Uplands,** taking their name from the Restigouche River, cover much of the northern part of the province. Five branches and numerous streams flow from the Restigouche through forested hills to reach the lowlands bordering the Baie des Chaleurs (Bay of Warmth). Mt Carleton Provincial Park is included in the area and contains one of the highest peaks in Atlantic Canada. It was in this region that the Micmac Indians first met with French settlers and later those from England, Scotland and Ireland. Main roads are Routes 17 and 11.

The **Southeast Shores** offer a contrast: there are sandy beaches and windswept dunes along the Northumberland Strait; there is the rocky tide-lashed shore of the Bay of Fundy. The region comprises three counties with rustic towns but also the bustling city of Moncton. There are

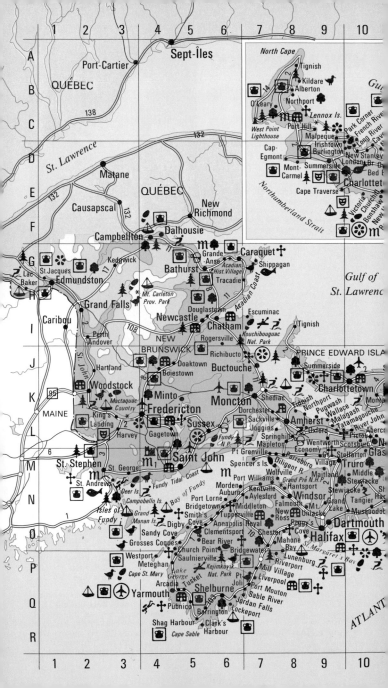

museums and historic properties here but there is equally the tranquillity of two national parks.

The focal point of the province is the **Saint John River Valley.** The river was the first route traveled by Indians then later by pioneers and explorers. New Brunswick people call it their 'Rhine'. It flows for some 725 km / 450 mi from inside northern Maine to the Bay of Fundy with lush vegetation along its banks.

Acadian Historical Village   G6

Just off Rte 11 between Grande-Anse and Caraquet. A major attraction re-creating the Acadian settlement in vivid detail. Acadian life and culture is depicted between 1780 and 1880 with costumed 'residents' demonstrating the old crafts: making soap and brooms, drying fish, weaving cloth, preserving vegetables. You can visit the local cobbler, wheelwright, printer and many others, plus a working grist mill, the Theriault home, a church, school, tavern and other buildings whose period-dressed occupants will tell you all about life in the 1800s.

On the site an old diking system or *aboiteaux* is in operation — built to reclaim marshy land for farming. The cafe features Acadian food and the gift shop, Acadian items. During the summer there are many special events. *Caraquet 11 km/7 mi.*

Bathurst   G5

(pop. 16,301). Situated at the mouth of the Nepisiguit River, this is the only city along the Acadian coast, and was the site of an early settlement established by Nicholas Denys, a regional governor. His book about the area was published in France in 1672 and a memorial has been erected where he is buried in the Gowan Brae section of the city. Bathurst is an industrial center with some of the world's largest zinc mines but it is also close to areas of scenic interest such as the *Tetagouche and Pabineau Falls* and the *Youghall Provincial Park.* In town, see the war museum on St Peter Ave. *Newcastle 80 km/50 mi.*

Boiestown   J4

At the center of the Miramichi Basin, the *Central New Brunswick Woodsmen's Museum* chronicles the history of those who worked in the woods. *Fredericton 64 km/40 mi.*

Campbellton   F4

(pop. 9282). The only city in the Restigouche Uplands, situated at the west of the

Baie des Chaleurs. Founded in 1773 it took its current name in 1832 from New Brunswick's lieutenant-governor, Sir Archibald Campbell. The last naval battle of the Seven Years War was fought just off Campbellton in 1790 and that battle is commemorated today at Riverside Park. The city's *Restigouche Gallery* serves as a national exhibition center but attractions for visitors are mostly in the surrounding area where there are numerous recreational possibilities. (Many outfitters are based in the city itself.)

A favorite excursion is to nearby *Sugarloaf Provincial Park* at Atholville, dominated by Sugarloaf Mountain rising 999 ft. In addition to hiking, jogging and nature trails, camping and tennis, there are bumper boats and Eastern Canada's only summer alpine slide. You take a chairlift up the mountain and slide down by chute, twisting and turning for 2486 ft. Sleds are equipped with brakes for your control and safety.
Bathurst 104 km/65 mi.

Lighthouse, Grand Manan Island

Campobello Island   N3
Off the Fundy Coast. Franklin Delano Roosevelt spent many pleasant summer holidays on this island which can be reached via a toll-free bridge from Lubec in Maine or by car ferry from Deer Island. The cottage owned by the former president can be visited in the **Roosevelt International Park.** The island was given to one Captain Owen in 1767 as compensation for an arm he lost in battle. The *Owens Home* is open to the public. You'll find a golf course, pebble beach and camping facilities in *Herring Cove Provincial Park.*
Saint John 92 km/57.5 mi.

Caraquet   G6
(pop. 3950). The heart of Acadia, this city

was founded in 1758 by those Acadians who had taken refuge in this area to avoid being deported. Today, this center boasts one of the province's largest commercial fishing fleets — visitors will find an abundance of fresh seafood wherever they go. Buy your own at the wharfside fish market or fish for your own — this is the central port for deep-sea fishing excursions, especially those in search of the enormous bluefin tuna. The town is also the home of the province's only fisheries school. Boat building is still carried on in the Caraquet area, often by families engaged in this work for generations.

Other sightseeing includes boat tours of the bay; a look at local history in the *Acadian Museum* and a visit to the *Sainte-Anne-du-Bocage Shrine* at the west end of town. *Bathurst 64 km/40 mi.*

Chatham   I6
(pop. 7601). Miramichi Basin. Former shipyards have been replaced by port facilities to export local wood products. It is one of the largest urban areas in the region whose share of famous residents has included Canada's only New Brunswick-born prime minister, R. B. Bennett. In town see the restored *Loggie House* (1879) and the *Miramichi Natural History Museum.* Also of interest are the genealogical and religious records housed in *St Michael's Historical Museum and Rectory. Fredericton 160 km/100 mi.*

Dalhousie   F4
(pop. 5640). A resort center with a Scottish influence. From the Renfrew Street Wharf, boat tours are available on the *Chaleur Phantom* giving magnificent views of the Bay and surrounding areas. Swimming can be enjoyed in both Inch Arran and Chaleur parks. Find out about local history at the *Restigouche Regional Museum.* For a picnic lunch with a difference, head out of town along the shores at Eel River Crossing where everyone digs for clams. A Scottish connection is notable inland from Dalhousie, where communities have names like Balmoral and Dundee. *Campbellton 24 km/15 mi.*

Deer Island   N3
Situated off the Fundy Coast, this island may be reached by a free ferry from Letete on New Brunswick's mainland. Traditionally, fishing has been the major occupation here and lobster canneries were established as early as 1873. You can also reach Campobello Island from here in summer on a toll ferry. Sport activities are the main attraction with opportunities for whale watching, scuba diving, hiking and rock-hounding. Offshore, the large whirl-

pool known as *'Old Sow'* clearly indicates the power of the Fundy tides. *Saint John 88 km/55 mi.*

Doaktown J5

(pop. 1022). Miramichi Basin. See the *Miramichi Atlantic Salmon Museum* which interprets the past, present and future of the salmon's struggle for survival. Conservation apart, salmon fishing is a mainstay in these parts. See also the *Doak Historic Park* with its restored Doak House. *Fredericton 88 km/55 mi.*

Dorchester L7

(pop. 1125). This southeast town was named after Canada's first governor-general, Sir Guy Carleton, 1st Baron of Dorchester. See the restored *Keillor House* which houses the Westmorland Historical Society Museum, and the *Bell Inn*, built in 1811 and believed to be the province's oldest stone building. Covered bridges and quiet side roads around town offer peaceful touring. *Moncton 36 km/22.5 mi.*

Douglastown I6

Miramichi Basin at the junction of Rtes 8 and 11. Formerly site of the Seaman's Marine Hospital, erected in 1829 to care for sailors visiting Miramichi ports and in need of medical attention. The stone structure is now a church hall. See the *MacDonald Farm Historic Park* which is a restored version of a typical 1830s working farm with stone manor house, outbuildings, fish shed, dock and orchards. *Newcastle 4 km/2.5 mi.*

Edmundston H1

(pop. 12,710). Capital of the Madawaska area, a 'republic' which originated in the 1800s when residents wanted to establish their own identity, and stop Canada and the US arguing over the area. See *The Madawaska Regional Museum* to find out more of the local history of this lively, French spirited city. Special exhibits are featured at the *Gallery Colline* on the campus of Saint-Louis College. Visitors may tour the pulp mill and forest nursery of Fraser Co., and there are many nature trails in the area. Also see the *Automobile Museum* in *Les Jardins de la Republique Provincial Park*. There is an annual midsummer festival, the *Fete de Brayonne*, and the *Lac Baker Provincial Park* (20 mi west on Rte 120) is a popular recreational area. *Fredericton 285 km/177 mi.*

Escuminac I7

Is the site of a monument paying tribute to 35 fishermen who lost their lives in a storm at sea in 1959. Sculpted by well known New Brunswick artist, Claude Rousell, its portrayal symbolizes the ocean's tremendous influence on those who depend on it for their livelihood. *Chatham 58 km/36 mi.*

Fredericton L4

(pop. 45,248). Capital of the province and called 'City of Stately Elms' and indeed, elm trees do line the city's gracious streets. It took its name in honor of the second son of King George III in 1785 and it became an important military town, as is still witnessed by *Officers Square*. The latter was the center for military activity during the time Fredericton was garrisoned by the British army 1785-1869, and by the Canadian army 1883-1914. The old Officers Quarters now house the *York-Sunbury Historical Society Museum* which houses many items connected with the city's past.

In the middle of the square is a statue of *Lord Beaverbrook*, a great benefactor of New Brunswick. One of his gifts to this city is the *Beaverbrook Art Gallery*, open year round, containing some outstanding British masterpieces and a Dali original. Stretching downriver from the gallery is *The Green*, a pleasant place for strolling along the bank of the Saint John River to the end of Waterloo Row. The marble fountain on The Green was another donation from Lord Beaverbrook in memory of his friend Sir James Dunn.

The center of Fredericton is compact enough for a walking tour — a five block square covers its most interesting historic sites. These include *City Hall*, *Justice Building*, *Soldiers Barracks* and the old stone *Guard House*. In the National Exhibition Centre, the N.B. *Sports Hall of Fame* exhibits trophies, photographs and memorabilia. In *Centennial Park* a metal obelisk marks the site of the old British American Coffee House which stood from 1785 to 1961 when it had to make way for the Playhouse. The Indian totem pole was donated by the British Columbian Indians.

The *Legislative Assembly Building* has been the seat of provincial government since 1882 and when it is not in session, visitors can see the Assembly Chamber. They are also welcome in the public gallery when it is in session. The city's finest church is *Christ Church Cathedral*, a prime example of decorated Gothic architecture. (Free guided tours available.) See also *Old York County Jail* (1840), *Loyalist Cemetery* and the *Old Burial Ground*.

Queen Street and King Street are the city's main shopping areas and Fredericton's top hotel, the Lord Beaverbrook is located on Queen St. There is also a craft area around Regent St. The main covered shopping areas are Regent St. Mall and Fredericton Mall. Not to be missed is breakfast under the elms at *Boyce Farmers' Market* on a Saturday morning. Located on George St. between Regent and John St., it operates year round selling fresh produce, flowers and bric-a-brac. One of the most elegant restaurants in town is Eighty Eight Ferry.

Not far from the center of Fredericton, *Odell Park* is where the residents go on a weekend for picnics, barbecues or to ride or walk through the many forest trails. The area is a unique example of primeval forest in New Brunswick and is part of the original land grant to Jonathan Odell, a Loyalist and early settler. Within the property, *Odell Arboretum* features a natural tree garden. *Saint John 109 km/68 mi.*

Fundy Tidal Coast   M5

The unique stretch of coastline that extends along New Brunswick's southern shore from Maine to the **Fundy National Park.** The biggest human influence in this region came from the thousands of United Empire Loyalists who settled here after the American Revolution. But the awesome 50 foot tides have more influence on this coast.

Fundy National Park   L6

Comprises a rugged coastline, with inland woods and lakes. It covers 80 square miles and sits on a plateau 1000 feet above sealevel. Wildlife is abundant so that bird watching and fishing are two prime activities. Other sport possibilities include camping, hiking on the 50 miles of trails, boating, tennis, lawn bowling and golf. A natural amphitheater is the setting for summer entertainment and salt water is piped in from the Bay of Fundy to create a heated salt water pool at Alma which is the service town and the park headquarters. *Saint John 140 km/87 mi.*

Gagetown   L4

(pop. 655). A tiny village in the St John Valley that has attracted artisans to settle here. For a number of years, for instance, the famous *Loomcrofters* (who have provided handwoven gifts for royalty) have maintained a studio in a former blockhouse, one of the oldest buildings on the river. In the *Queens County Museum,* once the home of Sir Leonard Tilley, one of the fathers of Canadian Confederation, local history is featured.

All around is a delightful area for tours. Like the popular one to the Kingston Peninsula, a pretty rural area, one of the first places to be settled by the Loyalists around 1783. Some of the province's earliest homes still survive on this peninsula along with other historic sites. *Fredericton 48 km/30mi.*

Grande-Anse   G6

(pop. 765). A French town on the Acadian Peninsula. There is a scenic lookout in the municipal park. See also the new *Popes' Museum and Art Gallery* on rue Acadie which relates to the history of the Roman Catholic Church. *Bathurst 40 km/25 mi.*

Grand Falls   H2

(pop. 6223). In the St John River Valley has 75 foot high falls which are among the biggest cataracts east of Niagara. The gorge is 1.5 km / 1 mi long. Interpretive displays explain the action of the falls and show their effect on the surrounding territory. You can walk down into the gorge via steps and several walking trails lead to a number of scenic vantage points. Officially this town is bilingual and when it was known as Grand-Sault it was a military post, as you can see by looking at Main Street which developed from a parade square. Today, it is a large agricultural center with potatoes its main crop. In summer, the fields of potato blossoms become subjects for painters and photographers. *Edmundston 58 km/36 mi.*

Grand Manan Island   O3

The largest and most remote of the **Fundy Isles,** reached by a 1½ hour ferry ride from the New Brunswick mainland. If you like the quiet, outdoor life, this island is a superb destination and excellent for bird watching — more than 275 species have been sighted. World-recognized ornithologist, James Audubon made many of his sketches while visiting here. Painters and photographers will find plenty of subject matter while whale watching, hiking and rock-hounding are other island pastimes. Boat tours and excursions can be arranged to reach the best vantage points. Amateur geologists might note the island is comprised of two types of rock and you can see a marked contrast between them in the cliff at Red Point. Fishing is the main occupation and seafood is on every menu. An edible seaweed called dulse is also harvested here for export around the world.

The island ferry terminal is located at North Head. In the local Grand Harbour museum you will find a first class maritime gallery plus the *Allan Moses* bird collection. Another community at Sea Cove has access to the *Anchorage Provincial Park* and a nearby bird sanctuary. To cross to *White Head Island,* take the free ferry. *Saint John 92 km/57.5 mi.*

Hartland   J2

(pop. 974). Site of the longest covered bridge in the world. It is 391 m / 1282 ft long and was originally built in 1897. Rebuilt in 1930, its seven spans link routes 103 and 105. *Fredericton 98 km/61 mi.*

Harvey   L3
In the St John River Valley, this town lies among agricultural and dairy farming land. Founded in 1840, its old woolen mill is still operating. Several horseback riding camps are in the area as are numerous freshwater lakes. *Fredericton 48 km/36 mi.*

Isles of Fundy   N3
These refer to the three tranquil islands off the Fundy Coast, situated at the western end of the Bay. They are: Campobello, Deer and Grand Manan.

Kings Landing   L3
A major attraction on an expansive riverside site, it was built when rising waters from Mactaquac Dam threatened several sites of historic interest. One of the best restorations of the Loyalist times in the province, Kings Landing can offer something for the whole family. The 'village' has about 60 buildings with costumed staff to tell you all about them. (Do wear comfortable walking shoes if you plan to tackle everything.) Among the buildings are:

Sleighride at King's Landing

Hagerman House, built in 1838, was originally on Bear Island. It is designed in neo-classical style and the furnishings feature one of the most complete collections of John Warren Moore (1812-1893), a St Stephen cabinetmaker. The red barn next door was part of the Rosborough Farm on the Barony Flats and is typical of barns in this part of New Brunswick.

The Joslin Farm (1790) used to be located three miles up river in Prince William on land granted to a Rhode Island Loyalist. Until it was acquired for Kings Landing, members of the Joslin family had worked on developing it. It is designed as a Classical Revival Home – some of the early 1790s trim can be found in the upper rooms. In the horse barn here (1860) there are several farm animals. The stock barn once belonged to the Ingrahams of Bear Island and is in English style, symmetrically laid out around two center bays. At one end of the garden fence is a smoke house for curing meat.

Jones House was built in 1828 for a family who came from the New Hampshire / Massachussetts area. A prominent farmer, Thomas Jones, built it and his son later became a wealthy brewer and was twice mayor of Saint John. It is unusual for its stone construction and has entrances on two levels.

The Sawmill is a new addition but built in the design of those typical in the area in the 1730s. *The Grist Mill*, on the other hand was built by a British immigrant in 1815 and has since been reconstructed. Typical of those grist mills operating in the valley in the 1800s it continues to produce buckwheat flour for use in the settlement today.

In the 1800s wooden boats worked the Saint John River, carrying huge cargoes of planks to the merchants of the port city. The *Brunswick Lion* you see here today is based on a woodboat registered in 1837 with an oak frame covered by black spruce planking and cotton sails dipped in red ochre to increase durability.

A popular stopping point on a tour of Kings Landing is the *Kings Head Inn*, originally a farmhouse built for Richard Holyoke at Longs Creek in 1855. From the 1850s stagecoaches changed horses in its yard and in the 1920s the building was used as a hotel. Nowadays you can have a snack, meal or a drink.

Lint House (1820s), built for Lawrence Lint, son of a New York Loyalist, used to be eight miles up river in Queensbury. The blacksmith shop on the site is based on the one at Jewett's Mills where most of the tools currently being used came from. It represents a shop typical of this area, small but open all year for business such as shoeing horses and maintaining farm implements.

Long House (1820s) was the home of a small farmer and sawmill owner, remaining in family hands until 1905. The design is neo-classical and its interior is interesting for its basement kitchen. Scottish carpenter, James Mitchell, built the *Heustis House* in 1845. Its distinguishing feature is the large central chimney which serves as a fireplace in the kitchen and a stove in the parlor.

St Mark's Church was located in Kingsclear, seven miles down river. This Gothic Revival Church was erected in 1858 and in 1894 a bell was donated and a belfry built. Typical of a mid-Victorian property is the *Perley House* (1866) with its Gothic Revival style, its front gable form and the rosette window in its peak. *Grant Store* is typical of the stores in the Saint John River Valley in the last quarter of the 19th century and was built, in the 1880s, up river at Middle Southampton. The little parish school (1835) housed 23 students back in those days while the *Killeen Cabin* looks like any of those first homes of Irish immigrants. Made of squared logs, it has one room with a large cooking fireplace and an overhead storage loft inside.

Light snacks are served today in the *Agricultural Hall*, originally constructed as a school in the 1890s and later serving as a meeting place. Typical of the austere Georgian architecture that Loyalist houses tended to feature, stands the *Morehouse House* (1812), though that simple exterior is far different from the spacious and colorful interior. One unusual feature is the use of a dummy chimney to heat one side of the house. The influential Ingraham family had the neo-classical *Ingraham House* built in the 1830s. Its adjoining octagonal privy seats four and is one of the oldest buildings at The Landing. Dating to 1795, it belonged to a prominent Virginia Loyalist and Chief Justice of New Brunswick. The *Fisher House* (1803-1809) is a Loyalist 'saltbox'.

Throughout the summer there is a full schedule of activities and events at Kings Landing that may vary from demonstrations of Scottish country dancing and tossing the caber to performances in the *Kings Theatre*, converted from an old barn. Open daily June-Oct. 1000-1700, July/Aug. to 1800. *Fredericton 35 km/21.8 mi.*

Kouchibouguac National Park   I6

A focal point of the Gulf of St Lawrence shore and New Brunswick's largest park covering 238 sq km/92 sq mi of forest, salt marshes, beaches and sand dunes that stretch along 25 km/15.6 mi of Northumberland Strait coast. Its name in Micmac means 'river of the longest tides'.

There is supervised swimming at *Kellys Beach*, fishing in its many rivers and lagoons, hiking, camping, windsurfing, biking, canoeing and bird watching. The network of hiking trails meander along the rivers and through the forests. Roadside picnic sites are established at scenic points and rental equipment for some of the sports is available. A nature interpretation program will help you understand the park's natural wonders. *Moncton 55 km/34.3 mi.*

Lac-Baker   H1

(pop. 325). In the Saint John River Valley and a popular summer resort area close to Edmundston. Activities include swimming, sailing, water skiing, board sailing and boating. In the area there are two provincial parks: *Lac-Baker Beach* and *Frontier*. In the nearby community of Clair, *Le Petit Musee* is a local history museum and

handicrafts are worth looking at in Saint-Francois-de-Madawaska. *Edmunston 40 km/25 mi.*

Mactaquac Country   L3

A well developed tourist area in the Saint John River Valley. The key to the area is the *Mactaquac Provincial Park*, an all seasons park that covers 1400 acres. Here you'll find camp facilities, two supervised beaches, marinas, a championship 18-hole golf course, nature trails, recreation programs and a lodge. Fishing and horseback riding are alternative activities and several craft studios in the area offer tempting buys. Holiday attractions and accommodations are also to be found on nearby Rte 105.

Moncton   K7

(pop. 55,934). Second largest city in New Brunswick and the major city in the southeast. It was named for Col. Robert Monckton, commander of the British forces which captured Fort Beausejour in 1775. It was only an accident that saw the 'k' dropped when the official designation was given by the provincial legislature.

This is quite a sophisticated city with good shopping and restaurants. For those interested in past history, visit the *Moncton Civic Museum*. The only French-language university in New Brunswick is also located in town with *The Acadian Museum and Art Gallery* located on its campus.

If you care to see one of the province's tidal phenomena, the *Tidal Bore*, go to *Bore Park* in downtown. If a beach or other recreation is on your mind, try *Centennial Park* at the western end of the city. An optical illusion makes you think cars can coast uphill at *Magnetic Hill* on the city's outskirts. (Fun to try at least twice!) Near the hill, there's a game farm with a small petting zoo for children.

A bridge from Moncton leads to Riverview across the Petitcodiac River while Rtes 112 and 2 lead to rural communities like Salisbury and Petitcodiac itself. Just east of the city at Dieppe, *Champlain Raceway* features good harness racing. Moncton is a good touring base as it is an important rail and distribution center for the Atlantic Provinces. *Saint John 144 km/90 mi.*

Mount Carleton Provincial Park   H3

A remote park in the Restigouche Uplands whose wilderness setting offers a full range of outdoor opportunities for boaters, bird watchers, fishermen and rockhounders. Whether you're a novice or an expert, you will find a hiking trail to suit you. For superb views, take the trail that winds up Mount Carleton itself. Camping sites and park headquarters are situated at *Nictau Lake*, but another point of access is St-Quentin on Rte 17, a popular hunting and fishing area. *Bathurst 100 km/62 mi.*

Newcastle I5

(pop. 6423). Located on Rte 8 and separated from Chatham by the Miramichi River, this town's greatest claim to international fame is that it was the boyhood home of Lord Beaverbrook who, of course, became a celebrity in the world of newspapers and politics. The monument containing his ashes is in the town square along with a gazebo made in Italy and other bequests from Beaverbrook. His former home is now the *Old Manse Library* which contains numerous volumes, including first editions taken from his personal collection. The *Enclosure Provincial Park* lies just outside Newcastle, where there is swimming and camping. *Fredericton 158 km/99 mi.*

Perth-Andover I2

(pop. 1973). A village in Saint John River Valley close to the *Maliseet Indian Reserve.* An international golf course on the outskirts is not only a challenge — the clubhouse is in the US and the course itself in Canada! From here you can head to *Mount Carleton Provincial Park* or to *Plaster Rock* on Rte 385, the site of an early plaster mill in the middle of a lumber area. This is prime hunting and fishing country. *Fredericton 169 km/105 mi.*

Richibucto J7

(pop. 1909). A small community on the St Lawrence Gulf shore. One of the churches here has a steeple resembling a lighthouse and a roof symbolic of waves — another reminder of the sea's influence over settlers here. Two attractions are *Kent Amusement Park* and the *World's Largest Map*, nearby is the *Jardine Provincial Park.* Not far away at *St-Louis-de-Kent*, an outdoor shrine with Stations of the Cross in landscaped grounds, is a replica of the famous Lourdes shrine. *Chatham 60 km/38 mi.*

Rogersville I6

(pop. 1138). A small community in the Acadian Coastal Region where a monument commemorates Acadians fleeing persecution. It was also the site of a Trappist monastery. Nowadays, it is known as the 'Brussels Sprouts Capital of Canada', set as it is in a rich agricultural area particularly noted for that crop. See the *G.M. & C. Antique Museum* for its collection of

antique cars, guns and household appliances. *Newcastle 32 km/20 mi.*

Sackville L7

(pop. 5755). A peaceful university town on the banks of the Cumberland Basin. Much of the land around it was reclaimed from the sea by an extensive dike system, the *'aboiteaux'*, created by the pioneer Acadians. Until 1920 when the course of the Tantramar River was changed by a landslide, this town was also a seaport. Now the marshes of the Tantramar are used for bird watching. Sackville's *Mount Allison University* was Canada's first to grant a woman a degree — in 1875, and these days is renowned for its arts programs. On its campus is the *Owens Art Gallery* which features a number of annual exhibits. As well as being a university town, this is an arts and crafts center. Its harness shop is the only one in North America still making hand-made horse collars, and there are many other craft shops of interest. *Moncton 43 km/27 mi.*

St Andrews N3

(pop. 1711). Possibly one of the prettiest resorts in New Brunswick. Situated on the Fundy Coast it has a New England type of charm and atmosphere, it is salt-weathered and picturesque. It is certainly one of the oldest settlements, dating from 1783 when the Loyalists founded it, bringing their homes with them aboard barges across the river from Maine, and

St Andrews

re-assembling them at their destination. Three of those originals still stand and many more lining the tree-flanked streets date to the 1700s or 1800s. I recommend a leisurely walking tour of this compact resort to admire the architecture with perhaps an overnight stay at the turreted *Algonquin Hotel* built in the early 1800s by Canadian railway magnate, William Van Horne.

It is a place to 'take the air' in an old

fashioned way, drop in at one of the pub terraces overlooking the sea for that lobster roll and glass of wine. Do not miss *The Huntsman Marine Laboratory and Aquarium* which will give an insight into marine life in the Bay of Fundy through displays, audio-visual presentations and live specimens. Children will find the 'Please Touch Tank' appealing and enjoy seeing the harbor seals. It is more serious next door at the *Federal Fisheries Research Station* where scientific research is carried out.

Summer activities include golf, tennis, sailing, hiking, swimming and fishing. The town's antique and craft shops are good for browsing through and at the *Sunbury Shores Arts and Nature Centre,* there are courses in arts, crafts and nature interpretation.

History buffs should take a look at the *Ross Museum,* Georgian architecture on the outside, and inside collections of fine antiques and porcelain. The *Greenock Church* has hand-carved green oak foliage on its steeple and at **St Andrews Blockhouse** is a National Historic Site.

St Andrews has a farmers' market and fish markets so food is as good a reason to come here as any and boat tours or other sightseeing cruises are easily arranged. *Saint John 96 km/60 mi.*

St George   M3
(pop. 1148). East of St Andrews and reputed to have its own 'monster'. It may or may not live in *Lake Utopia* but certainly a fish ladder below the dam allows the salmon to finish their journey upriver to their spawning grounds. Granite quarried here in 1875 was taken for building to cities as far away as Boston and Ottawa. *Saint John 64 km/40 mi.*

Saint-Jacques   G1
Coming from Québec to New Brunswick, this is the first community along the Trans Canada Hwy. Nature trails, an adventure playground, sports facilities, camping and an amphitheater can be found in the *Jardins de la Republique* here. Also a vintage *Auto Museum. Edmunston 10 km/6 mi.*

Saint John   M5
(pop. 85,956). New Brunswick's largest city and thanks to vast restoration projects, it is once again attracting people downtown. As it is Canada's oldest incorporated city, it can claim several 'firsts' — first police force in North America, first newspaper in Canada and first bank. Also Canada's first museum was founded in Saint John in 1842 — the present *New Brunswick Museum.* The museum has a series of model ships; preserved from the 1880s, including one of the *Marco Polo*

which was the fastest sailing ship of its day.

The waterfront is its focal point and its hub, revitalized these days with the building of a chic Hilton Hotel and the nearby dining/shopping complex of *Market Square.* The Loyalists arrived at the very same Market Slip in 1783. The Hilton and the Delta hotels are connected by an underground walkway and there are several other good hotels. Market Square tends to be the place to eat, recommended are Grannan's and The Continental, but there is also a food hall with different sections for different types of food where you can make your own selection.

Happily, many of the old homes which had been neglected have been, or are being, restored. *Barbours General Store,* stocked as it was in the year 1867 actually houses the tourist office. On a walking tour, you will see many historic sites including the *Loyalist House, the Pleasant Villa School*(1876), the old *Loyalist Burial Grounds, Chubbs Corner, Trinity Church.* (The tourist office suggests three city walking tours: Prince William's Walk, A Victorian Stroll, and the Loyalists Trail — each of which should take you about $1\frac{1}{2}$ hours.)

Another historic stop is at *Old City Market* (open every day but Sunday), where some of the stalls have been operated by the same families for years, selling all kinds of fresh produce, crafts and antiques.

You will need a car, or join a city sightseeing tour, to see the **Carleton Martello Tower,** a stone fortification which survived the War of 1812 and is now a National Historic Site. The British built it to guard against possible American attack and it overlooks the western end of Saint John Harbour and therefore gives an exceptional view over the city. Inside, artefacts from the 1800s are displayed and the upper floor houses items relating to the tower's own history. See also *Fort Howe Blockhouse,* a replica of one from 1777 and the *Telephone Pioneers Museum.*

Twice a day you can witness a strange phenomenon on the river when the Bay of Fundy tides rise so much they actually force the Saint John River to flow upriver, creating the *Reversing Falls Rapids.* The effects go on for 104 km/65 mi and there are two viewing points.

For outdoor recreation *Rockwood Park* in the city center is the best bet with a waterslide, golf driving range and zoo, though the area around Saint John is noted for boating and harbor tours are available from the Market Slip wharf. Weekly harnesss racing takes place at *Exhibition Park Raceway.*

Saint John Market Square

Because of its location, Saint John is always the suggested base for side and day trips within the valley. It is easy to take a river ferry to Kingston, for instance while Rte 7 leads into the valley by way of Grand Bay and Westfield. Take Rte 100 and you'll pass through small communities like East Riverside-Kinghurst, Renforth, Rothesay and Fairvale. Rte 121 will take you to Hampton and rural Norton and Rte 111 goes to the Bay of Fundy and the village of St Martins where *The Quaco Museum* shows the shipbuilding that used to be such an important industry here. *Fredericton 109 km/68 mi.*

Saint John River Valley   J2
Called 'oa-lus-tuk', the goodly river, by the Indians who travelled it. Starting in Maine, it wends its rolling way for 725 km/450 mi, harnessed here and there for power or recreation, to the Bay of Fundy. From Edmundston to Fredericton, it parallels the Trans Canada Highway and is known as 'the river road' on which Saint John sits. It has been infuenced by its original Indian inhabitants, by the settlers of three main French seigniories (now called Brayons), the Loyalists, and later by Scottish and Danish settlers.

St Stephen   M2
(pop. 5264). A town on the border of the US. Amusingly, during the War of 1812 St Stephen residents loaned their sup-posedly hostile neighbors across the river their own gunpowder for the Americans' July 4 celebrations. See the *Charlotte County Museum* for a glimpse of local history. *Oak Bay Provincial Park* offers horseback riding and a sheltered beach. And side trips find enchanting rural villages. *Fredericton 98 km/61mi.*

Shediac   K7
(pop. 4216). They call it 'Lobster capital of the world'. Don't miss the annual July *Shediac Lobster Festival.* One of the province's best sandy beaches is here, too, at *Parlee Beach Provincial Park.* A variety of water-sports can be arranged here along with regular boat tours and there is a nearby golf course. Sailing is popular along the Northumberland Strait. *Moncton 24 km/15 mi.*

Shippagan   G7
(pop. 2344). An important commercial fishing center, home of the *Marine Centre* which gives an in depth study of the Gulf of St Lawrence's marine life. It is a good base for deep sea fishing. Another major industry is the harvesting of peat moss — with tours available. Also visit *Shippagan Provincial Park.* (Peat moss is also gathered on Île Lameque, reached via a bridge. The wildlife park in town will be of interest to young travelers.) *Caraquet 28 km/17.5 mi.*

Sussex   L5
(pop. 3938). A dairy center and a notable potash mine site. Sussex is also well regarded for its crafts and there are many studios in the area. Just outside town, *Animalland* has unusual concrete sculptures of animals that include dinosaurs and a gargantuan lobster. *Saint John 68 km/42.5 mi.*

Tracadie   H7
(pop. 2591). On Rte 11, Acadian Coast. 'Tracadie' is an Indian word that actually means 'ideal place to camp'. So it is, as you will find out in *Val Comeau Provincial Park,* on the town's outskirts, where there's also a saltwater beach. See also the local history museum. *Caraquet 32 km/20 mi.*

Woodstock   K2
(pop. 4869). An entry point for US visitors who call it 'the hospitality town'. Canada's first automatic dial telephone was developed here in 1900. There are some lovely old homes and the *Old County Court House* (1833) is open to the public. For recreation, the area has a waterslide, horseback riding and a summer farmers' market. *Fredericton 101 km/63 mi.*

PRINCE EDWARD ISLAND

Prince Edward Island or P.E.I., to those who know it well, is a small crescent-shaped island lying in the Gulf of St Lawrence, just 170 km/106.25 mi long with a population of 123,000. Although it is Canada's smallest province it is important for its agriculture and noted for its rich verdant farmland, its red soil and its long sandy beaches.

The Micmacs called it 'the island cradled by the waves' and since 1864, it has also been known as 'the cradle of the Confederation', for it was here in Charlottetown the founding fathers met to discuss a united Canada. If the three county names — Prince, Queens and Kings, sound British, it is because the island was taken over from the French by Britain in 1763, its name being Anglicized to Island of Saint John. In 1799 its name was changed again to Prince Edward Island in honour of Prince Edward (later Duke of Kent).

Because of its fertile land it is often called 'The Million Acre Farm'. It is best for farmhouse holidays, best for potatoes, best for lobster. Its size gives the whole of the province a 'community' feel and small town friendliness, dare I say provinciality, whilst its waters are said to be Canada's warmest. Agriculture was not its only mainstay — in the 1800s, shipbuilding was important and later, silver fox farming was an economic mainstay.

Not only agriculture, but fishing filled the coffers — fishing villages dot the coastline and lighthouses are familiar landmarks. The land is as gentle as the atmosphere — no neon or brash cities here. Most of the residents live in the capital, Charlottetown, or in Summerside while the other communities, with their whitewashed houses and country churches, are much quieter and more picturesque.

P.E.I. is perhaps the most relaxed and delightful of the provinces, quickly seen, but best enjoyed at leisure. Basically, you should consider three scenic drives: the *Lady Slipper Scenic Drive* begins near Summerside in Prince County and will take you to the most historic section of the island in the west. Here there are the Micmacs of Lennox Island and Acadians in the Evangeline region. This was where shipbuilding and fox fur industries originated while today Irish moss is harvested for use in food, cosmetics and industrial products and Malpeque oysters are raked from the sea floor. The drive extends for 288 km/180 mi.

The *Blue Heron Scenic Drive* circles Queens County in the center of the island.

You will see those distinctive red shores in the south, white sandy dunes in the north. The drive of 190 km/120 mi starts and ends in the capital and includes landmark sites and the national park area.

The *Kings Byway Scenic Drive* is the longest, stretching for 375 km/234 mi round Kings County in the eastern part of the island. Stop at one of the beaches or harbors, look at the acres of berries and tobacco, look over to Nova Scotia from East Point and perhaps try for tuna at North Lake.

Alberton   B8
(pop. 1062). Prince County. A good place for handicrafts. In particular, visit the *Leavitts' Maple Tree Craft Shop* where skilled craftsmen produce fine gift items from Maritime wood, especially the bird's eye maple. You can watch artisans turn a rough piece of wood into an artistic masterpiece, look at the display of local and foreign woods. Open Mon.-Fri. year round 0800-1200, 1300-1700 and in summer on Sat. the *Alberton Museum* is on Church St., displays here concentrate on family life as it used to be, local history and also the silver fox industry which once thrived here. Open mid June-Labour Day, Mon.-Sat. 1000-1700. *Summerside 66 km/41 mi.*

Basin Head   D15
Kings County. Location of the *Basin Head Fisheries Museum* on Rte 16. Through photographs, artefacts and equipment, displays tell the story of the Maritime fisherfolk. The boat shed houses small craft and the canning factory features a marine aquarium. Among the other buildings to see are the smokehouse, fish-box factory and fishermen's sheds. The complex is situated next to one of the island's finest sand dune systems. Open in summer. *Souris 10 km/6 mi.*

Bear River D14

Kings County. Location of *Chaisson's Replicas* off Rte 2 west of Souris, on Rte 307. Replicas to be seen include St Alexis Church (1834-1931) the old hotel built in 1920 and Bear River settlement as it was in 1900, with log cabin, windmill and the old Chaisson family homestead. All in miniature. Guided tours are available. Open daily in summer 1100-1200. *Souris 9 km/ 5.5 mi.*

Bonshaw E11

Bonshaw 500 on the TransCanada Hwy is for go-carters of all ages, around a wide asphalt track. Visitors are free to use the playground and picnic areas and on Sun. there's a flea market. Open summer 0900-dusk. Also here are the *Car Life Museum; International House of Dolls; Strathgartney Homestead* and *Fairyland. Charlottetown 20 km/12.5 mi.*

Brackley E11

Queens County. Accommodations range from a campsite to tourist homes and a motel. At the junction of Rtes 15 and 220 you can take a farm tour to learn about the island's most important industry. A guide explains the dairy operation — visitors can see a proper working farm. Opens July/ Aug. *Charlottetown 5 km/3 mi.*

Brackley Beach D11

A seaside holiday area off Rte 15 with many cottage and tourist home accommodations plus a campsite. Activities include clam digging, watersports, nearby golf and lobster suppers. The **National Park** is within easy reach and of course, there is the beach itself. Lovers of handicrafts should drop into the *Dunes Studio Gallery* overlooking Brackley Bay, less than a mile from the park — it is a showcase for the island's best crafts including wooden wares, hand-woven items, art glass, embroidery. *Charlottetown 21 km/ 13 mi.*

Burlington D10

The 800 metre go-cart track is licensed by the Canadian Car Club Assn. Children have their own track and the amusement area also features what it terms an SR2 Simulator Ride. Open in summer 0930-sunset. On Rte 234 there are large scale models of famous homes, castles and cathedrals at *Woodleigh Replicas*, open summer 0900-1700, later some months. *Kensington 6 km/3.7 mi.*

Campbells Cove Provincial Park D15

A summer recreational area with a beach and a campground. *Elmira 5 km/3 mi.*

Cap-Egmont D8

A place you might stop at along the Lady Slipper Drive, to see *The Bottle Houses* on Rte 11. The main 18 ft × 24 ft building is entirely made of bottles — 12,000 different kinds. The chapel and gift shop here are also constructed of bottles and there

Church near Basin Head

are rock and flower gardens on the premises. Open summer daily 0900-2000. *Summerside 40 km/25 mi.*

Cape Traverse   E9
A summer beach area with several cottage accommodations. Activities include swimming and clam digging. *Borden 6 km/ 3.7 mi.*

Cavendish   D11
A seaside resort with plenty of accommodations from cottages to motels. In addition to the beach, all kinds of sport activities are possible in the vicinity from golf and tennis to horseback riding and fishing. There are also a number of family attractions close by, namely *The Enchanted Castle* on Rte 6 with its fairy tale scenes and *County Bear* musical show; *Rainbow Valley* which has water slides, a children's farm, boating lakes and playground; *Sandspit Fun Park* on Rte 6 with bumper boats. At the *Royal Atlantic Wax Museum,* yesterday's and today's celebrities are portrayed in wax, in suitable settings. A full size replica of Tutankhamen's tomb and its treasure is to be found at *King Tut's Tomb and Treasures* on Rte 6. Thanks to computer technology, lights and special effects, this is a realistically designed attraction of educational interest. Try your hand at archery or mini-golf at *Lincoln Green* next to the new entrance of the **Prince Edward Island National Park.** The most famous Cavendish attraction is *Green Gables House,* the farm home that

became famous as the setting for Lucy Maud Montgomery's best seller, *Anne of Green Gables.* The house (located in the park) has been fully restored and furnished in the period style. All these attractions close in winter. *Kensington 12 km/7.5 mi.*

Charlottetown   E11
(pop. 17,063). Capital of P.E.I. A compact pretty town which does not go in for neon lights. It was the 'Birthplace of the Confederation' since talks which led to the union of British North America were held in 1864 at *Province House* where today you can view the original meeting room and furniture.

Recently Charlottetown has been concentrating on restoring its old quarter, Old Charlottetown, where there are handsome houses on tree-lined streets lit by replicas of the original gas lamps. Historic wood and brick buildings have been restored as part of Project Harbourside, the waterfront restoration scheme. In this area you can find the town's only deluxe hotel, the Prince Edward Sheraton. Other hotels include The Charlottetown and Rod Royalty Inn.

Shopping is best at Confederation Plaza around Grafton, Queen and Richmond Sts. The largest indoor mall is the City Mall. There are many fine small restaurants dotted around town including Pat's Rose and Gray Room, a unique setting in a reconstructed 1920s drugstore. The Claddagh Room is considered one of the best places for seafood.

Cavendish

Charlottetown, aerial view

The cultural focal point is the *Confederation Centre of the Arts* which has two theaters, an art museum, provincial archives, a library and memorial hall. *St Dunstan's Basilica* is one of the largest buildings of its kind in Eastern Canada and contains many beautiful Italian carvings. *St Paul's* is the oldest Protestant church (1747) on the island while *St James'* has impressive stained-glass windows. *Charlottetown Driving Park* is the place to watch harness racing but the city's largest park is *Victoria*, covering 44 acres with pleasant walking trails. The official residence of P.E.I.'s Lieut. Gov. is *Fanningbank* (1833). One of the best ways to tour Charlottetown is in an authentic double decker, red London bus. One of the biggest annual events is the *Charlottetown Festival* which takes place in summer.

Churchill   E11

Queen's County, is the location of *Strathgartney Provincial Park* which has a nature trail, camping ground and golf. Alternative accommodation possibilities in the area are at tourist homes. *Charlottetown 20 km/12.5 mi.*

Dunstaffnage   D12

On Rte 2 in Queen's County. Stop in at the *Spoke Wheel Car Museum* to see the collection of cars from 1916 on. Among the special vintage models are a 1916 Buick, a 1921 490-Chevrolet touring car, a 1925 Studebaker and a 1929 Durant. Restaurant and snack facilities on site, open in summer daily 1000-1800, later some months. *Charlottetown 11 km/7 miles.*

Eldon   F12

Queen's County off Rte 1. Site of the **Lord Selkirk Pioneer Settlement** which contains one of Canada's largest collections of authentic log buildings. These hand-hewn constructions — weaving shed, smokehouse, stable barn, blacksmith shop, carpenter's shop, settler's home, outhouse and church — all date back to the 1800s. Open summer daily 0900-1600, later some months. Next to this complex is the *Lord Selkirk Provincial Park* with a beach campground. *Charlottetown 32 km/20 mi.*

Elmira   D15

Kings County. Visit *Elmira Railway Musem* which was a gift of Canadian National Railways, on Rte 16A. This used to be the eastern terminus of the island's railway system. Inside, different exhibits illustrate the development of the island's railways over the years. Open in summer. *Souris 16 km/10 mi.*

French River   C10

Queen's County. Site of *Anne's House of Dreams* on Rte 20, depicting the home that Anne and Gilbert, fictional characters from Lucy Maud Montgomery''s books, lived in. Furnished in turn-of-the-century style. Several housekeeping units and tourist homes in the vicinity. Open June-Sept. daily 1000-2000. *Cavendish 28 km/17.5 mi.*

Georgetown   E14

(pop. 732). A delightful small town in Kings County where you'll find a number of cottage and tourist home accommodations. It is most famous for the *Kings Playhouse* where summer plays and concerts take place. Although the original 86-year-old playhouse was destroyed by fire in 1982, it has since been rebuilt in the William Harris style. One of the province's oldest and prettiest churches, *Holy Trinity Church* is located nearby and anyone can have a go at brass rubbing in the crypt using facsimiles of medieval brasses found in English country churches. *Charlottetown 50 km/31 mi.*

Gladstone   F13
Kings County. *Fantasyland Provincial Park* on Rte 348 shows favorite storybook characters in statue form. Children's slides and swings, a miniature log fort and live deer complete the attraction. Bring your own barbecue. Open summer daily 0900-2100. *Montague 22 km/14 mi.*

Harrington   D11
Plenty of cottage accommodation and *Pinehills Playland* on Rte 15, a large theme park that features a maze, haunted cave and gallery, Indian area and dinosaurs. A miniature golf course and go-cart track are also on the premises. Open summer 0900-dusk. *Charlottetown 13 km/ 8 mi.*

Irishtown   D10
Queens County. Visit the optical illusion at *Woodland Heights Magnetic Hill.* Drive your car down a hill to a specific point and then put it in neutral and you appear to coast uphill. A playground, pool, nature trails and sightseeing tower are in the vicinity. Open June-Labour Day. *Cavendish 34 km/21 mi.*

Kildare   B8
Prince County. Site of *Prince Edward Island Miniature Railway* in a tranquil setting among the island's fields and forests. On or off the trail you will see the lovely Kildare River, ospreys fishing and beautiful wildflowers. Open June-Sept. At Kildare Capes, the *Jacques Cartier Provincial Park* provides a supervised ocean beach and camping. *Alberton 5 km/3 mi.*

Lennox Island Indian
Reservation   C9
On Rte 163, Prince County. A number of Indian families live on this Indian Reserve and its Roman Catholic church was built in 1869 by the Indians themselves. The arts and crafts store here displays the church altar railing and sells unusual jewelery, ceremonial Indian masks and headdresses, Huron dolls and moccasins. *Summerside 40 km/25 mi.*

Long River   D10
Queens County, not far from the Woodleigh Replicas. The *Long River Old Mill Museum* was built in 1820 and houses a private collection which gives you a glimpse into the past. Open summer daily 1000-1730. Several farmhouse accommodations in the area. *Kensington 3 km/1.6 mi.*

Malpeque   C9
Prince County. One of the places to stop on the Blue Heron Drive. The flowers in *Malpeque Gardens* are thought to be the loveliest in Atlantic Canada. Owned by the Mackay family, they feature 400 varieties and colors of dahlia, besides rose gardens and other brilliant flower beds. A wishing well, sunken gardens and children's mini farms are other attractions. Open summer daily 0900-1700, some months later. There's a choice of cottage accommodations in the area and camping in the *Cabot Provincial Park.* The park features interpretive programs, a supervised ocean beach and golf. *Kensington 16km/10 mi.*

Milltown Cross   F13
Kings County is the stop for *Buffaloland Provincial Park* where herds of buffalo and white-tailed deer graze contentedly in a 100-acre enclosure. Open daily year round. Also visit *Moore's Migratory Bird Sanctuary* which has nature trails and trout fishing. *Montague 6 km/3.7 mi.*

Montague   E13
(pop. 1827). A good-sized town in Kings County where you will find a selection of inns and b/b places to stay. The key attraction is the *Garden of the Gulf Museum* on Main St. S., where old farm implements and household items are on display. They all pertain to local history and pioneer farming. Collections of Indian stones, simple toys and guns are also included. Open summer Mon.-Sat. 0930-1700, Sun. 1300-1700. *Charlottetown 42 km/26 mi.*

Mont-Carmel   D8
Prince County. A stop not to be missed on the Lady Slipper Drive. This area is Acadian with the artisans in the **Acadian Pioneer Village** handicraft shop selling a variety of crochet and macrame work. The village itself is a reproduction of an early 1800s French Acadian settlement. It includes a church, store, priest's house, ordinary houses, shops and school. The log structures you see resemble those used as temporary dwellings for the original settlers. Authentic Acadian dishes are served in the restaurant. Open daily June-Sept. 1000-1900. *Summerside 24 km/15 mi.*

Murray Harbour F14
(pop. 419). Kings County. Noted for its *Log Cabin Museum* on Rte 18A. Among the antiques featured here are spinning wheels, crockery and gramophones and a doll collection dating to 1850. An authentically equipped kitchen of the era and farm tools are also displayed. Not far away at Murray River, *The Toy Factory* gives tours. Several b/bs and lots of craft shops in the general vicinity. *Montague 17 km/11 mi.*

New Haven E11
Queens County. Tourist homes in this area and *P.E.I. Fairyland* on Trans-Canada Hwy where young children will enjoy a huge playground, fairy tale forest, boating and miniature train rides. Open June-Sept., daily 0900-dusk. *Charlottetown 16 km/10 mi.*

New London D10
Queens County. The birthplace of authoress Lucy Maud Montgomery who wrote *Anne of Green Gables*. In her house, you can see a number of items made famous in her writings like the old blue chest, plus personal memorabilia. Open summer 0900-1800, some months later. *Cavendish 6 km/3.7 mi.*

North Cape A8
Prince County. *The Atlantic Wind Test* site is a national laboratory used for testing and evaluating wind generators. Audio-visual presentations are shown at frequent intervals at the visitor center. Open July-Sept. daily 1000-1800. *Tignish 13 km/8 mi.*

Northport B8
Prince County. See *Sea Rescue Park* on Rte 152, south of Alberton, featuring the rescue made in 1906 by Northport men as the sailing vessel *McKean* foundered in a raging storm. The park area on Cascumpec Bay has picnic areas, beaches and a children's play area. Open daily June-Oct. 0900-2200. *Alberton 1 km/0.6 mi.*

North Rustico D11
Queens County. An area for beach fans with a wide choice of accommodations from cottages to inns. Scenic with all the usual beach facilities. *Cavendish 6 km/3.7 mi.*

O'Leary C8
(pop. 805). Prince County. Site of the *O'Leary Museum* in Centennial Park. Here you can visit the log barn with its old farm tools and the potato museum. Another museum section displays local history and the small red schoolhouse was transplanted from Alaska, P.E.I. Open June-Sept. daily 1000-1600. *Summerside 56 km/35 mi.*

Beach at Murray Head

Orwell   E12

Queens County. There are several tourist homes near the beach here and goose hunting is possible in autumn. The attraction is the *Orwell Corner Rural Life Musem*, a recreation of a late 19th-century community. On the site you can see a general store, house and post office, farm machinery and barns, blacksmith's shop, shingle mill, school, church and community hall where summer concerts are given. Open in summer. *Charlottetown 30 km/19 mi.*

Oyster Bed Bridge   D11

Queens County. Plenty of farms which take guests in this area, all close to a beach and not far from Charlottetown. Youngsters can use the go-carts and children's playground at the intersection of Rts 223 and 6. On alternate weekends, May-Labour Day, there is drag racing here. *Charlottetown 10 km/6 mi.*

Panmure Island   E14

About an hour's drive from Charlottetown, best known for its provincial park where there is a bay beach and a supervised ocean beach plus campsite. A number of cottage and tourist home accommodations in the area. *Montague 16 km/10 mi.*

Park Corner   C10

Queens County. Site of *Anne of Green Gables Museum* at Silver Bush. Authoress Lucy Maud Montgomery married here in 1911 in a home that nestles by 'The Lake of The Shining Waters'. It is owned and operated by descendants of her aunt and filled with personal memorabilia. Open daily June-Oct. 0900-2100. *Kensington 12 km/7.5 mi.*

Pooles Corner   E13

At the junction of Rts 3 and 4 is the place to stop for an overall look at Kings County. The *Visitor Centre* here has displays and pictures of the county's early settlement and development and staff will assist with any of your questions. *Montague 6 km/3.7 mi.*

Port Hill   C9

One of the places to stay in this port-of-call on Lady Slipper Drive is *The Senator's House*, a restored 1901 mansion in a peaceful setting that has become a hotel with a highly recommended restaurant, specializing in Malpeque oysters. In Port Hill is *Green Park Historic Park*, once an active shipbuilding center and home of wealthy shipbuilder James Yeo Jr. Nowadays, the museum commemorates the shipping industry's heyday with the the help of artefacts and displays. Tours of the 1865 house itself are given and a 19th-century shipyard has also been recreated on the site. *Summerside 34 km/21 mi.*

Red Point
Provincial Park   D15

Provides a supervised ocean beach and camping. Open June-Labour Day. *Souris 13 km/8 mi.*

Rocky Point   E11

Queens County. Location of the **Fort Amherst/Port La Joie National Historic Park.** This was where the old French capital of P.E.I. was built in 1720 and where the British built Fort Amherst in 1758 after the French capitulated. Although only the earthworks of that fort remain today, it is worth taking in an audio-visual show at the visitor center. Open June-Oct. daily 0900-1700. On Rte 19 the *Micmac Indian Village* shows you how the former inhabitants of the Maritimes lived and survived, using birchbark for their wigwams and canoes and stone to make fishing and hunting tools. Take a walk along the trail and drop in to the craft shop if you like bear or wolf rugs and other Indian handicrafts. Open June-Sept. *Charlottetown 20 km/12.5 mi.*

Roseneath   E13

Kings County. A pleasant recreational area known for its *Brudenell River Provincial Park* which has an interpretive program and evening activities. Here you will find an 18-hole golf course, pool, tennis, lawn bowling, canoe/board sailing marina, river beach and horseback riding. There is also a recommended resort hotel. *Georgetown 5 km/3 mi.*

South Rustico   D11

A good holiday base with inns and motel accommodations, campgrounds and a resort overlooking ocean and golf course. On Rte 243 next to St Augustine Church the *Farmers' Bank of Rustico* is a museum commemorating Father Belcourt's works. Made of island sandstone, this building used to be a bank between 1864 and 1894 and it was also the island's first high school. Open June-Aug. daily 0930-1700. See also *Jumpin' Jack's Old Country Store Museum* on Rte 242 which dates back to the 1800s and features cracker and fish barrels, pot bellied stoves and loads of other bric-a-brac used by the pioneers. South Rustico is a base for taking a supervised horseback ride through fields and woods with great views of the Bay and Gulf of St Lawrence. Water thrills are available at *Summer Haven's Wild 'n' Wet Waterslide* on Rte 243 which has all kinds of curves and drops. *Charlottetown 26 km/16 mi.*

Stanhope   D12
Queens County. A great place for all kinds
of sports with numerous cottage accommodations. Near the beaches and good for
windsurfing — instruction and equipment
is on hand at the *Stanhope Beach Lodge*.
The annual windsurfing P.E.I. Championship takes place here in late August.
Charlottetown 18 km/11 mi.

Stanley Bridge   D10
Loads of tourist homes in this area where
activities include digging for clams, deep
sea fishing, tennis and golf and all beach
sports. Pedal boats can be rented from the
Seaview Marina on Rte 6 as can water skis
and sailboards. Take-out food service here
includes lobster burgers! The *P.E.I.
Marine Aquarium* displays all the area's
native fish. Learn, too, about oysters in
the oyster culture pond, see the display of
maritime furry animals and a particularly
fine private collection of mounted birds at
The Manor of Birds. Live seals play in their
own pool and there's a large display of
butterflies from around the world. Open
June-Sept. daily 0900-dusk. *Cavendish
6 km/3.2 mi.*

Summerside   D9
(pop. 14,145). A major town located in
Prince County. Visitors have their choice
of budget or better accommodations
including the Linkletter Inn which has a
convention center attached. It is also well
known for *'The Flyers Feast'* evening out at
Brothers Two Restaurant which also features a colonial evening when your waiters
and waitresses are also the stars of the
revue in which you participate. A fixed
price pays for the entertainment and the
food: steamed clams, lobster and other
types of seafood.

While in Summerside, go to the *Lady
Slipper Visitor Information Centre* in the
Wilmot area where you can have a preview
tour of Prince County. The region's
specialties are highlighted — from Irish
moss to Acadian culture — and of course
all your questions will be answered in the
friendly P.E.I. manner. Do not miss the
Acadian Museum of P.E.I. in the Mis-
couche area. It displays collections of
implements used by the Acadians at the
turn of the 18th century for farming,
woodworking, shoemaking, and around
the home. There are hand-spun and woven
flax and wool articles, church items and
ancestral pictures of 23 original Acadian
families, their land deeds and other details
from those times. Open June-Sept., weekdays 1000-1730, Sun. 1300-1700.

In the St Eleanors area, the *Argus Aircraft Memorial* stands on Rte 2 at the Canadian Forces Base. The Argus 739 is one of
30 anti-submarine maritime patrol aircraft that entered service in the 1960s.
Beside it is the Tracker Aircraft 131, used
for reconnaissance. On the Summerside
Waterfront you will find the *Eptek
National Exhibition Centre and P.E.I.
Sports Hall of Fame*. This features changing exhibits of historic and artistic interest
from the surrounding area and other parts
of Canada. Harness racing takes place
every Wed. in summer at *Summerside
Raceway* on Notre Dame St. and there are
nightly race cards during the July *Lobster
Carnival.*.

There are several recreational parks
with camping facilities: *Linkletter Provincial Park* is one, with a bay beach; *Rayner's
Park* is another and *Wagobak Park*, the
third. *Charlottetown 56 km/35 mi.*

Tignish   A8
(pop. 1077). A busy fishing village, Prince
County. The *Dalton Centre* on School St.
was a boys school built by pioneer silver
fox breeder Sir Charles Dalton in 1930. It
is now a community and cultural center
featuring local history exhibits and art
shows. Choice of accommodation in the
area.
Summerside 46 km/29 mi.

Victoria   E10
Queens County. Charming base with cottage and inns to stay overnight at. The
40 foot schooner *'Mirana'* will take you on
a two hour trip out of Victoria harbor in
summer, capturing the romance of a
bygone era. This is one of the last of the
traditional coastal working vessels. Or see
a play at the *Victoria Playhouse* on Main
St., often used for an evening out in combination with a lobster dinner at the Victoria
Village Inn or Lobsterland Restaurant.
Charlottetown 22 km/13.7 mi.

West Point Lighthouse   C7
Prince County on Rte 14. A stopping point
on Lady Slipper Drive next to *Cedar Dunes
Provincial Park* at P.E.I.'s southwestern
tip. Established in 1874, this lighthouse
was manned until 1963 and now has a
museum which documents all the island's
lighthouses. Open June-Sept. daily 0800-
2200. *Summerside 68 km/42.5 mi.*

York   E12
Queens County. There are several housekeeping units here, just a five minute ride
from Charlottetown. On Rte 25 is the family attraction, *Jewell's Gardens and Pioneer Village* comprising an original village,
an animal barn and an antique glass collection valued at $100,000. Beautiful gar-
dens, too. Open June-Oct. *Charlottetown
6 km/3.7 mi.*

NOVA SCOTIA

Before the first Europeans arrived, the inhabitants of this province were the Micmacs. Then there were 25,000 of them, now there are perhaps some 6000, most of whom live on reserves. The largest reserves are at Eskasoni, Whycocomagh and Nyanza on the Bras d'Or Lakes and Shubenacadie and Millbrook near Truro.

An English flag was the first to be planted here, though the first permanent settlement was established by the French. Today, most Nova Scotians are of British descent and only about ten per cent are of French or Acadian extraction. This is because, after many Anglo-French disputes over the territory, the British finally took complete possession in 1763. There are particularly strong Scottish links with this province which has annual Highland Games. The Highland Scots arrived here in large numbers in the 1800s, settling mostly in Cape Breton Island, Pictou and Antigonish counties.

Nova Scotia has always had a reputation for 'wooden ships and iron men', probably because no place on the island is more than 56 km/35 mi from the sea. In fact, four bodies of water wash the coastline: the Atlantic Ocean, the magnificent Bay of Fundy, the Northumberland Strait and the Gulf of St Lawrence. Nova Scotia is not quite an island since a very narrow isthmus connects it to neighboring New Brunswick and these days, Cape Breton Island is also linked by bridge.

The province is part of Atlantic Canada with a 7400 km/4625 mi long coastline and an area of 34,280 sq km/21,425 sq mi. The highest point is in the highlands of Cape Breton and most of the population is concentrated in the three main cities of Halifax, Sydney and Dartmouth.

It became a holiday destination in the 1860s when the railways and steamships brought the first visitors from Upper Canada and the eastern cities of the US. Today it is a highly popular Canadian ocean playground, noted for its sailboats, its lobster and the world's highest tides. The best beaches are along the Northumberland Shore and many scenic fishing villages lie along the province's coast. In the interior, a green blanket of orchards and farms covers the Annapolis Valley. Nova Scotians are known as 'Bluenoses' and here the famous *Bluenose* schooners were built but the origin of the name is uncertain.

If you wish to tour the province, the best way is to take one of the nine marked scenic routes: The *Evangeline Trail* takes you through the Annapolis Valley. It is a historic route, as you will see from the old forts, and an area rich in folklore and festivals.

The *Glooscap Trail* takes you along the

Fundy Tides at Halls Harbour, Nova Scotia

Fundy shore. According to legend, hundreds of years ago this area was claimed by Glooscap, a god worshiped by the Micmac Indians. When you gaze at the scenery today you will see a land almost as untouched as it ever was.

The *Sunrise Trail* is for the sun worshipers and beach fans, for it wanders along the warm Northumberland Shore. Here are some of sunniest and most popular beaches and you may meet Nova Scotians along the way who appear to be Scots!

The *Ceilidh Trail* travels along the northwestern shore of Cape Breton. You will pass by the Northumberland Strait and the waters of St George's Bay but also travel through communities originally settled by the Highland Scots whose traditional crafts and customs still prevail here today.

The *Fleur-de-lis Trail* through southwestern Cape Breton leads you into the Acadian villages and fishing communities. You will detect quite a difference in the coastline and in the colors of the Acadian dwellings. Eventually you will wind up at St Peter's Canal, and the entrance to the Bras d'Or Lakes (pronounced all in one, as Bradoor).

Perhaps the most scenic drive is the *Cabot Trail* which winds through the Cape Breton Highlands. Keep your fingers crossed for good weather to enjoy the splendid scenes of peaks, valleys and the coast.

Along the eastern shore runs the *Marine Drive* but take it slowly. You should give yourself time to stop for a spot of fishing or clam digging and be sure to visit the restored 19th-century Sherbrooke Village.

Halifax-Dartmouth Metro is for city fans. They are twin towns, one each side of the harbor, connected by bridge. The only real center in the province for good nightlife and shopping.

The *Lighthouse Route* along the south shore has been known by fishermen and shipbuilders for generations. Here are rocky bays, wave dashed headlands and picturesque fishing villages such as Peggy's Cove.

Abercrombie   L10
A small village on Pictou Harbour (Sunrise Trail), named for the General Abercrombie killed at Bunker Hill in 1775. In summer tours are given of the *Kraft Paper Mill.*

Amherst-Tidnish   L8, K8
(pop. 10,263). The major gateway to Nova Scotia. Known as Les Planches before New Englanders took over in 1764 and renamed the town in honor of Lord Amherst. It developed into a busy manufacturing center in the 19th century and continues to be one. It is the start of two of the province's scenic trails: Sunrise and Glooscap. It has a number of guest house and motel accommodations, good shops and recreational facilities including a golf course. See the *Cumberland County Museum* on Church St, located in the Grove Cottage (1831) former family home of Sen. R. B. Dickey. *Tatamagouche 97 km/69 mi.*

Annapolis County   O6
Covers an area of 1306 sq miles and is most famous for its apple orchards. Helping make the land fertile is the Annapolis River which flows through it, bordered by diked marshland. The wooded wilds in the southern part of the county are ideal for campers and sportsmen.

Annapolis Basin   O6
Overlooked by Annapolis Royal. At the eastern end is the *Annapolis River Causeway*—a fishing and boating area. In fact, a fishway was constructed so that bass can be caught above and below the causeway. It is here, too, that *Annapolis Royal Tidal Power Project*, the first project of its kind in North America, has been built. (The tides of the Bay of Fundy, the world's highest, vary from 12 ft at Yarmouth to 54 ft at Burtcoat Head in Minas Basin.) At the project there are displays of tidal power plant operation.

Annapolis Royal   O5
(pop. 738). The oldest permanent settlement in Canada (1605), overlooking the Annapolis Basin. (Evangeline Trail.) A picturesque and historic town with many delightful inns and also motel accommodation.

On Lower St George St. the *O'Dell Inn*

(1850) has been restored to its 19th-century appearance and contains a costume collection plus Victorian furnishings. (Open daily 0930-1700 mid May-Sept.) On the same street is the *Robertson-McNamara House* (1780) with items illustrating the area's social history. (Open daily 0930-1700 mid May-Sept.) Of architectural interest is the *Adams-Ritchie House* (1712) in Colonial-Georgian design, whose walls are mud-filled (the Acadian method for insulation). Also the *Farmer's Hotel*, a composite of two early 18th-century houses.

Saturday morning visitors should definitely drop in at *Farmers Market* (open May-Oct.) for a croissant and coffee. Local groups frequently entertain here. If you can, reserve a seat at the restored 1927 *King's Theatre*. Stroll the waterfront promenade behind the theater for one of the best loved views in the province — Granville Ferry village and the Annapolis Basin. On a good day when the village and mountains are clearly reflected in the Basin, the scene is postcard-pretty.

Two historic places not to be missed are: *Annapolis Royal Historic Gardens* (open 0800 to dusk, June-Oct. Admission fee.) You will find them on Upper St George St., ten acres worth of themed gardens. The Acadian Garden looks as it would have done in the days of the early pioneers; the Governor's Garden reflects the Georgian style of the 1740s; the Victorian Garden brought fame to the site in the late 19th century; the Rose Garden features a maze and 1600 rose bushes; the Garden of the Future illustrates new techniques in gardening. The garden's site used to be that of North America's first grist mill in 1607 and later what was thought to be the first dikeland. Over a mile of pathways wind through the plantings which also include a winter garden, spring garden, evergreen section and pine forest.

Also **Fort Anne National Historic Park** (open year round daily 0900-1800 May 15-Oct. 15 and rest of the year on weekdays 0900-1700.) The first fort here was erected in 1643 by d'Aulnay de Charnisay and part of one of its bastions is still visible. It was from here that d'Aulnay sailed three times to attack La Tour at Saint John. Col. Robert Sedgewick captured the fort in the name of Britain in 1654 but the Treaty of Breda restored it to the French in 1667. There were many more battles, takeovers and surrenders but the site has been a national historic park since 1917. Today you will find the old British field officers' quarters, a museum containing a Port Royal room, a Queen Anne room, a Loyalist room and a Garrison room. Also an Acadian room with utensils used in Acadian kitchens and other articles of everyday use in those time. *Digby 32 km/20 mi.*

Antigonish   L12

(pop. 5205). A major town (Sunrise Trail) with plenty of shops, hotels, inns and guest houses. It is the seat of the Roman Catholic Diocese with *St Ninian's Cathedral* (1868) built of blue limestone and granite from local quarries. It is also a university town since St Francis Xavier University moved here in 1855. In the Angus L. MacDonald Library, near the campus, the *Hall of The Clans* is dedicated to the founding Scottish families of the region. *Annual Highland Games* are held here every July. Not far away from Antigonish is the *Keppoch Mountain Ski Resort. New Glasgow 50 km/31 mi.*

Antigonish County   L12

Occupies 562 sq miles in the northeast of Nova Scotia with farms and extensive lumber tracts and land that is good for hunting and fishing. The name stems from a Micmac Indian word meaning 'the place where branches were broken off the trees by bears gathering beechnuts'. (That's what we're told anyway!)

Arcadia   Q5

(pop. 481). Sited at the head of the Chebogue River (Lighthouse Route) very near Yarmouth, it was named for the brig *'Arcadia'* which was built here in 1817. Among the many old houses is the one where New England patriot, Paul Revere, took his mark degree in Free Masonry. *Yarmouth 5 km/3 mi.*

Auburn   N6

A fruit growing center (Evangeline Trail), particularly apples and cranberries. *St Mary's Church* here was built in 1790, its walls plastered with powdered mussel shells. *Kentville 30 km/19 mi.*

Auld Cove   L12

A fishing settlement on the Strait of Canso (Sunrise Trail). This area of St George's Bay is especially good for tuna fishing. A record catch here weighed 1496 lb. *Port Hastings 1.6 km/1 mi.*

Aylesford   N7

(pop. 687). Center for agriculture (Evangeline Trail). Numerous fruit farms and *Oaklawn Farms* which has domestic, plus some exotic, animals and fowl — welcome visitors. Named for the fourth Earl of Aylesford, the town was settled in 1784. The assistant rector of New York's Trinity Church, Bishop Charles Inglis, had a residence close by. *Kentville 26 km/16 mi.*

Baddeck   K13

(pop. 965). Notable village on the Cabot Trail with numerous pleasant places to stay, particularly Inverary Inn Resort. It takes its name from the Micmac word 'Abadak' meaning 'place with an island near'. (The island in Baddeck Harbour is Kidston's.) This is a very Gaelic part of Nova Scotia — you will hear it spoken and find old Scottish customs still carried on throughout the district.

One of the most famous Scotsmen to come to these parts was *Alexander Graham Bell* and the **Alexander Graham Bell Museum National Historic Park** honoring him, at the eastern end of Baddeck, is a most worthwhile place to visit. Bell spent 35 years here and died here and the superb museum contains hundreds of original items telling his life story. Although the inventor is best known for the telephone, this museum concentrates on other inventions like his hydrofoil which in 1919 skimmed across Bras d'Or Lake at 113 km/67.8 mph. (The original hull of this craft is housed in the museum.) Also Bell's flight experiments — the first powered flight in the British Empire took place in Baddeck in Bell's plane, *the Silver Dart* in 1909. Film clips add to the pleasure in this museum (open year round, daily 0900-2100 July 1-Sept. 30, 0900-1700 rest of the year).

Sailing on Bras d'Or Lake

Baddeck is an excellent base for touring the western part of Cape Breton Island. It is the start of the Cabot Trail, the road which winds around northern Cape Breton, as well as other scenic routes. Waters in the area are famous for yachting and fishing. *Port Hastings 75 km/43 mi.*

Barrington   Q5

(pop. 424). One of the earliest English settlements (Lighthouse Route). One of La Tour's forts once stood on the beach here, which is 3.2 km/2 mi long. The village the French built on the present site of Barrington was called La Passage which in 1755 during the expulsion of the Acadians, was a flourishing settlement. When the New Englanders attacked, they razed the lot. The first English settlers came from Cape Cod and Nantucket in 1760, descendants of Mayflower colonists. They named the town Barrington in honor of the second Viscount Barrington (1717-1793), Secretary for War.

See the *Barrington Meeting House* (1766), the oldest non-conformist church building in Canada and Nova Scotia's only surviving New England style meeting house. Also *Barrington Woollen Mill* built in 1884, and now a provincial museum. Inside there is an interesting collection of looms, spinning machines etc. History apart, the area around town provides opportunities for yachting, fishing, deer hunting and duck shooting. *Yarmouth 87.5 km/54 mi.*

Bear River   O5

(pop. 716). Locally known as 'Nova Scotia's Switzerland' (Evangeline Trail). A pretty village settled in the 18th century with an 'olde worlde' shopping district. An annual July *Cherry Carnival* sees a number of festivities taking place here and the river itself is one of the finest for stripe bass. The community has attracted several artisans, look for candles especially.
Annapolis Royal 19.2 km/12 mi.

Beinn Bhreagh   K14

This was the place where Alexander Graham Bell had his summer estate and where he and his wife were buried. The name is Gaelic for 'beautiful mountain'. It is not open to the public (Bell's descendants still live here), but it may be easily viewed from the **Bell Historic Park.**

Bible Hill   M9

This was an early supplies center for Colchester County (Glooscap Trail) and a stagecoach stop. Now it is best known for the *Nova Scotia Provincial Exhibition* which takes place yearly during the third week in August.
Truro 1.6 km/1 mi.

Bridgetown   N6

(pop. 1047). A manufacturing center at the head of the Annapolis River (Evangeline Trail). See *James House* on Queen St, built in 1835 by a successful merchant and now a tearoom cum museum. *The Tolmie Gallery* houses paintings depicting typical rural life in Annapolis County. From Bridgetown you can take a riverboat tour of historic dikelands. *Halifax 177 km/ 111 mi.*

Bridgewater   N6

(pop. 6010). A thriving town on the banks of the LaHave River (Lighthouse Route), with a good variety of lodges and motels, plentiful restaurants and shops. Locals say that salmon fishing on the LeHave River at *Cooks Falls* is the county's best. See the *Des Brisay Museum and Park* which gives the history of Lunenburg County. The museum also operates the *Wile Carding Mill* built in 1860. *Yarmouth 235 km/ 145 mi.*

Cabot Trail   J13-J14

Possibly the most beautiful scenic route in the Maritimes, named for navigator and explorer John Cabot who first sighted Cape Breton Island in 1497.

Canso   N13

(pop. 1173). Located at the entrance of Chedabucto Bay, a stop on Marine Drive, this has always been a center for fishing and fish processing. Its name comes from the Indian 'Kamsok' meaning 'opposite the lofty cliffs'. One of the first attempts at settlement was in 1518 by Baron de Lery and Nicholas Denys built a fort here in the 17th century. It has had its fair share of turbulent history including being the rendezvous point for Pepperell's fleet which first captured Louisbourg. Visit *Whitman House* which gives the history of a prominent fish-packing family and features a special marine exhibit and widow's walk (open summer Mon.-Thurs. 1200-1800, Fri. 1200-2100, weekends 1300-1700). *Guysborough 56 km/35 mi.*

Cape Breton Highlands National Park   I14

On the Cabot trail, it covers 370 sq mi between the Gulf of St Lawrence and the Atlantic. (See Parks.)

Beach near Ingonish, Cape Breton

Cape St Mary   P4

Off Rte 1 (Evangeline Trail). From here you have marvelous views of sea, rock, sand and fishing villages. Below the cape is *Mavillette Beach*, now developed as a provincial picnic park behind whose dunes bird-watching is ideal. Along the cliff top is a 13 km/8 mi hiking trail from the cape to Bear Cove.

Chester   O8

(pop. 1119). A scenic summer resort on a peninsula at the head of Mahone Bay (Lighthouse Route). Opportunities for outdoor sports include yachting and fishing and in summer there are art galleries and craft shops open. Chester was first settled in 1759 by New Englanders and was then known as Shoreham. For defence purposes a blockhouse was mounted with 20 cannon and in olden days pirates haunted the harbors and coves of Mahone Bay. *Halifax 57.6 km/36 mi.*

Cheticamp   J13

(pop. 1027). An Acadian fishing village on the Gulf of St Lawrence (Cape Breton Trail) that is today a busy fishing and tourist center with a variety of places to stay and eat. It is an ideal base for visiting **Cape Breton Highlands National Park.** The Acadians here are descended from those who first landed in 1755, expelled by the British during the Seven Years War. In the Acadian Museum on the Cabot Trail, there is a small display of Acadian relics and *Les Trois Pignons* Society has been set up to preserve the area's Acadian heritage. *Baddeck 86 km/53 mi.*

Church Point   P5

(pop. 377). A village on the Evangeline Trail, dominated by North America's largest and tallest wooden church — *St Mary's.* The church is part of the campus of *Université St Anne,* Nova Scotia's center of Acadian culture and the province's only French university. *Yarmouth 61 km/38 mi.*

Clare   P4

An Acadian community (Evangeline Trail). The bilingual inhabitants are descendants of the first white settlers who arrived from France in the early 1600s. This district boasts several typical Acadian settlements although older homes reflect New England style architecture.

Clark's Harbour   R5

(pop. 1077). An old fishing town (Lighthouse Route). After the French, pioneers from Nantucket arrived here in 1760 and today it is considered one of the province's finest ocean fishing spots. *Shelburne 48 km/30 mi.*

Clementsport   R5

(pop. 428). A farming, fruit growing and fishing area (Evangeline Trail). It was settled by United Empire Loyalists in 1784 and the old Loyalist Church of *St Edward* (consecrated in 1788) is one of Canada's earliest museums. Built with hand-hewn timber and fastened with wooden pegs, this church was used for many years as a lighthouse to guide ships through Digby Strait. In Upper Clements there is a small wildlife park. *Digby 16 km/10 mi.*

Cumberland County   L8

One of Nova Scotia's largest counties (Glooscap Trail). It covers 1679 sq mi with 280 km/175 mi of scenic coastline. It possesses rich and varied resources and offers streams, lakes and forests for outdoor enthusiasts.

Digby   O5

(pop. 2542). A port of entry overlooking the Annapolis Basin and Digby Gut which opens out into the Bay of Fundy. There are three daily ferry services between here and Saint John (New Brunswick). The town was named in honor of Robert Digby, the British admiral who commanded the *HMS Atlanta* which brought 1500 Loyalist refugees from New England in 1799.

There are a number of places to stay, among the most notable, the *Pines Resort* overlooking Digby Gut which has deluxe facilities including an 18-hole golf course. Other sports which can be enjoyed here include deep sea fishing for pollock, haddock and cod. The town is home to one of the world's largest scallop fleets and you can watch from fishermen's wharf when the fleet comes in. Try some, along with smoked herring known as 'Digby chicken'.

One of the attractions is the old *Admiral's Well,* dug on the Cannon Bank in the early 19th century. In the *Admiral Digby Museum,* old maps, ship models and photographs illustrate Digby's marine history. *Yarmouth 106 km/66 mi.*

Digby County   O5

Covers 1020 sq mi with a 376 km/235 mi coastline. The county has many fruit farms and its network of streams and lakes offer impressive fishing. In season, you may also hunt bear, deer and woodcock.

Diligent River   M8

(pop. 208). The area was named by Gov. John Parr for the diligence of its settlers (Glooscap Trail). At *Salter's Confederation Farm,* a museum shows old farming implements and there's a horseshoe-shaped beach at nearby *Diligent Harbour. Ward's Brook Hiking Trail* at Wharton runs for

4 km/2.5 mi through a forested area. *Amherst 90 km/56 mi.*

Economy   M8
A lumber and farming community where the Economy River enters the Minas Basin (Glooscap Trail). The name is a corruption of the Micmac name 'Kenomee' meaning 'a long point jutting out into the sea'. It is best known for its annual *Clam Festival. Truro 60 km/36 mi.*

Englishtown   J14
The first permanent European settlement on Cape Breton, commemorated by a monument on the site of the 1629 fort erected by Capt. Daniel of France. This is also the site of Cape Breton's first Jesuit Mission. *Baddeck 30 km/18 mi.*

Falmouth   N8
(pop. 1095). Center of fruit growing and dairy area (Evangeline Trail). Many fruits and veg are produced year round under glass. The town was settled in 1760 by people from Connecticut and named in honor of Admiral Boscawen, son of the first Viscount Falmouth. *Windsor 3.3 km/2 mi.*

Glace Bay   K15
(pop. 21,836). A Cape Breton mining town whose mines extend for miles out under the Atlantic. It was here that French troops dug coal in 1720 to supply their Louisbourg garrison and it was they who named the town 'Glace Bai' because of ice in the harbor, even if the Indians had called it 'Wosekusegwon' ('Home of Glory'). At the *Miners Museum* there is a 'village' showing miners' dwellings from the 1850-1900 period. *Sydney 21 km/13 mi.*

Grand Lake   N9
The place to catch land-locked salmon (grayling) and trout. A federal fish hatchery is located here and there are campsites. *Halifax 33.3 km/20 mi.*

Grand Narrows   K14
A 24-hour motor ferry operates from here (Cape Breton Grail) across the Barra Strait to Iona, site of the *Nova Scotia Highland Village* and annual *Highland Village Day* in August. The Highland Village devotes itself to the life of early Scottish settlers with replicas of a carding mill, log cabin, schoolhouse, blacksmith forge and pioneer home. *Sydney 72 km/43 mi.*

Grand Pré   M8
(pop. 305). Site of one of the province's earliest French settlements (Evangeline Trail). The name means 'the great

meadow' and it was the setting for Longfellow's poem 'Evangeline'. One incident leading to the British expelling the Acadians was the Battle of Grand Pré in 1747 — a monument here tells the story. See **Grand Pre National Historic Park,** site of the Acadian village in 1675, open daily 0900-1800 June 1-Oct. 15. New England planters built the nearby old church of the *Covenanters* (1790) on a hillside. *Wolfville 5 km/3 mi.*

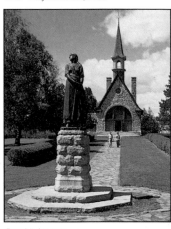

Grand Pré N.H.P.

Great Village   M9
(pop. 394). This village used to be famous for shipbuilding. Shipwrights built the *St James United Church* in 1884, whose Marine Room now features ships' logs, letters, models and paintings etc. *Truro 30 km/18 mi.*

Grosses Coques   P5
(pop. 357). Famous for giant clams (Evangeline Trail), which is what its name means. At one time they were so bountiful that settlers existed on them through a whole winter. Just past Grosses Coques River bridge is the site of the first Acadian cemetery (1774). Beachcombing and clam digging can be done on the beach at Major's Point. *Digby 40 km/24 mi.*

Guysborough   M12
(pop. 514). Situated at the head of Chedabucto Bay, originally called Chedabucto by the Indians, meaning 'the great long harbor'. On the Marine Drive, the town was founded in 1654 by Nicholas Denys who built Fort St Louis here. You might visit the restored *Court House* (1843) and local museum. *Canso 49 km/31 mi.*

Halifax O9

(pop. 117,882). Capital of Nova Scotia and the largest city in Atlantic Canada. A naval and military base, it was founded by Gov. Edward Cornwallis in 1749 making it Canada's first town to be settled primarily by the British. It can boast the continent's first newspaper, post office and public school plus the first elected public assembly. Today the twin city of Dartmouth stands across the harbor.

Halifax, Tallis map circa 1800

There are many hotels including Chateau Halifax on Scotia Square, Citadel Inn, the Lord Nelson and the Holiday Inn in Dartmouth, plus a new Sheraton on the harbor front. The waterfront is a focal point of downtown Halifax which is compact enough to enjoy a walking tour. In many ways it is reminiscent of San Francisco right down to the summer mists. Halifax also has a major convention center.

Shopping is good along Spring Garden Road which was a 'hippie' area in the 60s but is now a trendy street for browsing in boutiques. The streets off this one are also to be recommended. Spring Garden road starts at Robie Street and runs to Barrington Street. At Spring Garden Place there are more than 30 retail outlets. Of the malls, Scotia Square is the main one but there is also Barrington Place, both are connected by covered walkways to the major hotels. Also try the Maritime Centre, Quinpool Centre and Halifax Shopping Centre across from Simpson's Mall.

Eating out in Halifax poses no problem as there are many fine restaurants and pubs. Down at the waterfront, Clipper Cay has a good view over the water. Fat Frank's is considered the most elegant eatery in town and on Argyle Street you will find a number of interesting restaurants and bars, notably Applause, Five Fishermen and The Newsroom. Many lounges and restaurants, like Privateers Warehouse, provide live music and Misty Moon and The Palace are both cabaret clubs.

In addition to city sightseeing tours, you can join a guided walking tour of Halifax and Dartmouth waterfronts between June and Sept., take a carriage ride through downtown Halifax or a rickshaw tour. Daily cruises are available on the *Bluenose II* departing from Historic Properties and several other boats also tour the harbor. Helicopter tours are possible from the Waterfront Heliport.

Start at the **Historic Properties National Historic Site** on the waterfront. Some 40 buildings have been converted into shops, bars and restaurants, recapturing the 19th century days of privateering. *The Old Red Store*, for instance (1812) was the place where captured privateer prizes were auctioned off. The *Bluenose II* is moored by the Properties.

Drop into *Fishermen's Market* by the ferry wharf where there is everything from salt cod to flounder. Not far away is the *Maritime Museum* which contains a variety of seafaring exhibits including Queen Victoria's barge and the prismatic light from the old Sambro Lighthouse. There is a restored chandler's shop, scale models of ships and figureheads from old sailing vessels. At the back of the museum is the *C.S.S. Acadia* is moored. Open year round, summer hours Mon.-Sat. 0930-1730, Sun. 1300-1730. Also on the waterfront is the *Brewery Market* complex of shops and restaurants, and also the *Nova Scotia Sport Heritage Museum*.

Halifax has many museums worth seeing: The *Nova Scotia Museum* on Summer St. is one of the largest with exhibits on social and natural history of the area including Micmac quillwork. (Open year round, summer hours Mon.-Sat. 0930-1730, Sun. 1300-1730.) The *Maritime Command Museum* is at Admiralty House (1814) and contains naval artefacts. (Open year round, Sept. 1-June 30 Mon.-Fri. 0930-1530, July 1-Aug. 31 Mon.-Fri. 0930-2030.) In the *Halifax Police Museum*, collections of weapons, memorabilia and insignia date back to the establishment of the police department in 1841. (Open by appointment.) *The Public Archives of Nova Scotia*, which can be found on University Ave, consist of a museum and art gallery with all kinds of paintings, prints, coins, stamps etc. (Open year round, Mon.-Fri. 0830-2200, Sat. 0900-1800, Sun. 1300-2200.) Also visit *McCulloch Museum* in Dalhousie University, the *Mount Saint Vincent University Art Gallery* and *Province House* on Granville St. which is

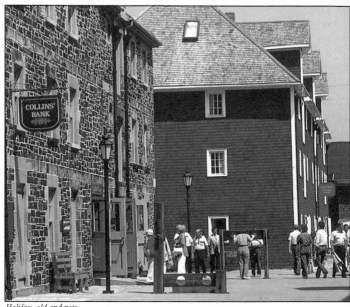

Halifax, old and new

Canada's oldest provincial legislative building (1811-1819).

In Dartmouth, *Whaler's House*(1785) is associated with Nantucket Whalers. In the suburbs at Forest Hills, *Cole Harbour Heritage Farm Museum* holds a weekly farmers' market on Sat. 0830-1200 June-Sept. The farm itself is open Mon.-Fri. 1000-1600. The *Shearwater Aviation Museum* is an official Armed Forces Museum dedicated to the history of this military base. (Open May-June/Sept.-Oct., Tues.-Thurs. 0900-1600, July 1-Aug. 31 weekdays 0900-1600.)

Dominating Halifax is the **Citadel National Historic Park.** Although Halifax was never actually attacked, this is the fourth citadel to be built on this site whose original fortifications dated to 1749. Begun in 1828, it was finished in 1856, the ramparts have been restored and you will also see barrack rooms, the powder magazine, the defence casemate and garrison cell, the musketry gallery, exhibits on communications and an audio-visual presentation about the citadel's history. Guided tours are available in summer. (Open year round, June 15-Labour Day 0900-2000, rest of the year 0900-1700.)

The other famous landmark is *York Redoubt* standing high on a bluff overlooking the harbor. It was established in 1793 at the outbreak of the Revolutionary War between France and Britain as a first attempt to defend the harbor. When it had been expanded and strengthened it became a key defense element during the second half of the 19th century. Canadian troops trained here during both World Wars. You will see rifled, muzzle-loading guns, a photo display and an excellent harbor view. (Open daily June 15-Labour Day 1000-1800, but grounds open year round.)

On the subject of landmarks, do not miss the *Prince of Wales Martello Tower* in Point Pleasant Park, erected 1796/97 by Prince Edward, as part of Halifax's coastal defense network to protect British batteries from a French attack. (Open June 15-Labour Day 1000-1800.) *Point Pleasant Park* itself has plenty to recommend it with forested areas, beaches and many hiking trails.

Other parks are: *Sir Sanford Fleming Park*, a prime recreational area covering 137 acres with a bandstand, hikers trails, seawall and beach. For a good view, climb the 122 steps of the Dingle Tower. In the heart of downtown, the *Halifax Public Gardens* are laid out Victorian style with an array of plants and trees and a duck pond. There are band concerts in summer. A relaxing spot is *Flyn Park* at the waterside with grassy knolls and a wading pool. Also at the waterfront, the small *Seaview Park* offers a magnificent view of Bedford Basin. Down the road from the Citadel, The *Halifax Commons* offers tennis courts and a swimming pool, while *Wanderer's Grounds*, surrounding the Nova Scotia Museum, has a running track and riding stables. *Fort Needham Memorial Park* commemorates the victims of the Great Halifax Explosion of 1917. If you want 'wilderness' go to *Hemlock Ravine Park*, a natural forest which was once the private summer estate of Loyalist Lieut. Gov. John Wentworth. The latter lent the property to Prince Edward and his mistress, Julie St Laurent in 1794. Today the park is superb for hiking and nature walks or for cross-country skiing in winter.

Also see the Halifax War Memorial at *Grand Parade Square*, one of the best examples of sculpture by Scottish artist John Massey Rhind. Just south of Grand Parade is Canada's oldest Anglican church, *St Paul's* (1750). Its interior is lined with relics and many an illustrious man is buried in its vaults.

The twin city of *Dartmouth* (pop. 65,341) is located on the eastern side of the harbor, it was incorporated with Halifax in 1961 and is known as the city of lakes, there are 23 within its boundaries. It was founded in 1750 and named after England's Dartmouth as well as Sir William Legge, second Earl of Dartmouth. From 1785-1792 it was a whaling headquarters. Ferries operate between the two cities daily. While here visit the *Dartmouth Heritage Museum* which tells the city's story from Indian times to the present, and see the *Old Geary Street Cemetery* where many Indians were buried.

Hantsport   N8

(pop. 1423). Once a shipbuilding center (Evangeline Trail). Artefacts of the wooden sailing ship era are displayed at the *Churchill House Marine Memorial Room* on the grounds of the community center. Today this is the hub of a large farming region. *Windsor 19 km/12 mi.*

Head of St Margaret's Bay   O8

Notable for its scenery (Lighthouse Route), the adjacent rivers and lakes are good for anglers. Not far away is the start of the *Bowater Mersey Hiking Trail* which can be used by cross-country skiers in winter. French explorer Champlain named the bay in 1631. *Halifax 26 km/16 mi.*

Indian Point   O8

Formerly an important Micmac area — an old Indian burial ground is located here and many relics have been discovered in its vicinity. (Lighthouse Route.) *Bridgewater 23 km/14 mi.*

Ingonish   I14
(pop. 407). A Scottish influenced village
with a beautiful location on Warren Lake.
There was a thriving French settlement
here in the 17th century. The name is said
to be of Portuguese origin since before the
French, they had a fishing settlement here
in 1521. Ingonish Beach is the main
entrance to **Cape Breton Highlands
National Park,** one of the east coast's
finest anchorages. Between Middle Head
and Ingonish Harbour there's a sandy
beach and between the beach and the
mainland, a freshwater lake. A choice of
hotels includes *Keltic Lodge,* one of the
Maritimes' best resort properties. In the
surrounding area all the favorite outdoor
sports may be enjoyed. *Baddeck 175 km/
105 mi.*

Inverness County   J13
Land mostly settled by the Scots, this
county covers the western side of Cape
Breton. A native of Inverness-shire suggested the name. The Margaree Valley in
this county is renowned for salmon and
trout fishing.

Isle Madame   L13
An island named for the Queen of France
by the Acadians (Fleur-de-lis-Trail). It is
connected to the mainland by the Lennox
Passage Bridge, with its main commercial
center at Arichat. Arichat is one of Nova
Scotia's oldest settlements — landmarks
include an 1838 cathedral and *the Bishop's
Palace* (now a hospital). Also visit *Le Noir
Forge Museum.* The island's most important fishing center is Petit de Grat,
founded by Acadians from Louisbourg in
1713. One of the most delightful harbors is
Little Anse — from here take the hiking
trail to Cap Rouge for a view of Green
Island, gateway to the Strait of Canso.
Other stopoff points on Isle Madame are
Martinique, Port Royal and Janvrins Har-
bour. *Port Hawkesbury 33 km/20 mi.*

Joggins   L7
(pop. 692). Noted for its fossil fields and
cliffs (Glooscap Trail). You may well find
prehistoric relics along the beach or in the
fields and you will certainly see fossilized
trees and other plants embedded in the 150
ft sandstone cliffs.
Amherst 33 km/20 mi.

Jordan Falls   Q6
Situated on the Jordan River (Lighthouse
Route). From here roads lead to Jordan
Ferry and Jordan Bay where many a
rewarding catch of fish has been made.
The 48 km/30 mi long Jordan River has
good trout fishing almost all season long.
Shelburne 10 km/6 mi.

Judique   L12
A district on the Ceilidh Trail comprising
Judique South, Judique itself, Judique
North, Judique Intervale and Little
Judique. These communities were founded
in 1775 by families from the Scottish
Hebrides, though the name is of French
origin meaning, it is said, 'where the waters
turn swiftly forming eddies'. In the past
the region was noted for the Highlanders
who brought their love of highland dancing
with them. *Port Hawkesbury 38 km/23 mi.*

Kejimkujik National
Park   P6
381 sq km/238 sq mi of wilderness with
many lakes and primitive campsites on the
canoe routes. Formerly a Micmac reservation it can be reached from Hwy 8 between
Liverpool and Annapolis Royal. *Liverpool
68 km/42 mi.*

Kentville   N7
(pop. 5056). The largest Annapolis Valley
community (Evangeline Trail), it was
named in honor of the Duke of Kent. Following the Acadian expulsion, New England planters settled here in the mid
1700s. Good shopping areas, motels and a
golf course are among the facilities. Most
of the major events of the annual spring
Annapolis Valley Apple Blossom Festival
take place in Kentville, including parades,
concerts and sporting events. *Middleton
52 km/33 mi.*

Kings County   N7
Forms the core of the Annapolis Valley,
covering 861 sq mi. It is one of Canada's
best orchard regions exporting vast quan-
tities of apples in particular. It is also Nova
Scotia's main poultry producing area.
Pick your own strawberries in summer at a
variety of farms and take in fishing or
hunting.

Lake Charlotte   N10
On the Marine Drive is in one of the province's best hunting and fishing areas and
experienced guides are available. Not far
away Clam Bay used to be unusually plentiful in clams and at Clam Harbour, there
is a long, hard, white sand beach. *Dartmouth 53 km/32 mi.*

Lake George   P4
Provides the water for Yarmouth and its
islands are nesting points for thousands of
black-backed gulls. Visitors are welcome
at the Lake George fish hatchery; fishermen can head for lakes Killam, Brizil and
Bird. *Yarmouth 20 km/12 mi.*

Liscomb   N11
(pop. 106). This town took its name from
Liscomb House in Buckinghamshire. The
district's Indian name meant 'splendid eel-

ing place'. One of Atlantic Canada's finest resorts — *Liscomb Lodge* nestles at riverside. Spanish Ship Bay, between Liscomb Mills and Liscomb Village, is a good fishing area. *Dartmouth 146 km/88 mi.*

Liverpool P7

(pop. 3336). A major industrial town on the Lighthouse Route, with tourist accommodations, restaurants and shops. Located on the Mersey River, it was named for Lord Liverpool, head of the London Board of Trade and Plantations, and was settled by New Englanders in 1759. Since privateering is very much a part of this town's history, it holds a special July celebration each year. Many old homes date back to privateering days, like the *Simeon Parkins House* (1776). Now a provincial museum, it contains colonial furnishings and other items. Next door is the *Queens County Museum* which has historical exhibits about the area. *Trinity Church* here was erected in 1822; the Anglican rectory in 1820; and the *County Court House* was completed in 1854. *Yarmouth 189.5 km/117 mi.*

Lockeport Q6

(pop. 1030). (Lighthouse Route) named for one of the Plymouth, Mass. settlers who came here in 1755, the town suffered a great deal from privateers. Today, it depends on its fishery for income, exporting fresh, frozen, smoked and tinned fish. Visit the local schoolhouse museum. *Shelburne 30 km/18 mi.*

Louisbourg K15

(pop. 1519). Lies within Canada's largest National Historic Park. The original lighthouse here (1730-1733) was damaged first by fire and then in the 1758 Siege of Louisbourg. It has always played an important role in this 18th-century French stronghold since its light was visible from as far away as 29 km / 18 mi at sea. Today a new lighthouse stands near the ruined original.

The fortress stood on the southwestern part of the harbor and it was the administrative, commercial and military epicenter of a colony that included Cape Breton Island and Prince Edward Island. It was such a vast fort, it took 20 years to build and was only just finished when war broke out. Its size alone was a constant threat to the New England colonies and this was partially the reason for their attack in 1745 under the command of William Pepperell. After a 45 day siege, the fort was conquered. The Treaty of Aix-la-Chapelle gave Louisbourg back to the French in 1748 only to see it recaptured by the British in 1758 under the command of James Wolfe. In 1760 William Pitt ordered the fort's demolition.

Guard at Fort Louisburg

Fortress of Louisbourg National Historic Park covers a large area and includes partial reconstruction of the 18th-century town. Go first to the visitor center where you will be bused to the fortress. Among the reconstructed buildings are the *King's Bastion Barracks*, two operating 18th-century taverns, homes of soldiers, and warehouses of merchants and fishermen. There are also craft shops. Costumed guides, films and displays bring the era to life and guided tours are available throughout the day. (Outdoor walking tours are possible from May to Oct.) Other significant places within the park include *Lighthouse Point, Careening Point, the Royal Battery* and *Kennington Cove.* (Open June 1-Sept. 30 daily, 1000-1800, June and Sept., 0900-1900 July 1-Aug. 31.)

Also of interest to visitors is the *Sydney and Louisbourg Railway Museum*, a restored 1895 station. From 1895 to 1968, the railway carried coal and fish between the two points. Open June 15-Sept. 30 0900-1800. *Sydney 37 km/22 mi.*

Lunenberg P8

(pop. 3014). A fishing port built on a peninsula on the Lighthouse Route, former home of the *'Bluenose'* schooner. Comfortable accommodations, good shops and restaurants can be found in town along with art galleries. Do not miss the *Fisheries Museum of the Atlantic* on Lunenberg Waterfront (open May 15-Oct. 15 0930-1730 daily). The museum is in three vessels which are moored there: *Cape North*, a dragger, the *Reo II*, a rum runner, and the *Theresa E. Connor*, whose exhibits tell the *Bluenose* story. This was the last schooner to fish the Grand Banks. An aquarium and industrial displays are equally part of the museum complex. Films on the past and present of the fishing industry are screened in *The Ice House Theatre.* The replica of the *Bounty* used for the film *'Mutiny on the Bounty'* was also built in Lunenburg shipyards.

Like many sites this one in ancient times was an Indian encampment. It subsequently became a French fishing station before Swiss and German immigrants founded the town in 1751. *St John's Church* came about by Royal Charter in 1754 and has communion vessels presented by King George III, the choir still wears scarlet cassocks and the Queen Anne pewter chalice used in 1754 is still on view here. Another interesting antique is the bell taken from Louisbourg which is now in the *Zion Evangelical Lutheran Church*, built in 1776.

The *Nova Scotia Fisheries Exhibition and Fishermen's Reunion* is held every Sept. Twice weekly yacht races are held at Prince's Inlet just outside of town, an area which also has boating and swimming facilities. The old blockhouse is a public park with a good view of town and harbor. *Yarmouth 159 km/99.4 mi.*

Mabou   K13

(pop. 377). A Cape Breton farming center whose name comes from the Indian one, 'Malaboo'. In the little church here (with the interior of a miniature cathedral) there is a pioneer shrine known as *Mother of Sorrows Pioneer Shrine*. From here, it is a short distance to the Mabou Highlands where a number of hiking trails follow the coast. *Port Hood 13 km/8 mi.*

Mahone Bay   O8

(pop. 1236). A town at the head of Mahone Bay (Lighthouse Route) with a lovely view

of ocean, islands and coves, and noted for its craft shops. The Indians called the site 'Mush-a-mush', a name which was later given to the river flowing into the harbor. The word 'Mahone' is thought to be derived from the old French word 'Mahonne', a craft used by pirates. The town was founded in 1754 by Capt. Ephraim Cook. Names of other places in the vicinity will remind you of piratical and Indian days: Sacrifice Island, Murderers Point and Indian Point. *Yarmouth 248 km/153 mi.*

Maitland   M9

(pop. 217). A little township named for Sir Peregrine Maitland, Nova Scotia's governor in 1828. The natural timber resources made it an important shipbuilding center, bringing a great deal of prosperity, something reflected in the charming properties you can still see here today. Visit *Lawrence House* which contains a host of memorabilia connected with the *'William D. Lawrence'* — the largest wooden ship ever built in Canada. (Open May 15-Oct. 15 Mon.-Sat. 0930-1730, Sun. 1300-1700.) *Shubenacadie 33 km/20 mi.*

Malagash   L9

A holiday resort on the Malagash Peninsula (Sunrise Trail) with a fine view of the Northumberland Strait. The name comes from the Indian word meaning 'the place of games', but in fact Malagash is renowned for its lobster and oysters. In the vicinity are Malagash Centre, Malagash Salt Mines, Malagash Point and Malagash

Bluenose II, the famous schooner

Station where salt was discovered in 1916. This obviously aided the fishing industry which uses tons of salt yearly. *Truro 53 km/ 32 mi.*

Mapleton L8
The maple sugar industry center (Glooscap Trail) where thousands of pounds is manufactured each year. The maple groves are situated in the hills of the Cobequid range. It was the Indians who discovered the advantages of maple syrup when they happened to boil some potatoes in maple sap and found the sap became sweet and thick with the boiling. *Springhill 11 km/7 mi.*

Margaree Forks J13
(pop. 296). The junction of the Ceilidh and Cabot Trails, settled originally by Irish immigrants in 1815, who were joined later by Scottish highlanders. It was the home of Dr Moses Coady and Dr J. J. Tompkins, founders of the Antigonish Movement. Visitors will find a variety of restaurants and a nine hole golf course here, but fishing is the big attraction. In addition to salmon, the Margaree River provides trout and *gaspereaux.* There is a fish hatchery at *Frizzelton* and a salmon museum at *North East Margaree. Baddeck 53 km/32 mi.*

Martinique M13
An Acadian settlement (Fleur-de-lis

Maple syrup making

Trail). During the expulsion the Acadians were deported to France and then journeyed to the West Indies, hence the name of this spot. There is a park with a beach here and several short hiking trails.

Meteghan P4
(pop. 761). The busiest port on the Acadian shore (Evangeline Trail). The name is derived from the Indian word 'mitihkan' (blue stone) and it was settled by the Acadians in 1785. *La Vieille Maison,* one of the oldest homes, is now a museum. Meteghan is the region's largest lobster fishing center.
Yarmouth 43 km/26 mi.

Middle Stewiacke and Upper Stewiacke M10
Are both situated in the Stewiacke Valley (Glooscap Trail), popular with the Micmac Indians for its streams and forests. Acadian farmers came in the 18th century, followed by New England and Irish settlers. Visit the natural land bridge on Dawson Mountain at *Upper Stewiacke and Burnside Park* where there are also waterfalls.
Truro 16 km/10 mi.

Middleton N6
(pop. 1824). Situated half way between Annapolis Royal and Kentville (Evangeline Trail). It was formerly called Gates Ferry after Capt. Oldham Gates, a New England planter who came here in 1760. *Holy Trinity Church* (1788) in Lower Middleton is well preserved with original box pews fitted with doors and it also has a 1783 Bible and prayer book. Also see the *Annapolis Valley Macdonald Museum,* showing the history of the area and a collection of antique clocks and watches. (Open June 14-Sept. 15 Mon.-Sat. 0900-1700, Sun. 1300-1700; Sept. 16-June 13 Tues.-Sun. 1300-1700.) *Kentville 52 km/ 33 mi.*

Mill Village P7
Situated on the Medway River (Lighthouse route), a very fine salmon stream. Hunting for moose and deer is possible in the area. At nearby Charleston you can tour the *satellite tracking station. Liverpool 15 km/9 mi.*

Monastery L12
(pop. 454). (Sunrise Trail) A monastery was established here in 1825 which is now run by the Augustinian monks, and welcomes visitors. See the *Outdoor Shrine of Our Lady of Grace.* Trout fishing is good in the Tracadie River. *Antigonish 31 km/ 19 mi.*

Morden N6

Located on the Bay of Fundy (Evangeline Trail), it was once called French Cross because of the cross commemorating the death of several Acadian refugees in 1756 who died in hiding. Others escaped to the opposite side of Minas Channel to a place now called Refugee Cove. The present name of Morden is taken from a Kings County family. *Kentville 40 km/25 mi.*

Mount Uniacke N8

(pop. 1145). Named for Richard John Uniacke, an Irish aristocrat who became Attorney General of Nova Scotia in 1797. His handsome colonial mansion in a 5000-acre estate is today a museum housing an excellent collection of original furnishings. Inside the grand home are four-poster beds, cook's quarters in a basement kitchen and a huge fireplace. The exterior is considered one of Canada's prime examples of colonial architecture. (Open May 15-Oct. 15 Mon.-Sat. 0930-1730, Sun. 1300-1700.) *Halifax 43 km/26 mi.*

Musquodoboit Harbour N10

(pop. 495). The largest community on the western part of the Marine Drive, with accommodations and restaurants. The Musquodoboit River (noted for its trout and salmon) bisects the town. See the *Musquodoboit Railway Museum* in an old railway station, many of whose exhibits will interest children. *Dartmouth 38 km/23 mi.*

Musquodoboit Valley N10

An area geared to sport with plenty of hiking and cross-country ski trails. Europeans first settled this district in 1692. The name is Indian, meaning 'rolling out in foam'. *The Musquodoboit Valley Provincial Park* is popular for a day out.

New Glasgow L10

(pop. 10,672). On the East River (Sunrise Trail). An area of interesting drives and *Melmerby Beach* a little way out of town; also an 18-hole golf course. *Halifax 166 km/104 mi.*

New Ross O7

(pop. 516). Named in honor of Lord Mulgrave's son in 1863. See *Ross Farm*, a provincial museum emphasizing early rural life. Restored to its 19th-century appearance, it features farm animals including oxen and horse-drawn wagons, a cooperage, blacksmith's forge and an exhibit of farm implements. *Chester 28 km/17 mi.*

Northport L8

A community on the Northumberland Strait (Sunrise Trail) where clam digging is popular along the wide beaches, especially at low tide in spring. The beach and

warm water make it a pleasant summer destination. *Amherst 30 km/18 mi.*

North Sydney K14

(pop. 8319). A port on the north side of Sydney harbor. Ships sail daily to Port-Aux-Basques and Argentia (Newfoundland). Along the harborfront are three parks: *Indian Beach* with sands and playground; *The Ballast Grounds Park* with boardwalk and gardens; and *Munroe Park* with tennis courts and beach. The Northern Yacht Club's marina is located in Munroe Park. *Sydney 21 km/12.5 mi.*

Oxford L8

(pop. 1498). A pretty town in the center of Cumberland County (Sunrise Trail). The River Philip, good for trout and salmon fishing, runs through it while the extra salty lake in town has been developed as a swimming resort. Fishing is good in several lakes only a few miles away. *Springhill 21 km/13 mi.*

Parrsboro M8

(pop. 1857). A sporting center on the northern shore of the Minas Basin (Glooscap Trail), with boating, bathing, trout fishing and bear hunting all available. From nearby Partridge Island you get a lovely view of the Basin and Blomidon. The region is rich in folklore about Glooscap — the Indian man-god who was both a warrior and magician.

The Indian name for this place was 'Owokum' (crossing over); the present name was acquired in 1784 to honor Lieut-Col. John Parr, then governor of Nova Scotia. At Partridge Island you will see the ruins of the old *Parrsboro Blockhouse*. Along the shores it is often possible to pick up amethysts and agates — every August a *Rockhound Roundup* takes place. *Hidden Falls* are a 125 ft waterfall a few miles east of town. *Amherst 81 km/50 mi.*

Peggy's Cove O8

A resort on the Lighthouse Route which still retains its fishing village charm. It attracts artists and crafts people every summer and there are several places to stay in and to shop. Walk to '*Whale's Back*' *Rock*, visit *Lighthouse Point*, look at the William de Garthe murals inside *St John's Anglican Church*. Peggy's Cove is located on a particularly picturesque route which passes through several other similar hamlets. *Yarmouth 325 km/200 mi.*

Pictou L10

(pop. 4588). A major town on the Sunrise Trail on the site of a very early Micmac settlement. The name comes from the Indian 'Pictools' (big harbor) and a large harbor it has with three rivers emptying into it. The town has a number of tourist amenities including a marina, a golf course, an entertainment center and places to stay ranging from bed and breakfast to motels. It is also an entry point for Nova Scotia with a colorful and historic harbor front, where the first wave of Scottish immigrants arrived on the *Hector* in 1773.

Every July there is a two day *Lobster Carnival* worth being here for, immediately followed by a *Strawberry Festival*. Music, theater and dance are available year round at the *DeCoste Entertainment Centre*, but if you wish to tour the *Grohman Knives* plant, it must be during summer months. Also see *First Presbyterian Church* (1786) in the heart of town which displays two centuries of church history via artefacts, documents and audio-visual displays. (Open June-Sept. Mon.-Sat. 0900-1800, Sun. 1300-1800.) The *Hector National Exhibit Centre* is open all year round. *Northumberland Fisheries Museum* in the former Pictou railway station is open in the summer months. The most important museum is the *Thomas McCulloch House* built in 1806 as the home of Rev. McCulloch, founder of Pictou Academy. (Open Mon.-Sat. 0930-1730, Sun. 1300-1730, May 15-Oct. 15). *Tatamagouche 53 km/31 mi.*

Pictou County   M10

Covers 1116 sq mi with three scenic river valleys, the East, Middle and West rivers, all flowing into the Northumberland Strait.

Pleasant Bay   I14

(pop. 248). A village given its present name in 1873 (Cabot Trail). Until 1927, it could only be reached by foot or water. The inhabitants, of English and Scottish descent, earn their keep from fishing for lobster, herring, salmon *etc.* The area around the village is the site of Atlantic Canada's largest maple stand. Four miles east *The Lone Shieling* represents the crofter huts in Scotland. *Cheticamp 30 km/18 mi.*

Port Greville   M7

Named for English diarist Charles Greville (Glooscap Trail), this village is situated on Minas Channel one of the headwaters of the Bay of Fundy. A place for deep sea fishing. *Parrsboro 20 km/13 mi.*

Port Hawkesbury   L13

(pop. 4008). An entry point on the Strait of Canso and a major industrial center. The completion of the Canso Causeway in 1955 prevented ice from flowing through

the Strait and created a deepwater port large enough for the biggest supertankers. There are several hotels, motels and restaurants and a small museum at Port Hastings. During the last week in June, *The Festival of the Strait* takes place. This is a week of sporting events that includes a sailing regatta, parades and concerts. *Port Hastings 6 km/3.5 mi.*

Port Hood   K12

(pop. 769). A popular beach and swimming area on the Ceilidh Trail, named for Admiral Hood, commander-in-chief in North America in 1767. Stone used to build Fort Louisbourg was quarried out of the southern end of Port Hood Island. *Port Hawkesbury 54 km/34 mi.*

Port Joli   Q6

'Beautiful Port' on the Lighthouse Route, it was called Port Noir by the French and Baya Formose by the Portuguese. In autumn and winter large numbers of Canadian geese can be seen here and the place has been established as a federal bird sanctuary. *Liverpool 25 km/16 mi.*

Port Lorne   N6

A summer hideaway (Evangeline Trail) with a good view of the Bay of Fundy. The small fishing village with its pretty beach was named for the Marquis of Lorne, Canada's Governor General 1883-1888. *Bridgetown 20 km/13 mi.*

Port Mouton   Q7

A fishing village on the Lighthouse Route named by the DuMonts in 1604 when a sheep was accidentally lost overboard. There are beaches around here and the two fishing villages of Central Port Mouton and South West Port Mouton. *Liverpool 19 km/12 mi.*

Port Royal   O5

A **National Historic Park** (Evangeline Trail) where the habitation of Champlain and de Monts (1605) has been reconstructed. It was here that North America's first Social Club, *the Order of Good Cheer*, was founded by Champlain. All the buildings have been built as they would have been in the 17th century. On this site Canada's first cereal crops were grown, the first bricks made, the first drama produced, *The Theatre of Neptune* (1606), and the first conversions to Christianity took place. The park is open year round, the buildings June 1-Oct. 15 daily 0900-1800. The settlement was destroyed in 1613 by an expedition from Virginia and Acadia eventually became British territory. It was reconstructed by the Canadian Government in 1938-39 from the writings of

Champlain, Lescarbot and the Jesuits. *Annapolis Royal 3.2 km/2 mi.*

Port Williams   M8
A shipping port for apples and potatoes (Glooscap Trail) — interesting in autumn when the steamers load up. Nearby is the site of the French settlement 'Boudro Point'. *Kentville 8 km/5 mi.*

Pubnico   Q5
The name is derived from the Indian word 'Pogomkook' which means 'land that has been cleared for cultivation.' (Lighthouse Route.) There are actually seven Pubnicos. West, Middle West and Lower West were all settled by Acadians in 1651, making them the province's oldest Acadian settlement. In the area are several wharves, breakwaters, fishing fleets and fish processing plants. *The Acadian Museum of Yarmouth County* is located at Lower West Pubnico. See also *St Peter's Church* (1892) in Middle West Pubnico and the oldest home (1779) in Lower West Pubnico which once belonged to the first Acadian magistrate and shows the typical high, steep central gable. Below Pubnico Harbour, *Subsea City* is used by scuba divers who want to see an abundance of marine life.
Yarmouth 38 km/24 mi.

Pugwash   L9
(pop. 746). Summer resort on the Sunrise Trail noted for its good climate and fine sandy beaches. The area caters for boating, golfing, fishing and hunting and the community is one of the sites for the July 1 **Gathering of the Clans.** *Tatamagouche 36 km/22 mi.*

River John   L10
(pop. 681). A fishing village on the River John (Sunrise Trail). Lobster is the main catch and this village's community lobster suppers are well worth sampling in May, June and July. Chicken barbecues are held on *Canada Day* (July 1) and in August. There are some good beaches on the Cape John Road just outside of the village. *Tatamagouche 19 km/12 mi.*

Riverport   P8
(pop. 387). A village at the mouth of the LaHave River (Lighthouse Route). In the **Ovens National Park** here there are a series of caverns in the rocky cliffs, created by the sea. In the 19th century Riverport saw a gold rush so there are lots of old pits and tunnels on the site. After gold was found in 1861, parcels of land by the shore were sold for thousands of dollars. Between June and December of that year, The Ovens yielded $120,000 in gold which was recovered without using machinery. *Lunenburg 12 km/8 mi.*

Sable River   Q7
Adjacent to first class hunting grounds (Lighthouse Route). Little Harbour and Louis Head, two small fishing villages here, are both scenic and have sandy beaches. *Shelburne 25 km/16 mi.*

St Peter's   L14
(pop. 705). A service center for Richmond County, situated on a narrow strip of land separating the Atlantic Ocean from Bras d'Or Lake (Fleur-de-lis Trail). It has hotels, restaurants, shops and craft stores. Prior to the arrival of Europeans the Micmacs used it as a portage. Nicholas Denys established an important fishing and fur trading post here in 1650 and carried on a number of commercial enterprises for 19 years. His project to cut a channel across the isthmus in order to haul boats from sea to lake, was completed many years later when the St Peter's Canal was built.

By 1737, the French had made St Peter's a strong point and a supply center for **Fort Louisbourg.** Remains of a later fortification can be seen on *Mount Granville* above Battery Park on the canal's east bank. *Port Hawkesbury 38 km/24 mi.*

Sandy Cove   O4
One of the prettiest villages in Nova Scotia (Evangeline Trail) and an excellent place for deep sea fishing. *Digby 32 km/20 mi.*

Saulnierville   P5
(pop. 395). A typical Acadian village (Evangeline Trail). Visit the *Sacred Heart Church* (1880). *Yarmouth 54 km/34 mi.*

Scotsburn   L10
(pop. 342). A village on the Sunrise Trail noted for its summer church suppers and barbecues. *Pictou 11 km/7 mi.*

Shag Harbour   Q5
The name 'shag' is derived from a bird called the shag or cormorant (Lighthouse Route). Visit *Chapel Hill Museum*, located in a former church, for a panoramic view. What was the belfry provides an observation tower and at night you can see the lights of five lighthouses from this point. *Shelburne 49 km/31 mi.*

Sheet Harbour   N11
(pop. 782). A tourist center on Marine Drive with accommodations, restaurants *etc.* Salmon catches are good from Sheet Harbour East and West rivers. The East River road leads to *Lochaber Mines* and *Malay Falls* for more good fishing. *Dartmouth 102 km/64 mi.*

Shelburne Q6

(pop. 2511). A major tourist base on the Lighthouse Route with inns and motels and a variety of visitor services. Known as 'The Loyalist Town' since in 1783 about 3000 United Empire Loyalists settled here. Many of its houses date from that period like the *Ross Thompson House* (1784), now a museum with period artefacts and furnishings. (Open May 15-Oct. 15, Mon.-Sat. 0930-1730.) It is also the only surviving Loyalist 'store' — its shelves are stocked with goods that were necessary and fashionable in the 1780s. *The Rudolph-Williams House* (1787) is also a museum with exhibits on shipbuilding, fire fighting and the Loyalist heritage and is open year round. Drop in at the *J. C. Williams Dory Shop* on Dock St., opened by Prince Charles and Princess Diana on their 1983 visit. The shop features exhibits on dory making and examples of the craft.

The Islands Park is on the western edge of town and at the entrance to Shelburne Harbour is *McNutt's Island*, another favorite picnic place, which can be reached by motorboat. There are no residents apart from the lighthouse keeper. The *Cape Roseway Lighthouse* (1788) still operates. You might also go to the *Tobeatic Game Sanctuary*, an area for canoeing and fishing — fishing is allowed if accompanied by a registered guide. *Yarmouth 120 km/ 74 mi.*

Sherbrooke M12

(pop. 380). A small resort on Marine Drive, situated on the banks of St Mary's River where there is prime salmon fishing. Originally a fur trading post, built by French trader La Giraudière in 1655, the site was settled in 1800. The village took its name from Sir John Coape Sherbrooke, Lieut. Gov. of the province in 1813.

You will find accommodations, eating places and shops. The river is good for spring and early summer salmon but the other main attraction besides sport is *Sherbrooke Village Restoration*, an area of the town renovated and looking as it did in the 1860-1880 period when Sherbrooke was a center for lumber, shipbuilding and gold mining. Costumed guides take you through some 20 buildings, including a general store, a blacksmith's shop, the post office and a woodworking shop. Here you can also try your hand at some of the tasks and crafts of that era. *Country Harbour Ferry 37 km/23 mi.*

Smith's Cove O4

(pop. 469). A holiday resort (Evangeline Trail), where cherries and strawberries are grown. See *Smith's Cove Historical Museum*. Many explorers sailed through Digby Gap here, a narrow strait that has seen the likes of Champlain and the DeMonts. Look also at the unique little chapel of *St Anne's Birchbark* in the grounds of Harbour View House. *Digby 4.8 km/3 mi.*

Soldier's Cove L14

Near this point (Fleur-de-lis Trail) is Chapel Island with its Indian shrine. The chapel was built in 1792 by Micmac chiefs, Francis Bask and Michael Tomma. Each July there is a three day religious festival here for the Micmac Indians. *Sydney 70 km/44 mi.*

South Gut St Ann's K14

First settled by the Highland Scots (Cabot Trail). Between here and North Gut St Ann's is the only Gaelic college in North America where not only the Gaelic language is taught, but also traditional Highland arts and crafts. In the *Highland Pioneers Museum* you will see many familiar

Sherbrooke Village

tartans and also the personal possessions of Giant MacAskill. The *Gaelic Mod* seven day festival of Celtic culture takes place usually the first full week of August. Drive round *St Ann's Harbour*, a notable beauty spot in the vicinity. *Baddeck 19 km/12 mi.*

Spencer's Island   M7

(Glooscap Trail). The mystery ship *'Mary Celeste'* was built here in 1861. First named the *'Amazon'* it was driven ashore at Cow Bay, Cape Breton Island. An American firm bought it and renamed it and in 1872 it left New York bound for Genoa. Weeks later, a Nova Scotia brig came upon the *Marie Celeste* with nothing out of place but no people on board. No storm, no leak, no fire. The mystery of what happened has become a classic among strange sea tales. A short distance from Spencer's Island's fine beach is Glooscap's Kettle, an island resembling an overturned pot or kettle. *Parrsboro 8 km/5 mi.*

Springhill   L8

(pop. 5220). Location of what was once Canada's deepest coal mine, the 4000 feet Number 2 mine. A series of disasters in 1891, 1916, and 1956 occurred in the mines, culminating in the 'bump' of 1958 in which 76 men died. Visit the *Miners Museum* on Black River Rd, and take a mine tour. *Amherst 35 km/22 mi.*

Starr's Point   M8

On the Glooscap Trail, location of *The Prescott House* (1814) built for Charles Ramage Prescott who introduced the Gravenstein apple to Nova Scotia. The house and well manicured grounds are now a museum. From those grounds you can see the Wellington dyke, which took seven years to build, one of the main dykes in Kings County. *Kentville 10 km/6 mi.*

Stellarton   M10

(pop. 5366). Canada's pioneer coal mining center and rail road town (Sunrise Trail), located on East River. Coal was found here in 1798 and mined until quite recently. You will find a small but interesting miners' museum here and an early locomotive, *'Albion'* (1854) in *Albion Park. New Glasgow 3 km/2 mi.*

Stewiacke   N9

(pop. 1174). Located on the Stewiacke River in the middle of the province. Locally made crafts are offered by the *Cottage Crafts Shop* and in season there is fishing for trout, salmon, bass etc. A popular place to picnic, canoe or fish is *Stewiacke River Park* where a canoe route runs south for 48 km/30 mi. *Truro 27 km/17 mi.*

Sydney   K14

(pop. 30,645). A city, with an excellent harbor, built on a peninsula in the industrial Cape Breton area. There is a good choice of motels and shops but the city showplace is *Wentworth Park.* The city was founded in 1785, and was known then as Spanish Bay. The current name honors British Colonial Secretary, Lord Sydney. The first settlers came from the Scottish Highlands to the area around *St George's Church* (1786), Canada's fourth oldest Anglican church. A chair from Nelson's ship *'Victory'* can be found inside. *Cossitt House*, a provincial museum on Charlotte St (1787) is Sydney's oldest house. *Port Hastings 142 km/85 mi.*

Tancook Islands   O8

Big and Little Tancook Islands (Lighthouse Route) are just a short ferry ride from Chester. Apart from their natural beauty they are famed for the schooners built here and also known for their cabbages, sauerkraut and seafaring traditions.

Tangier   N10

Gold mining was developed in this town which lies on Marine Drive. Few traces of the mining remain now though the celebrated Kent shaft lies capped just beside the road. Try smoked fish here — it's famous — salmon, mackerel or eel. *Sheet Harbour 20 km/13 mi.*

Tatamagouche   L9

(pop. 636). Situated at the mouth of the French and Waugh rivers (Sunrise Trail). The Indian name means 'meeting place of the waters'. The place was settled early on by the French but nothing remains now of old Fort Franklin built by DesBarres in 1768 or the wells, mill, dam, dikes and cemetery used by the Acadians. However you will find arts and crafts displays in *The Fraser Culture Centre* on Main St, and a number of good bathing beaches along the Tatamagouche shore. *Amherst 97 km/69 mi.*

Tidnish   K8

A town near the border with New Brunswick and on the Northumberland Strait. Along the Tyndale Rd McLellan Pond and McLellan Brook afford good trout fishing — geese and brant are also found along this shore. At Tidnish Dock there are three parks: *Lorneville* with a fine sand beach; *Amherst Shore*, a summer colony, and *Northport* also with a good beach. *Amherst 18 km/11 mi.*

Tupperville   O6

Named in honor of Sir Charles Tupper,

the Canadian statesman (Evangeline Trail). See *Tupperville School Museum* with school items of over 100 years old. Also the nearby waterfalls. *Bridgetown 3 km/2 mi.*

Tusket   Q5
(pop. 400). A Loyalist village on the Lighthouse Route and the county seat of Argyle. The name comes from the Indian word meaning 'the great forked tidal river'. At one time the largest ships were launched here on their way to trade with South America and the West Indies. The old *Tusket Court House* dates to 1805. See also *Reynardson* on the Tusket River and Surrette Island, one of the Tusket Islands. *Yarmouth 16 km/10 mi.*

Wallace   L9
(pop. 322). (Sunrise Trail) named for onetime Nova Scotia treasurer Michel Wallace and birthplace of Simon Newcomb, leading American scientist and astronomer in his time (1835). There are many beaches near Wallace. *Tatamagouche 19 km/12 mi.*

Wentworth   L9
A farming community in the Wentworth Valley (Sunrise Trail). Scenically the valley is beautiful year round and in winter this is a popular ski resort. The town name honours Sir John Wentworth, Lieut. Gov. of Nova Scotia in 1792. *Tatamagouche 29 km/18 mi.*

Westport   P4
(pop. 341). Located on Brier Island (Evangeline Trail). The scenery here can be compared with Giant's Causeway in Ireland. The island is recommended for bird-watchers and lapidary enthusiasts. *Digby 64 km/40 mi.*

Whycocomagh   K13
(pop. 437). A community on the western side of Bras d'Or Lake. The Skye River separates a Micmac Indian Reserve and a Highland Scottish village. In 1853, 5000 Scottish immigrants joined in Cape Breton's largest church communion and an outdoor ecumenical service continues to be held on the third Sunday in June in the hills of Salt Mountain. A hiking trail from this park leads to a vantage point atop the mountain, overlooking the lake. An annual summer festival here features arm wrestling. *Port Hastings 50 km/31 mi.*

Windsor   N8
(pop. 3702). A scenic town where two rivers meet. Early French settlers built miles of dikes to hold back the tides of the Bay of Fundy, reclaiming acres of land from the sea by doing so. The English changed the original Indian name of Piziquid (meeting of the waters) to Windsor in 1764. Parts of old *Fort Edward* (1750) can still be seen and the blockhouse still stands. Bonnie Prince Charlie's friend, Flora Macdonald, spent the winter of 1779 in this very blockhouse.

Windsor native, Judge Thomas Chandler Haliburton and his fictional character, Sam Slick, you may not have heard about, but you will know the phrases that moved from the pages of his books into everyday language: 'raining cats and dogs', 'quick as a wink', 'truth is stranger than fiction'. The judge's home is now the *Haliburton Memorial Museum*, an interesting representation of 19th century Nova Scotia culture, with many of his personal belongings. (Open May 15-Oct. 15 Mon.-Sat. 0930-1730, Sun. 1300-1730.) You might also walk through the *Old Parish Burying Ground* on King St., where the tombstones date back to the 1760s. *Halifax 62 km/ 38 mi.*

Wolfville   N7
(pop. 3073). Situated where the Cornwallis River opens into the Minas Basin (Evangeline Trail) and the center for Longfellow's *'Evangeline'* country. Settled in the 1760s by New England Planters and named for Judge Elisha DeWolfe. See *Randall House* on Main St, built in 1836 and now a museum featuring items pertaining to the New England Planters and Loyalists. It is also the home of *Acadia University*, founded by Baptists in 1838, and the beach nearby, called *Evangeline Beach*, offers bathing in water noted for its warmth. *Kentville 14 km/9 mi.*

Yarmouth   Q4
(pop. 7801). A port of entry and the largest town in southern Nova Scotia, often called a gateway to the province as it is the terminus for car ferries arriving from Portland and Bar Harbor, Maine. It boasts good shops, restaurants and hotels and has its own airport. Yarmouth has great shipping traditions, back in the 1800s its port had the world's highest per capita ship tonnage. Items relating to the seafaring past may be seen at *The Yarmouth County Historical Society Museum* on Collins St., including one of Canada's largest collections of ship paintings. (Open year round.) Also visit the *Firefighters Museum*.

CN Marine operates a ferry *'Bluenose'* between Yarmouth and Maine May-mid Oct., and Prince of Fundy Cruises offer daily trips to Portland from early May to the end of Oct. *Digby 106 km/66 mi.*

NEWFOUNDLAND

The Vikings were the first Europeans to discover Newfoundland and this may indeed be the location of the land they called 'Vinland'. The current name was given by John Cabot who thought he had discovered new territory — hence new-found-land. It was his discovery of the vast fishing grounds that brought other explorers and fishermen, such as the Basque whalers who set up stations on Newfoundland's shores, to Atlantic Canada.

Together, Newfoundland and Labrador are larger than the other three Atlantic provinces combined, and could quite easily contain several American states. There is space and wilderness here with only four people to every square mile, and only two major cities. The province's forests and rivers teem with wildlife, one reason why it is a paradise for sportsmen, particularly those who like fishing.

What is interesting is that the land is closer to Europe than any other part of North America. Newfoundland is midway between British Columbia and Italy. Severe winters and stormy seas contrast with brilliant sunsets and pleasant temperatures in summer.

Nature lovers will have the time of their life here with two national parks and 47 provincial parks to choose from; endless sporting activities from climbing and canoeing to whale watching and gem collecting. And because of the unique history of the territory, the visitor will find more folklore and legend than anywhere else in Canada. The communities each have their own words and sayings, their recipes and remedies, old songs and handicrafts. The place names alone are worth a postcard or two — Jerry's Nose, Blow-me-down, Ha Ha Bay to name only three.

Basically there are five sections to the province: *Western Newfoundland* offers rugged **Gros Morne National Park,** but also the Cordroy Valley farmlands. It is an area dominated by the Long Range Mountains, from Port-aux-Basques to the tip of the Great Northern Peninsula. The *Central* region is for the most part unspoiled forest, crossed by the Watershed of the two main rivers, Humber and Exploits. *Eastern* Newfoundland lives for its seafaring traditions, dominated as it is by the ocean. *Avalon*, is connected to the rest of the island by a narrow barren isthmus, but is the most historic portion of the province. *Labrador* shares a border with Québec and covers almost 113,000 sq mi of great wilderness. High mountains, fjords, empty coastal plains, huge lakes and immense forests are found here.

Argentia   O9
A ferry terminal for North Sydney N.S. and for trips along the South Coast of the island to Channel-Port-aux-Basques. Located on the west coast of the Avalon Peninsula, there is also a US naval base dating from World War II. *St John's 131 km/82 mi.*

Baie Verte Peninsula   I5
In Central Newfoundland, situated between White Bay and Green Bay. Near the town of Baie Verte is *Flatwater Pond Park* on the site of what used to be a logging camp. There are many tiny communities on the peninsula worth exploring — the most northerly is Fleur-de-Lys. *Corner Brook 208 km/130 mi.*

Western Brook Pond, Gros Morne

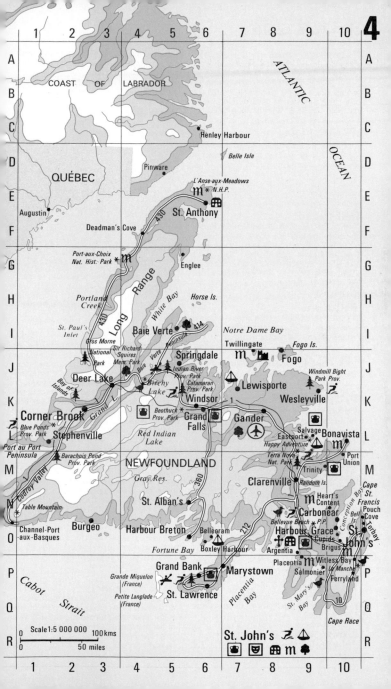

Barachois Pond   M2

Newfoundland's largest provincial park is situated in the southwest at the base of the Long Range escarpment. In summer, guided tours along the park trails are offered in addition to other recreational facilities.
Corner Brook 77 km/48 mi.

Bay of Islands   K2

A photogenic area in the southwest best viewed from the lookout trail and tower in *Blow Me Down Provincial Park.* From here you will see Guernsey, Tweed and Pearl Islands rising high out of the surrounding sea.
Corner Brook 47 km/29 mi.

Bell Island   O10

Named for an offshore rock near Freshwater on the western coast of the island which lies in Conception Bay. An excellent base for views of Conception Bay, Little Bell Island and Kelly's Island which (they say) used to be the site of a pirate's fort. This is also the site of recent iron-ore mining.

Belleoram   O6

A picturesque fishing community on the south coast. There was a settlement here from 1759 and the name is thought to refer to a 'meeting or calling together of troops'. The area was greatly influenced by the Loyal Orange Brotherhood and the Society of United Fishermen. *Grand Falls 216 km/135 mi.*

Bellevue Beach Provincial Park   O9

On the Trinity Bay shore of the Avalon isthmus. Ideal for observing sea birds, beach combing and shell collecting. Come in late June or early July and you will be able to do the easiest fishing ever when schools of spawning caplin are washed ashore. They can be scooped up in any handy receptacle.
St John's 134 km/84 mi.

Beothuck Provincial Park   K5

Located in central Newfoundland, this park should not be missed. It has a logging exhibit that recreates the early logging days of Newfoundland. *Windsor 7 km/4 mi.*

Birchy Lake   J4

This is a haven for wildlife, close to the Baie Verte Peninsula. Thousands of caribou migrate through here. *Corner Brook 104 km/65 mi.*

Blue Ponds Provincial Park   L1

Southwest Newfoundland. Limestone-based subterranean springs feed two freshwater ponds here which have a distinctive blue-green color. Nice for a swim and an afternoon's relaxation. *Corner Brook 30 km/19 mi.*

Bonavista   L10

(pop. 4299). Supposedly the place where Cabot first landed in 1497 which is why it takes its name from the Italian 'buonavista' meaning 'good sight'. The town was not actually settled until the 1600s but by 1681 was frequented by French fishing fleets and by 1690 boasted a population of 1000. It was fortified in 1696 to prevent French attacks. The lighthouse here, first used in 1843, has reopened as a provincial historic site.
St John's 301 km/188 mi.

Boxey Harbour   O6

In colonial times, this was famous for a 'spy hole' in the rock formation, used to navigate safely through the rocks to the St John Harbour area. Coax someone to take you fishing in the waters of Fortune Bay from any of the communities on Hwy 363.
Grand Falls 219 km/137 mi.

Brigus   O10

Avalon Peninsula. This was the birthplace of Capt. Bob Bartlett (1875-1946), an explorer who made 30 Arctic expeditions including three attempts to reach the North Pole. His former home, *Hawthorne Cottage,* still stands and has been designated an historic site. Because of its 'olde worlde' atmosphere and picturesque appeal, American artist Rockwell Kent established a studio here at the early part of this century.
St John's 81 km/50 mi.

Carbonear   N10

(pop. 5026). An interesting historic town which may have taken its name from the corruption of 'Cape Carveiro' or perhaps from the French for charcoal pot. Although it was razed by the French in 1696, the inhabitants successfully defended a small fortified island in its harbor against further attack. Not far up the coast you'll find two sandy beaches.
St John's 109 km/68 mi.

Cape St Francis   N10

Reached via Hwy 20 was on a map as early as 1527 and is believed to have been named by Portuguese explorer Gaspar Corte Real on his voyage to Newfoundland in 1501. The road to the Cape looks rough but is navigable by car.
St John's 24 km/15 mi.

Catamaran Provincial Park K5

In this area the two last known Beothucks were found and brought back to civilization. Most of today's knowledge of the tribe was gained from these women's words and drawings. There is a sandy beach and pool here. *Windsor 42 km/26 mi.*

Channel-Port-aux-Basques O1

(pop. 6817). The suggested starting point for a tour along Hwy 470 on Newfoundland's southern coast. Most of the communities along the way were originally French, like Foxroost — Fox Rouge or Red Fox, and Rose Blanche named for the white granite not white roses. It is the principal ferry port for the province with links to North Sydney N.S. and there are beaches nearby at *J. T. Cheeseman Provincial Park. Corner Brook 248 km/136 mi.*

Churchill Falls *see map p. 23*

(Labrador). This is the site of a huge hydro-electric plant which supplies power to the eastern USA.

Clarenville M9

(pop. 2807). Once a wood camp, this is now a bustling commercial town serving the whole Bonavista Peninsula. It is a good start for a tour of the peninsula with its scenic wilderness and trout-filled lakes. At Southern Bay Junction there is a 57.6 km/36 mi scenic drive that is one of the peninsula's most photographed. *St John's 184 km/115 mi.*

Codroy Valley N1

One of the west coast's earliest settled areas. The French arrived in the early 1700s and were later joined by Scottish settlers, Channel Islanders and Micmac Indians from across the Gulf of St Law-rence. The land in this fertile valley, south of the Anguille Mountains, proved to be some of the island's best farming land. Visitors will find good swimming, canoeing and fishing facilities at the *Grand Codroy Provincial Park* in this vicinity. *Channel-Port-aux-Basques 45 km/28 mi.*

Conception Bay O10

Was named by Gaspar Corte Real. Easily reached from St John's, it is surrounded by several picturesque and historic towns. In the Bay itself you will frequently see whales.

Corner Brook K2

(pop. 25,198). Newfoundland's second city is situated at the mouth of the *Humber River* and is an ideally located base for salmon fishing enthusiasts. Until the 1920s, Corner Brook was only a small town but the Bowater pulp and paper mill changed that and turned it into a busy industrial center, tours of the mill are available. *St John's 687 km/429 mi; Channel-Port-aux-Basques 240 km/150 mi.*

Cupids O10

When John Guy sailed from Bristol, he attempted to establish his 'Sea Forest Plantation' here at what was known as Cuper's Cove in 1610. Although his colony was not successful in itself, it did pave the way for future colonization of the area.
Carbonear 30 km/18 mi.

Deadman's Cove F4

A northern fishing community. Due to heavy Arctic ice flows each spring, the wharf here has to be dismantled every autumn and rebuilt the following year. Just south, *Three Mile Lake* and *Castor's River* offer anglers good sport. *Corner Brook 265 km/165 mi.*

Salmon leaping on the Humber River

Eastport   L9
A farming center and supplies base. Provisions for fishing and camping trips may be picked up from the town's supermarkets and general stores and its own beach is equipped with changing places and picnic tables. A few miles away at St Chad's and Burnside, arrangements may be made with local fishermen to see the islands in Bonavista Bay. *Clarenville 96 km/60 mi.*

Ferryland   P10
On the southern shore. It was Sir David Kirke's base in the 1600s when its high rocky cliffs were fortified to protect the settlement from attack. The name is thought to be a corruption of the word 'farehao' meaning rocky or 'Forillon' as John Guy called it in 1611. *St John's 75 km/46 mi.*

Fogo Island   J8
(pop. 1103). Reached by daily ferry from Carmanville. This small picturesque island only measures 25.6 km/16 mi long and 14.5 km/9 mi wide. It was first settled in the 1680s by fishermen seeking refuge from French raiders and Beothucks. Later there were English settlers in Elizabethan times. You can still hear traces of the old dialect on the island today and the inhabitants continue to keep up old customs like *Christmas Mummering*. The name Fogo is believed to derive from the Portuguese 'fuego' (fire), something seen by early settlers warning of Beothuck encampments.

On the way to the village of Fogo, see *Barred Islands* and *Joe Batts Arm* (named for one of Capt. Cook's deserters). Sandy Cove is notable for its beaches and is the most northeasterly point in Notre Dame Bay. Keep an eye out for the caribou which roam on Fogo. *Gander 77 km/48 mi from Carmanville.*

Gander   K7
(pop. 9031). Best known for its international airport. Its low incidence of fog made it an air base in the mid thirties, as a site to handle seaplanes on Gander Lake, but it was its strategic position that made it invaluable in World War II and turned it into a major military air base. The town of Gander is modern with good accommodations and shops and is surrounded by some of North America's finest fishing and hunting territory. *Glenwood Park,* for picnics, is just 20 km/13 mi away to the west of Hwy 1. *Grand Falls 91 km/56 mi.*

Grand Bank   P6
On the Burin Peninsula. It was the excellent fishing grounds of Newfoundland's continental shelf, 'Grand Banks', that first drew 16th-century fishermen here. Maritime historic exhibits are on view at the *Southern Newfoundland Seamen's Museum. St John's 359 km/224 mi.*

Grand Falls   *see map p. 23*
(Labrador). 350 mi from the coast the Hamilton River drops 250 ft and the Bowdoin Canyon here has walls 400 ft in height.

Grand Falls   K6
(pop. 8729). Two Britons, Lord Northcliffe and Lord Rothmere established Newfoundland's first pulp and paper mill here which led to the development of this town. Visit the *Mary March Museum,* named after the last of the Beothuk Indians. *Corner Brook 272 km/170 mi.*

Gros Morne National Park
Situated in Bonne Bay. (See Parks.)

Happy Adventure   L9
The middle cove of three, particularly safe for children. Buy fresh live lobster here in season, which extends until late July. Not far away, *Sandy Cove,* is one of Newfoundland's best beaches. *Clarenville 98 km/61 mi.*

Happy Valley-Goose
Bay   *see map p. 23*
(pop. 8075). (Labrador). Established in the Second World War as an airforce base, it is now largely a supply center and is on the ferry run from Newfoundland Island. It is also a starting point for fly-in fishing and hunting trips.

Harbour Grace   O10
(pop. 2937). The French gave this site its name — Harve de Grace — in 1505. Situated on Conception Bay, it was once the island's second largest town with major seal and cod fisheries. Pirate captain, Peter Easton used Harbour Grace as his headquarters and his fort stood on the site of the present day museum in the old *Customs House.* See the island's oldest stone church, *St Paul's* (1835) and Canada's oldest jail (1830). Many early attempts at transatlantic flying took place at Harbour Grace. In 1938, Amelia Earhart, the first woman to fly solo across the Atlantic, left from here on her record-breaking attempt. *St John's 108 km/68 mi.*

Heart's Content   N10
(pop. 634). Named by optimistic early settlers, its fame outweighs its size. The first successful transatlantic cable was landed here in 1866, transforming the community into a major relay station. Visit the *Cable Station,* open as a provincial historic site in summer. Just

Gros Morne National Park

beyond Heart's Content you'll discover Heart's Desire and Heart's Delight and across the bay is Little Heart's Ease. *Carbonear 21 km/13 mi.*

Indian River Provincial Park   J5

Caribou hunters followed Indian River to Birchy Lake, still popular with canoeists. The scenery here has changed little from the days when the Beothuck Indians lived in the area. *Windsor 100 km/60 mi.*

Labrador City Wabush   *see map p. 23*

(Labrador). Two newer towns on the border with Québec. Half of Canada's total iron-ore output comes from here and is shipped out by rail to Sept-Iles in Québec. The area has one of the best cross-country ski ranges in the world and international competitions are sometimes held here. The Smokey Mountain Ski Club also attracts cross-country skiers.

Lance Cove   O10

A fertile valley in the west of Bell Island, infrequently visited until Bell Island proved to be a source of iron-ore in 1892. That led to a bustling mining community at Wabana whose operation was forced to close down only in 1966.

L'Anse aux Meadows

L'Anse-aux-Meadows   E6

The northern tip of Newfoundland, and a famous national historic park. It was here that archaeologists discovered evidence that the Vikings had established a settlement around 1000 A.D. Reproductions of collected items are displayed at the visitors center and three sod houses have been reconstructed. Guides are on the site June 1-Labour Day. The park is now on the UNESCO World Heritage List. *St Anthony 50 km/31 mi.*

La Manche   P10

Is best reached on foot via *La Manche Valley Provincial Park* (where there are camping facilities). Noted for its waterfall. *St John's 57 km/36 mi.*

Lewisporte   K7

(pop. 3782). A commercial shipping port on Notre Dame Bay. A particularly good base for deep sea fishing — several boats are available for charter out on the bay in search of tuna. Also a good place for buying/eating lobster. This is also the main ferry port in the north with links to Labrador and the outports on White Bay. *Grand Falls 61 km/38 mi.*

Marine Drive   N10

For some excellent views, take this road on the east coast from St John's to Pouch Cove, passing Logy Bay, Outer Cove and Middle Cove. The first of these took its name from the lethargic species of fish caught there — the word 'logy' in Newfoundland means 'sluggish'. The last two take their names from their location on the coast.

Placentia   P9

(pop. 2209). Formerly called Plaisance, it was a French fishing base in 1662. You will see evidence of French occupation in the tombstones in the old graveyard near the Anglican Church, but there are only remains of fortifications on *Castle Hill*. There is a superb view from Castle Hill across the Gut of Placentia. A path leads to the old French redoubt of *Le Gaillardin* (1692) from which there are also superb views. Placentia Bay was the meeting place for drafting the 'Atlantic Charter' in 1941. *Argentia 8 km/5 mi.*

Port au Choix   G3

A National Historic Park. Just off the main road is a 'Maritime Archaic' Indian burial ground which, according to the archaeologists dates back to 2340 B.C. Recent discoveries in the area place the Dorset Eskimo communities at Port au Choix some time after the Maritime Archaic group disappeared. *Corner Brook 280 km/175 mi.*

Port au Port Peninsula   L1

Part of 'The French Shore' used for fishing. Just offshore, Red Island was considered France's most important North American fishing base. Today's community is Newfoundland's only French one. Residents of Port au Port itself can fish both in Port au Port Bay and St George's Bay due to their location on the isthmus. *Stephenville 6 km/3.7 mi.*

Portland Creek   H3

A notable area for fishing. To the north, River of Ponds is another good region with a number of trout pools. *Corner Brook 202 km/126 mi.*

St. John's

Port Union M10

Site of the monument and tomb of Sir William Croaker who founded the Fishermen's Protective Union Party. *Bonavista 16 km/10 mi.*

Pouch Cove N10

(pop. 1543). Site of one of Newfoundland's oldest settlements founded around 1611. Strangely enough it was chosen for its dangerous harbor since it was illegal to reside permanently in the island during the 17th and 18th centuries and the harbor kept ships away. *St John's 21 km/13 mi.*

Random Island M9

A logging community on the Trinity Shore, settled in 1799, at Hickmans Harbour. One of the few places where fishing comes second.

St Anthony E6

(pop. 2987). Largest town on the Northern Peninsula and home of the *Grenfell Mission* which provides medical services for those in isolated areas. Be sure to visit the Mission's handicraft center where hand embroidered parkas are for sale. *Corner Brook 493 km/308 mi.*

St John's O10

(pop. 83,770). Capital of the province and eastern terminus of the Trans Canada Highway. They say that as Cabot discovered Newfoundland on St John's Day (June 24, 1497), the town was named in honor of the Saint. For many years the

French and the British wrangled for its possession until there was a final British victory in 1762. Steeped in history, *St John's Annual Regatta* (usually held the first Wednesday in August) is recognized as North America's oldest organized sporting event.

High above the city is **Signal Hill National Historic Park,** one of the largest in Canada, and the site of the last Anglo-French battle for the Atlantic Coast. Only remnants of the once heavy fortifications remain but at the Interpretative Centre you can see an audio visual presentation of Newfoundland's history. There are superb views from the *Queen's Battery* and a Military Tattoo takes place here annually in mid-July and mid-August. Below *Cabot Tower* built in 1897 to commemorate the 400th anniversary of the discovery of Newfoundland, a monument marks the spot where Marconi received the first transatlantic wireless signal in 1901.

In the city, visit *The Newfoundland Museum* on Duckworth St. which contains a first class collection of prehistoric Indian and Eskimo artefacts. The *Commissariat House* on King's Bridge Rd, has been restored and furnished in the style of 1830. Limestone was imported from Ireland to build *The Colonial Building* on Military Rd, an 1850 building which served as the seat of government until 1960 and now houses the Provincial Archives. Nearby is Government House, built in 1830, a pleasant Georgian stone building in attractive grounds. At the eastern end of Military Rd, St Thomas *'Old Garrison Church'* was opened in 1836 for use by the Garrison at nearby Fort William. Other interesting churches include the Anglican Cathedral on Church Hill and the Roman Catholic *Basilica of St John the Baptist*, built in the shape of a Latin cross, with a fine carving before the altar and a statue of Our Lady of Fatima donated by Portuguese sailors.

See also *Quidi Vidi Battery*, a Provincial Historic site at the eastern edge of the city, overlooking the village of the same name. It is here that the annual Regatta is held. The *Arts & Culture Centre* on Prince Philip Drive is focal point for all of St John's performing arts with an art gallery, museum and major theater. In July it is used for the *Summer Festival of The Arts.*

The city's most attractive park is *Bowring Park*, a land parcel donated to the city by one of the province's most prominent families. Visiting heads of state and Royals plant a tree here as a traditional reminder of their visit. The park contains several statues including an exact replica of Kensington Gardens' Peter Pan. Two striking bronzes — a caribou and a soldier in battle kit — act as memorials to the war dead of the Royal Newfoundland Regiment in World War I. For recreation, Bowring has picnic sites, a swimming pool and boating pool. *Channel-Port-aux-Basques 905 km/ 565 mi.*

St Paul's Inlet   I2
Jacques Cartier anchored near here at Cow Head in 1534. Also nearby, Shallow Bay's miles of scenic coastline offers relaxing beaches. *Corner Brook 151 km/94 mi.*

Salmonier Nature Park   P10
A 3000 acre Wilderness Reserve on the Avalon Peninsula which contains a 100 acre exhibit area so that summer visitors can study the natural environment at close range. You will find at least 30 species of animal and birdlife indigenous to Newfoundland and Labrador within the enclosed area.
St John's 67 km/42 mi.

Salvage   L9
An old settlement with a museum. In this village, salmon and caplin are both smoked locally and are well worth trying. *Clarenville 116 km/72.5 mi.*

Sir Richard Squires
Memorial Park   J4
Situated along the Humber River. At *Big Falls* the large Atlantic salmon attempting to scale the white water, a feat which often takes them hours to achieve, are the main attraction. *Corner Brook 90 km/56 mi.*

Stephenville   L1
(pop. 10,284). Next to Harmon Air Force Base. Until 1844 the settlement was named Indian Creek, after which Acadians renamed it for one of their party, Stephen LeBlanc. *Corner Brook 77 km/48 mi.*

Table Mountain   N1
A 1700 ft high geological oddity near Channel-Port-aux-Basques which has been known to raise windy gusts on the area below at over 160 km/100 mph.

Terra Nova
National Park   M9
Situated on the shores of Bonavista Bay. (See Parks.)

Torbay   N10
(pop. 2908). Probably named by English fishermen for their own bay of this name. It was here that Col. Amherst and his British forces landed in 1762 to recapture St John's from the French. *St John's 8 km/5 mi.*

Trinity   M9
(pop. 367). Discovered on Trinity Sunday by Gaspar Corte Real in 1500. North America's first Court of Admiralty convened here in 1615. Like other settlements, Trinity suffered pirate and French attacks and was fortified in 1706 though the original guns you can see today at the harbor entrance were never used in defense. The town's museum contains an interesting history of the area. *Clarenville 74 km/46 mi.*

Twillingate   J7
For many years the trade center for Labrador and shore fisheries. In the gravel pits alongside the road you may well find good specimens of jasper. There is also a 3500 year old Red Paint Indian burial ground here and a bell which was cast in 1862 to mark a large kill of seals. The animals drifted near the shore on an iceberg and around 30,000 were killed. *Gander 85 km/53 mi.*

Windmill Bight Park   J9
Features a sandy beach and fresh water lagoon. The Bight is also a scheduled salmon river for serious angling.

Witless Bay   P10
The place to make arrangements with local fishermen to reach the *Seabird Sanctuary*. The sanctuary comprises three islands: Gull Island, Green Island and Great Island, where during the nesting season thousands of seabirds can be viewed in their natural environment from the boat. Among the species you will see are gannets, puffins, kittiwakes and razorbills. *St John's 40 km/25 mi.*

Puffin (top left), Gannet (top right), Kittiwakes (bottom)

INDEX

All main entries are printed in heavy type. Map references are also printed in heavy type. The map page number precedes the grid reference. Abbreviations used: Co. = County; Is. = Island.